# 500
## Best-Loved
# Song Lyrics

Collected and Edited by
**RONALD HERDER**

D0828914

**DOVER PUBLICATIONS, INC.**
Mineola, New York

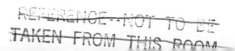

# DOVER MUSICAL ARCHIVES

*Copyright*

Copyright © 1998 by Dover Publications, Inc.
All rights reserved under Pan American and International Copyright Conventions.

*Bibliographical Note*

*500 Best-Loved Song Lyrics* is a new work, first published by Dover Publications, Inc., in 1998.

*Library of Congress Cataloging-in-Publication Data*

500 best-loved song lyrics / compiled and edited by Ronald Herder.
        p.      cm.
    ISBN 0-486-29725-X (pbk.)
    1. Songs—Texts.   I. Herder, Ronald.
    ML54.6.A15   1998 <Case>
    782.42164'0268—dc21                                98-34608
                                                           CIP
                                                            MN

Manufactured in the United States of America
Dover Publications, Inc., 31 East 2nd Street, Mineola, N.Y. 11501

# NOTE

This collection of song lyrics touches on the great, wonderfully varied, sometimes sad, sometimes nutty song lyrics that seem to sum up who we are by what we like to sing. There are somber hymns and rollicking comedy songs, charming children's pieces, show tunes and love-sick ballads, deeply felt spirituals and patriotic songs born in conflicts that stretch back to our revolutionary colonial days. A lot of territory to cover, to be sure, although the great bulk of these best-loved lyrics falls in that enormously fertile period from the turn-of-the-century to about 1922.

Lyrics and credits come directly from the original sheet music—when such prized gems were available to us—or from sources that have proven exceptionally reliable over the years. James J. Fuld's encyclopedic *The Book of World-Famous Music: Classical, Popular and Folk** has been a particularly valuable treasury of important credits and background information. There is nothing quite like it on any library shelf, and our occasional footnotes dip deeply and often into Mr. Fuld's well-stocked pond.

The charm of many an old-fashioned song—depending on your mood of the moment—may or may not extend to how it was punctuated in the original publication. In their rush to riches, Tin Pan Alley publishers (a major force of the period) were notoriously nonchalant about *any* editorial aspect of their song lyrics. Commas come and go; semi-colons abound; capitalization is merrily hit-and-miss; and quotation marks (where somebody in a song actually *says* something quotable) are noticeably absent.

Since that productive band of composers, lyricists and publishers are now long gone and far away, we've exercised the right of the well-meaning latecomer to supply a bit of order where none existed. So the way lines are typeset in this collection, and how they are punctuated, is our responsibility—or fault—depending on how you feel about such things.

*Third Edition: Dover, 1985 (0-486-24857-7)

iii

A word, finally, about completeness.

Many a folk song defies completeness in any forum short of a doctoral dissertation. There are endless verses in countless variants. Narratives of the roaming cowboy or the roving young lover seem to go on and on into a meandering eternity. Short of producing a staggering bookshelf of lyrics, we've made every effort to reproduce that text that is most memorable, that captures the spirit of the original song the way we remembered it, that is truly "best-loved."

Ronald Herder

# CONTENTS
*Titles arranged alphabetically*

v

vi

# G

# H

# I

# The Aba Daba Honeymoon

W&M: ARTHUR FIELDS & WALTER DONOVAN (1914)

1. 'Way down in the Congoland
   Lived a happy chimpanzee,
   She loved a monkey with a long tail,
   (Lordy, how she loved him!)

   Each night he would find her there,
   Swinging in the cocoanut tree,
   And the monkey gay, at the break of day,
   Loved to hear his Chimpie say:

   > *Chorus:*
   > "Aba, daba, daba, daba, daba, daba, dab,"
   > Said the Chimpie to the Monk,
   > "Baba, daba, daba, daba, daba, daba, dab,"
   > Said the Monkey to the Chimp.

   > All night long they'd chatter away,
   > All day long they were happy and gay,
   > Swinging and singing
   > In their hunky, tonkey way.

   > "Aba, daba, daba, daba, daba, daba, dab,"
   > Means "Monk, I love but you,"
   > "Baba, daba, dab," in monkey-talk,
   > Means "Chimp, I love you too."

   >> *1st time:*
   >> Then the big baboon, one night in June,
   >> He married them, and very soon
   >> They went upon their aba, daba honeymoon.

   >> *2nd time:*
   >> One night they were made man and wife,
   >> And now they cry, "This is the life,"
   >> Since they came from their aba, daba honeymoon.

2. Well, you should have heard that band
   Play upon their wedding day,
   Each Chimp and Monkey had nutshells,
   (Lordy, how they played them!)

   And now it is ev'ry night,
   High up in the cocoanut tree,
   It's the same old thing, with the same old swing,
   When the Monk and Chimpie Sing:

   > [*to Chorus*]

1

# Abide with Me

W: HENRY F. LYTE (1847) / M: WILLIAM H. MONK (1861)

1. Abide with me! Fast falls the eventide,
   The darkness deepens—Lord, with me abide!
   When other helpers fail, and comforts flee,
   Help of the helpless, oh, abide with me!

2. Swift to its close ebbs out life's little day;
   Earth's joys grow dim, its glories pass away;
   Change and decay in all around I see;
   O Thou, who changest not, abide with me!

3. I need Thy presence every passing hour,
   What but Thy grace can foil the tempter's pow'r?
   Who, like Thyself, my guide and stay can be?
   Thro' cloud and sunshine, oh, abide with me!

4. Hold Thou Thy cross before my closing eyes;
   Shine thro' the gloom, and point me to the skies;
   Heav'n's morning breaks, and earth's vain shadows flee!
   In life, in death, O Lord, abide with me!


# Ach, du Lieber Augustin

AUSTRIAN DRINKING SONG

Ach, du lieber Augustin,
    Augustin, Augustin,
Ach, du lieber Augustin,
    Alles ist weg:
Bock ist weg, Stock ist weg,
    Auch ich bin in dem Dreck,
Ach, du lieber Augustin,
    Alles ist weg.

# After the Ball

W & M: CHARLES K. HARRIS (1892)

1. A little maiden climbed an old man's knee,
   Begged for a story, "Do, uncle, please!
   Why are you single, why live alone?
   Have you no babies, have you no home?"

   "I had a sweetheart years, years ago,
   Where she is now, pet, you will soon know;
   List to the story, I'll tell it all:
   I believed her faithless after the ball."

   *Chorus:*
   "After the ball is over, after the break of morn,
   After the dancers' leaving, after the stars are gone,
   Many a heart is aching, if you could read them all,
   Many the hopes that have vanished after the ball."

2. "Bright lights were flashing in the grand ballroom,
   Softly the music playing sweet tunes.
   There came my sweetheart, my love, my own:
   'I wish some water; leave me alone.'

   "When I returned, dear, there stood a man
   Kissing my sweetheart as lovers can.
   Down fell the glass, pet, broken, that's all,
   Just as my heart was after the ball."

   [*to Chorus*]

3. "Long years have passed, child, I've never wed,
   True to my lost love, 'though she is dead.
   She tried to tell me, tried to explain,
   I would not listen, pleadings were vain.

   "One day a letter came from that man.
   He was her brother, the letter ran.
   That's why I'm lonely, no home at all,
   I broke her heart, pet, after the ball."

   [*to Chorus*]

# After You've Gone

W & M: HENRY CREAMER & TURNER LAYTON (1918)

1. Now, won't you listen, honey, while I say
   How could you tell me that you're going away;
   Don't say that we must part,
   Don't break your baby's heart.

   You know I've loved you for these many years,
   Loved you night and day.
   Oh, honey baby, can't you see my tears?
   Listen while I say:

   *Chorus:*
   After you've gone and left me crying,
   After you've gone, there's no denying
   You'll feel blue, you'll feel sad,
   You'll miss the bestest pal you've ever had.

   There'll come a time, now don't forget it,
   There'll come a time when you'll regret it;
   Oh! Babe, think what you're doing,
   You know my love for you will drive me to ruin,
   After you've gone,
   After you've gone away.

2. Don't you remember how you used to say
   You'd always love me in the same old way;
   And now it's very strange
   That you should ever change.

   Perhaps some other sweetie's won your heart,
   Tempted you away.
   But let me warn you tho' we're miles apart,
   You'll regret some day:

   [*to Chorus*]

# Ah! Sweet Mystery of Life

W: RIDA JOHNSON YOUNG / M: VICTOR HERBERT
[from *Naughty Marietta*, 1910]

Ah! Sweet mystery of life, at last I've found thee,
Ah! I know at last the secret of it all;
All the longing, seeking, striving, waiting, yearning,
The burning hopes, the joy and idle tears that fall!

For 'tis love, and love alone, the world is seeking;
And 'tis love, and love alone, that can repay!
'Tis the answer, 'tis the end and all of living,
For it is love alone that rules for aye!

For 'tis love, and love alone, the world is seeking;
For 'tis love, and love alone, that can repay!
'Tis the answer, 'tis the end and all of living,
For it is love alone that rules for aye!


# Ah! Vous Dirai-je, Maman

FRENCH FOLK SONG
*(same melody as "Twinkle, Twinkle, Little Star")*

Ah! vous dirai-je, Maman,
Ce qui cause mon tourment!

Papa veut que je raisonne
Comme une grande personne;

Moi, je dit que les bonbons
Valent mieux que la raison.

# Alexander's Ragtime Band

W & M: IRVING BERLIN (1911)

1. Oh, ma honey, oh, ma honey,
   Better hurry and let's meander;
   Ain't you goin', ain't you goin'
   To the leader man, ragged meter man?

   Oh, ma honey, oh, ma honey,
   Let me take you to Alexander's
   Grandstand, brass band,
   Ain't you comin' along?

   *Chorus:*
   Come on and hear, come on and hear
   Alexander's Ragtime Band;
   Come on and hear, come on and hear,
   It's the best band in the land.

   They can play a bugle call like you never heard before,
   So natural that you want to go to war;
   That's just the bestest band what am,
   Honey lamb.

   Come on along, come on along,
   Let me take you by the hand
   Up to the man, up to the man
   Who's the leader of the band.

   And if you care to hear the "Swanee River"
   Played in ragtime,
   Come on and hear, come on and hear
   Alexander's Ragtime Band.

2. Oh, ma honey, oh, ma honey,
   There's a fiddle with notes that screeches,
   Like a chicken, like a chicken,
   And the clarinet is a colored pet.

   Come and listen, come and listen
   To a classical band what's peaches,
   Come now, somehow,
   Better hurry along.

   [*to Chorus*]

# Alice Blue Gown

W: JOSEPH McCARTHY / M: HARRY TIERNEY
[from *Irene*, 1919]

1. I once had a gown, it was almost new,
    Oh, the daintiest thing, it was sweet Alice Blue;
   With little forget-me-nots placed here and there,
    When I had it on, I walked on the air.
   And it wore, and it wore, and it wore,
    Till it went and it wasn't no more.

   *Chorus:*
   In my sweet little Alice Blue gown,
   When I first wander'd down into town,
     I was both proud and shy
     As I felt ev'ry eye,
   But in ev'ry shop window I'd primp passing by;

   Then in manner of fashion I'd frown,
   And the world seemed to smile all around,
     Till it wilted I wore it,
     I'll always adore it,
   My sweet little Alice Blue gown.

2. The little silkworms that made silk for that gown,
    Just made that much silk and then crawled in the ground;
   For there never was anything like it before,
    And I don't dare to hope there will be any more.
   But it's gone 'cause it just had to be,
    Still it wears in my memory.

   [*to Chorus*]


# All God's Children Got Shoes

SPIRITUAL

1. I got a shoe, you got a shoe,
   All God's children got shoes,
   When I get to heaven gonna put on my shoes,
   I'm gonna tromp all over God's heaven,
     Heaven, heaven,
   Ev'rybody talkin' 'bout heaven ain't goin' there,
     Heaven, heaven,
     Gonna tromp all over God's heaven.

2. I got a robe, you got a robe,
   All God's children got robes,
   When I get to heaven gonna put on my robe,
   I'm gonna shout all over God's heaven,
       Heaven, heaven,
   Ev'rybody talkin' 'bout heaven ain't goin' there,
       Heaven, heaven,
       Gonna shout all over God's heaven.

3. I got a harp, you got a harp,
   All God's children got harps,
   When I get to heaven gonna play on my harp,
   I'm gonna play all over God's heaven,
       Heaven, heaven,
   Ev'rybody talkin' 'bout heaven ain't goin' there,
       Heaven, heaven,
       Gonna play all over God's heaven.


# All Night, All Day
SPIRITUAL

> *Chorus:*
> All night, all day,
> Angels watchin' over me, my Lord,
> All night, all day,
> Angels watchin' over me.

1. Now I lay me down to sleep,
       *Angels watchin' over me, my Lord,*
   Pray the Lord my soul to keep,
       *Angels watchin' over me.*

   [*to Chorus*]

2. If die before I wake,
       *Angels watchin' over me, my Lord,*
   Pray the Lord my soul to take,
       *Angels watchin' over me.*

   [*to Chorus*]

# All Through the Night

WELSH FOLK SONG

1. Sleep, my love, and peace attend thee
All through the night;
Guardian angels God will lend thee,
All through the night.

   Soft the drowsy hours are creeping,
Hill and dale in slumber steeping,
Love alone his watch is keeping,
All through the night.

2. Though I roam a minstrel lonely,
All through the night,
My true harp shall praise thee only,
All through the night.

   Love's young dream, alas, is over,
Yet my strains of love shall hover
Near the presence of my lover,
All through the night.

3. Hark! a solemn bell is ringing,
Clear through the night.
Thou, my love, are heav'nward winging
Home through the night.

   Earthly dust from off thee shaken,
Soul immortal thou shalt waken
With thy last dim journey taken,
Home through the night.


# Alouette

FRENCH-CANADIAN CHILDREN'S "ACCUMULATION" SONG

[*Lark, sweet lark, I'll pluck your feathers . . .
. . . and your head . . . and your beak . . .
and your eyes . . .* (etc.)]

1. Alouette, gentille alouette, alouette, je te plumerai.
Je te plumerai <u>la tête</u>, je te plumerai la tête,
   Et la tête, et la tête,
   *Alouette, alouette—ah!*
Alouette, gentille alouette, alouette, je te plumerai.

**2.** Alouette, gentille alouette, alouette, je te plumerai.
Je te plumerai le bec, je te plumerai le bec,
    Et le bec, et le bec,
    Et la tête, et la tête,
    *Alouette, alouette—ah!*
Alouette, gentille alouette, alouette, je te plumerai.

**3.** Alouette, gentille alouette, alouette, je te plumerai.
Je te plumerai les yeux, je te plumerai les yeux,
    Et les yeux, et les yeux,
    Et le bec, et le bec,
    Et la tête, et la tête,
    *Alouette, alouette—ah!*
Alouette, gentille alouette, alouette, je te plumerai.

**4.** Alouette, gentille alouette, alouette, je te plumerai.
Je te plumerai les ailes, je te plumerai les ailes,
    Et les ailes, et les ailes,
    Et les yeux, et les yeux,
    Et le bec, et le bec,
    Et la tête, et la tête,
    *Alouette, alouette—ah!*
Alouette, gentille alouette, alouette, je te plumerai.

**5.** Alouette, gentille alouette, alouette, je te plumerai.
Je te plumerai le dos, je te plumerai le dos,
    Et le dos, et le dos,
    Et les ailes, et les ailes
    Et les yeux, et les yeux,
    Et le bec, et le bec,
    Et la tête, et la tête,
    *Alouette, alouette—ah!*
Alouette, gentille alouette, alouette, je te plumerai.

**6.** Alouette, gentille alouette, alouette, je te plumerai.
Je te plumerai les jambes, je te plumerai les jambes,
    Et les jambes, et les jambes
    Et le dos, et le dos,
    Et les ailes, et les ailes,
    Et les yeux, et les yeux,
    Et le bec, et le bec,
    Et la tête, et la tête,
    *Alouette, alouette—ah!*
Alouette, gentille alouette, alouette, je te plumerai.

**7.** Alouette, gentille alouette, alouette, je te plumerai.
Je te plumerai les pieds, je te plumerai les pieds,
    Et les pieds, et les pieds,
    Et les jambes, et les jambes

Et le dos, et le dos,
Et les ailes, et les ailes
Et les yeux, et les yeux,
Et le bec, et le bec,
Et la tête, et la tête,
*Alouette, alouette—ah!*
Alouette, gentille alouette, alouette, je te plumerai.


# The Alphabet Song
CHILDREN'S PLAY SONG
*(same melody as "Twinkle, Twinkle, Little Star"*
*as well as "Ah! Vous Dirai-je, Maman")*

A B C D E F G,
H I J K L-M-N-O-P,
Q R S and T U V,
Double-U [W] and X Y Z.

Now you've heard my A B C's,
Tell me what you think of me.


# Amazing Grace
AMERICAN FOLK SONG

1. Amazing grace! How sweet the sound
That saved a wretch like me!
I once was lost, but now am found,
Was blind but now I see.

2. 'Twas grace that taught my heart to fear
And grace my fears relieved,
How precious did that grace appear
The hour I first believed!

3. Through many dangers, toils and snares,
I have already come.
'Tis grace hath brought me safe thus far,
And grace will lead me home.

4. When we've been there ten thousand years,
Bright shining as the sun,
We've no less days to sing God's praise
Than when we first begun.

# America
## (My Country! 'Tis of Thee)

W: SAMUEL FRANCIS SMITH (1831)

M: ANON. *(from the English anthem "God Save the King,"
itself possibly based on an unknown English ballad)*

1. My country! 'tis of thee,
   Sweet land of liberty,
     Of thee I sing;
   Land where my fathers died,
   Land of the pilgrim's pride,
   From every mountain side,
     Let freedom ring.

2. Our fathers' God! to thee,
   Author of liberty!
     To thee we sing;
   Long may our land be bright
   With freedom's holy light;
   Protect us by thy might,
     Great God, our King!

3. My native country! thee,
   Land of the noble free,
     Thy name I love;
   I love thy rocks and rills,
   Thy woods and templed hills:
   My heart with rapture thrills,
     Like that above.

4. Let music swell the breeze,
   And sing from all the trees
     Sweet freedom's song;
   Let mortal tongues awake;
   Let all that breathe partake;
   Let rocks their silence break,
     The sound prolong.

# America the Beautiful

W: KATHERINE LEE BATES (1895)
M: SAMUEL A. WARD (1882)
*(melody originally known as "Materna")*

1. Oh, beautiful for spacious skies,
   For amber waves of grain,
   For purple mountain majesties
   Across the fruited plain,

   *America! America!*
   God shed His grace on thee,
   And crown thy good with brotherhood
   From sea to shining sea.

2. Oh, beautiful for Pilgrim feet
   Whose stern impassioned stress
   A thoroughfare for freedom beat
   Across the wilderness.

   *America! America!*
   God mend thine every flaw;
   Confirm thy soul in self-control,
   Thy liberty in law.

3. Oh, beautiful for heroes proved
   In liberating strife,
   Who more than self their country loved,
   And mercy more than life.

   *America! America!*
   May God thy gold refine
   Till all success be nobleness
   And ev'ry gain divine.

4. Oh, beautiful for patriot dream
   That sees beyond the years,
   Thine alabaster cities gleam
   Undimmed by human tears.

   *America! America!*
   God shed His grace on thee,
   And crown thy good with brotherhood
   From sea to shining sea.

# Anchors Aweigh

SONG OF THE UNITED STATES NAVY
W & M: CAPT. ALFRED H. MILES, U.S.N. (Ret.)
& CHARLES A. ZIMMERMAN (1907)

1. Stand, Navy, out to sea,
   Fight our battle cry;
   We'll never change our course,
   So vicious foe, steer shy-y-y-y.

   Roll out the T.N.T.,
   Anchors aweigh,
   Sail on to victory,
   And sink their bones to Davy Jones, hooray!

2. Anchors aweigh, my boys,
   Anchors aweigh,
   Farewell to college joys,
   We sail at break of day-day-day-day.

   Through our last night on shore,
   Drink to the foam,
   Until we meet once more,
   Here's wishing you a happy voyage home.

3. Stand, Navy, down the field,
   Sail set to the sky!
   We'll never change our course,
   So, Army, you steer shy-y-y-y.

   Roll up the score, Navy,
   Anchors aweigh,
   Sail, Navy, down the field,
   And sink the Army, sink the Army gray.


# Angels, from the Realms of Glory

W & M: JAMES MONTGOMERY (19th c.)

1. Angels, from the realms of glory,
   Wing your flight o'er all the earth;
   Ye who sang creation's story,
   Now proclaim Messiah's birth.
      *Come and worship,*
      *Come and worship,*
      *Worship Christ, the newborn King!*

2. Shepherds, in the fields abiding,
   Watching o'er your flocks by night,

14

God with man is now residing;
Yonder shines the infant Light.
*Come and worship,*
*Come and worship,*
*Worship Christ, the newborn King!*

3. Sages, leave your contemplations;
Brighter visions beam afar;
Seek the great Desire of Nations;
Ye have seen his natal star.
*Come and worship,*
*Come and worship,*
*Worship Christ, the newborn King!*

4. Saints, before the altar bending,
Watching long in hope and fear,
Suddenly, the Lord descending,
In his temple shall appear.
*Come and worship,*
*Come and worship,*
*Worship Christ, the newborn King!*


# Angels We Have Heard on High

TRADITIONAL FRENCH NOEL
*(anonymous English translation)*

1. Angels we have heard on high,
Sweetly singing o'er the plains,
And the mountains in reply,
Echoing their joyous strains.
*Gloria in excelsis Deo;*
*Gloria in excelsis Deo.*

2. Shepherds, why this jubilee?
Why your joyous strains prolong?
What the gladsome tidings be
That inspire your heav'nly song?
*Gloria in excelsis Deo;*
*Gloria in excelsis Deo.*

3. Come to Bethlehem and see
Him whose birth the angels sing;
Come, adore on bended knee,
Christ the Lord, the newborn King.
*Gloria in excelsis Deo;*
*Gloria in excelsis Deo.*

# Annabel Lee

W: EDGAR ALLAN POE (1849-50) / M: ANON.

It was many and many a year ago,
    In a kingdom by the sea,
That a maiden there lived whom you may know
    By the name of Annabel Lee.
And this maiden lived with no other thought
    Than to love and be loved by me.

I was a child and *she* was a child,
    In this kingdom by the sea:
But we loved with a love that was more than love—
    I and my Annabel Lee.
With a love that the winged seraphs of heaven
    Coveted her and me.

And this was the reason that, long ago,
    In this kingdom by the sea,
A wind blew out of a cloud, chilling
    My beautiful Annabel Lee;
So that her high-born kinsman came
    And bore her away from me,
To shut her up in a sepulchre
    In this kingdom by the sea.

The angels, not half so happy in heaven,
    Went envying her and me—
Yes!—that was the reason (as all men know,
    In this kingdom by the sea)
That the wind came out of the cloud by night,
    Chilling and killing my Annabel Lee.

But our love it was stronger by far than love
    Of those who were older than we—
    Of many far wiser than we—
And neither the angels in heaven above,
    Nor the demons under the sea,
Can ever dissever my soul from the soul
    Of the beautiful Annabel Lee,

For the moon never beams, without bringing me dreams
    Of the beautiful Annabel Lee;
And the stars never rise, but I feel the bright eyes
    Of the beautiful Annabel Lee;
And so, all the night-tide, I lie down by the side
Of my darling—my darling—my life and my bride,
    In the sepulchre there by the sea,
    In her tomb by the sounding sea.

# Annie Laurie

W: WILLIAM DOUGLAS(?) (18th c.)
M: LADY JOHN SCOTT (1835)

1. Maxwellton braes are bonnie,
   Where early fa's the dew,
   And it's there that Annie Laurie
   Gie'd me her promise true.

   Gie'd me her promise true,
   Which ne'er forgot will be;
   *And for bonnie Annie Laurie,*
   *I'd lay me doon and dee.*

2. Her brow is like the snowdrift,
   Her neck is like the swan,
   Her face it is the fairest
   That e'er the sun shone on.

   That e'er the sun shone on,
   And dark blue is her e'e;
   *And for bonnie Annie Laurie,*
   *I'd lay me doon and dee.*

3. Like dew on the gowan lying,
   Is the fa' o' her fairy feet;
   And like winds in summer sighing,
   Her voice is low and sweet.

   Her voice is low and sweet,
   And she's a' the world to me,
   *And for bonnie Annie Laurie,*
   *I'd lay me doon and dee.*


# The Ash Grove
WELSH FOLK SONG

The ash grove, how graceful,
   how plainly 'tis speaking,
The harp through it playing
   as language for me.
Wherever the light
   through its branches is breaking,
I see the kind faces of friends,
   of friends dear to me.

The friends of my childhood
again are before me,
Each step brings a mem'ry
as freely I roam.
With soft whispers speaking,
its leaves rustle near me,
The ash grove, the ash grove
alone is my home.

# As I Walked Out in the Streets of Laredo

AMERICAN COWBOY SONG

1. As I walked out in the streets of Laredo,
   As I walked out in Laredo one day,
   I spied a poor cowboy wrapped up in white linen,
   Wrapped up in white linen and cold as the clay.

2. "I see by your outfit that you are a cowboy,"
   These words he did say as I boldly stepped by.
   "Come sit down beside me and hear my sad story;
   I was shot in the breast and I know I must die.

3. "Let sixteen gamblers come handle my coffin,
   Let sixteen cowboys come sing me a song,
   Take me to the graveyard and lay a sod o'er me,
   For I'm a poor cowboy and I know I've done wrong.

4. "It was once in the saddle I used to go dashing,
   It was once in the saddle I used to go gay.
   'Twas first to drinking and then to card playing,
   Got shot in the breast, I am dying today.

5. "Get six jolly cowboys to carry my coffin,
   Get six pretty girls to carry my pall;
   Put bunches of roses all over my coffin,
   Put roses to deaden the clods as they fall.

6. "O beat the drum slowly and play the fife lowly
   And play the dead march as you carry me along,
   Take me to the green valley and lay the sod o'er me,
   For I'm a young cowboy and I know I've done wrong."

7. We beat the drum slowly and played the fife lowly,
   And bitterly wept as we bore him along;
   For we all loved our comrade, so brave, young and handsome,
   We all loved our comrade although he'd done wrong.

# Asleep in the Deep
W: ARTHUR J. LAMB / M: H. W. PETRIE (1897)

1. Stormy the night and the waves roll high,
   Bravely the ship doth ride;
   Hark! while the lighthouse bell's solemn cry
   Rings o'er the sullen tide . . .

   There on the deck see two lovers stand,
   Heart to heart beating and hand in hand,
   Tho' death be near, she knows no fear,
   While at her side is one all most dear.

   *Chorus:*
   Loudly the bell in the old tower rings,
   Bidding us list to the warning it brings . . .
   Sailor, take care! Sailor, take care!
   Danger is near thee, Beware! Beware!
   Beware! Beware!

   Many brave hearts are asleep in the deep,
   So beware! Beware!
   Many brave hearts are asleep in the deep,
   So beware! Beware!

2. What of the storm when the night is o'er?
   There is no trace or sign!
   Save where the wreckage hath strewn the shore,
   Peaceful the sun doth shine . . .

   But when the wild raging storm did cease,
   Under the billows two hearts found peace,
   No more to part, no more of pain,
   The bell may now toll its warning in vain . . .

   [*to Chorus*]


# At a Georgia Campmeeting
## (A Song in Black)
W & M: KERRY MILLS (1897)

1. A campmeeting took place by the colored race,
      'Way down in Georgia;
         There were blacks large and small,
         lanky, lean, fat and tall,
      At this great black campmeeting.

19

When church was out, how the "Sisters" did shout,
    They were so happy;
    But the young folks were tired
    and wished to be inspired,
    And hired a big brass band.

2. The old "Sisters" raised sand when they first heard the band,
    'Way down in Georgia;
    The preacher did rare
    and the deacons did stare
    At the young darkies prancing.

The band played so sweet that nobody could eat,
    'Twas so entrancing;
    So the church folks agreed
    'twas not a sinful deed,
    And joined in with the rest.

# Au Clair de la Lune

FRENCH FOLK SONG

1. Au clair de la lune,
    Mon ami Pierrot,
    Prête-moi ta plume
    Pour écrire un mot.

    Ma chandelle est morte,
    Je n'ai plus de feu;
    Ouvre-moi ta porte
    Pour l'amour de Dieu.

2. Au clair de la lune
    Pierrot répondit:
    Je n'ai pas de plume,
    Je suis dans mon lit.

    Va chez la voisine,
    Je crois qu'elle y est,
    Car, dans sa cuisine,
    On bat le briquet.

3. Au clair de la lune
    Pierrot se rendort,
    Il rêve à la lune,
    Son cœur bat bien fort:

    Car toujours si bonne
    Pour l'enfant tout blanc,
    La lune lui donne
    Son croissant d'argent!

# Auld Lang Syne

W: ROBERT BURNS (late 18th c.)

M: ANON. *(from various sources,
including "The Duke of Bucclugh's Tune," 1687)*

1. Should auld acquaintance be forgot,
   And never brought to mind?
   Should auld acquaintance be forgot
   And auld lang syne!

   *Chorus:*
   For auld lang syne, my dear,
   For auld lang syne,
   We'll tak a cup o' kindness yet
   For auld lang syne!

2. And surely ye'll be your pint-stowp,
   And surely I'll be mine,
   And we'll tak a cup o' kindness yet
   For auld lang syne!

   [*to Chorus*]

3. We twa hae run about the braes,
   And pou'd the gowans fine,
   But we've wander'd monie a weary fit
   Sin' auld lang syne.

   [*to Chorus*]

4. We twa hae paidl'd in the burn
   Frae morning sun till dine,
   But seas between us braid hae roar'd
   Sin' auld lang syne.

   [*to Chorus*]

5. And there's a hand, my trusty fiere,
   And gie's a hand o' thine,
   We'll tak a right guid-willie waught
   For auld lang syne.

   [*to Chorus*]

# Auprès de Ma Blonde

FRENCH MARCHING SONG

1. Dans les jardins d'mon père
   Les lilas sont fleuris,
   Tous les oiseaux du monde
   Vienn't y faire leurs nids.

   *Chorus:*
   Auprès de ma blonde
   Qu'il fait bon, fait bon, fait bon,
   Auprès de ma blonde
   Qu'il fait bon dormir.

2. Tous les oiseaux du monde
   Vienn't faire leurs nids,
   La caill', la tourterelle
   Et la joli' perdrix.

   [*to Chorus*]

3. La caill', la tourterelle
   Et la joli' perdrix
   Et ma joli' colombe
   Qui chante jour et nuit.

   [*to Chorus*]

4. Et ma joli' colombe
   Qui chante jour et nuit,
   Ell' chante pour les filles
   Qui n'ont pas de mari.

   [*to Chorus*]

   [*plus numerous verses*]

# Aura Lea

W: W. W. FOSDICK / M: GEORGE R. POULTON (1861)
*(In 1956, Elvis Presley and Vera Matson wrote
"Love Me Tender," new lyrics set to the same melody.)*

1. When the blackbird in the spring,
   On the willow tree
   Sat and rocked, I heard him sing,
   Singing Aura Lea.

   *Chorus:*
   Aura Lea, Aura Lea,
   Maid of golden hair;
   Sunshine came along with thee,
   And swallows in the air.

2. On her cheek the rose was born,
   'Twas music when she spake,
   In her eyes, the rays of morn
   With sudden splendor break.

   *Chorus:*
   Aura Lea, Aura Lea,
   Maid of golden hair,
   Sunshine came along with thee,
   And swallows in the air.

3. Aura Lea, the bird may flee,
   The willow's golden hair
   Swing through winter fitfully
   On cold and stormy air.

   *Chorus:*
   Yet if thine eyes I see,
   Gloom will soon depart,
   For to me, sweet Aura Lea
   Is sunshine through my heart.

4. When the mistletoe was green
   Amidst the winter's snows,
   Sunshine in thy face was seen
   And kissing lips of rose.

   *Chorus:*
   Aura Lea, Aura Lea,
   Take my golden ring.
   Love and light return with thee
   And swallows in the spring.

# Ave Maria

W: LATIN HYMN / M: VARIOUS SETTINGS:

*(The best-known musical setting is by Charles Gounod, 1853,*
*originally entitled "Méditation sur le 1<sup>er</sup> Prélude de Piano de S. Bach"—*
*an instrumental piece to which words were later added.*
*Franz Schubert's "Ave Maria," 1825, is set to a German text*
*based on English words by Sir Walter Scott,*
*bearing no relation to the Roman Catholic prayer.)*

Ave Maria,
gratia plena,
Dominus tecum!
Benedictus tu in mulieribus!
et benedictus fructus ventris tui, Jesus.

Sancta Maria,
Ora pro nobis,
nobis peccatoribus,
nunc et in hora mortis nostrae!
Ave! Ave!


# Away in a Manger

TRADITIONAL CHRISTMAS SONG

1. Away in a manger, no crib for his bed,
   The little Lord Jesus laid down his sweet head.
   The stars in the sky looked down where he lay,
   The Little Lord Jesus, asleep on the hay.

2. The cattle are lowing, the poor baby wakes,
   But little Lord Jesus, no crying he makes.
   I love thee, Lord Jesus, look down from the sky,
   And stay by my cradle till morning is nigh.

3. Be near me, Lord Jesus, I ask thee to stay
   Close by me forever and love me, I pray!
   Bless all the dear children in thy tender care,
   And take us to heaven, to live with thee there.

# Baa! Baa! Black Sheep

NURSERY SONG
*(same melody as "Twinkle, Twinkle, Little Star")*

> Baa! Baa! Black sheep,
> Have you any wool?
> Yes, sir! Yes, sir!
> Three bags full.
>
> One for my master
> And one for my dame,
> And one for the little boy
> Who lives down the lane.
>
> Baa! Baa! Black sheep,
> Have you any wool?
> Yes, sir! Yes, sir!
> Three bags full.


# Ballin' the Jack

W: JAMES H. BURRIS / M: CHRIS SMITH (1913)

1. Folks in Georgia's 'bout to go insane
   Since that new dance down in Georgia came;
   I'm the only person who's to blame,
   I'm the party introduced it there, so!

   Give me some credit to know a thing or two,
   Give me credit for springing something new;
   I will show this little dance to you,
   When I do, you'll say that it's a bear.

   *Chorus:*
   First you put your two knees close up tight,
   Then you sway 'em to the left, then you sway 'em to the right;
   Step around the floor kind of nice and light,
   Then you twis' around and twis' around with all your might;

   Stretch your lovin' arms straight out in space,
   Then you do the Eagle Rock with style and grace;
   Swing your foot 'way 'round, then bring it back,
   Now that's what I call "Ballin' the Jack."

2. It's being done at all the cabarets,
   All society now has got the craze;
   It's the best dance done in modern days,
   That's why I rave about it so.

   Play some good Rag that will make you prance,
   Old folks, young folks, all try to do the dance;
   Join right in now while you got the chance,
   Once again the steps to you I'll show.

   [*to Chorus*]


# La Bamba
MEXICAN FOLK SONG

Para bailar la Bamba,
Para bailar la Bamba
Se necesita una poca de gracia,
Una poca de gracia y otra cosita.

*Ay arriba y arriba,*
*Ay arriba, ay arriba y arriba iré.*
Yo no soy marinero,
Yo no soy marinero
Por ti seré, por ti seré, por ti seré.

Una niña en un baile se lamentaba
Zapatito de raso,
Zapatito de raso que le apretaba.

*Ay arriba y arriba,*
*Ay arriba, ay arriba y arriba iré.*
Yo no soy marinero . . .

# The Band Played On
W & M: JOHN F. PALMER (1895)

1. Matt Casey formed a social club that beat the town for style
And hired for a meeting place a hall.
When payday came around each week they greased the floor with wax,
And they danced with noise and vigor at the ball.

Each Saturday you'd see them dressed up in Sunday clothes,
Each lad would have his sweetheart by his side.
When Casey led the first grand march they all would fall in line
'Behind the man who was their joy and pride.
  For—

  *Chorus:*
  Casey would waltz with a strawberry blonde
  And the band played on.
  He'd glide 'cross the floor with the girl he adored
  And the band played on.

  But his brain was so loaded it nearly exploded,
  The poor girl would shake with alarm.
  He'd ne'er leave the girl with the strawberry curls
  And the band played on.

2. Such kissing on the corner and such whisp'ring in the hall
And telling tales of love behind the stairs.
As Casey was the favorite and he that ran the ball
Of the kissing and love-making did his share.

At twelve o'clock exactly they all would fall in line
Then march down to the dining hall and eat,
But Casey would not join them although ev'rything was fine
But he stayed upstairs and exercised his feet.
  For—

  [*to Chorus*]

3. Now when the dance was over and the band played "Home Sweet Home,"
They played a tune at Casey's own request.
He thanked them very kindly for the favors they had shown
Then he'd waltz once with the girl that he loved best.

Most all the friends are married that Casey used to know
And Casey too has taken him a wife,
The blonde he used to waltz and glide with on the ballroom floor
Is happy Missis Casey now for life.
  For—

  [*to Chorus*]

27

# Barbara Allen

ENGLISH FOLK SONG

1. In Scarlet Town, where I was born,
   There was a fair maid dwellin',
   Made ev'ry youth cry well-a-day!
   Her name was Barb'ra Allen.

2. All in the merry month of May,
   When green buds they were swellin',
   Sweet William on his death-bed lay,
   For love of Barb'ra Allen.

3. He sent his servant to the town,
   He sent him to her dwelling,
   Sayin', "Master's sick, he's very sick,
   For the love of Barb'ra Allen."

4. Then slowly, slowly she got up,
   And slowly she came nigh to him;
   And all she said when she got there,
   "Young man, I think you're dyin'."

5. When he was dead and in his grave,
   Her heart was filled with sorrow,
   "Oh, mother dear, go make my bed,
   For I shall die tomorrow."

6. And as she on her death-bed lay,
   Begged to be buried by him,
   And she repented of the day
   That she did e'er deny him.

7. "Farewell, farewell, ye maidens all,
   And shun the fault I fell in;
   So now take warning by the fall
   Of cruel Barb'ra Allen."

8. They buried her in the churchyard,
   And William's buried by her;
   A red rose grew from William's breast,
   And from her feet there grew a briar.

9. They grew as high as the church top,
   They could not grow any higher;
   There they tied in a lover's knot,
   For all true lovers to admire.

# The Battle Cry of Freedom

W & M: GEORGE F. ROOT (1862)

1. Yes, we'll rally 'round the flag, boys, we'll rally once again,
Shouting the battle cry of freedom,
We will rally from the hillside, we'll gather from the plain,
Shouting the battle cry of freedom.

   *Chorus:*
   The Union forever, hurrah, boys, hurrah!
   Down with the traitor, up with the star;
   While we rally 'round the flag, boys, rally once again,
   Shouting the battle cry of freedom.

2. We are springing to the call for three hundred thousand more,
Shouting the battle cry of freedom,
And we'll fill the vacant ranks of our brothers gone before,
Shouting the battle cry of freedom.

   [*to Chorus*]

3. We will welcome to our numbers the loyal true and brave,
Shouting the battle cry of freedom,
And altho' he may be poor he shall never be a slave,
Shouting the battle cry of freedom.

   [*to Chorus*]

4. So we're springing to the call from the east and from the west,
Shouting the battle cry of freedom,
And we'll hurl the rebel crew from the land we love the best,
Shouting the battle cry of freedom.

   [*to Chorus*]


# Battle Hymn of the Republic

W: JULIA WARD HOWE (1862)
M: "GLORY, HALLELUJAH" (Anon., 1857?)
*(same melody as "John Brown")*

1. Mine eyes have seen the glory of the coming of the Lord:
He is trampling out the vintage where the grapes of wrath are stored;
He has loosed the fateful lightning of His terrible swift sword:
His truth is marching on.

   *Chorus:*
   Glory! Glory, Hallelujah!
   Glory! Glory, Hallelujah!

29

Glory! Glory, Hallelujah!
His truth is marching on.

2. I have seen Him in the watch-fires of a hundred circling camps,
   They have builded Him an altar in the evening dews and damps;
   I can read His righteous sentence by the dim and flaring lamps:
   His day is marching on.

   [*to Chorus*]

3. I have read a fiery gospel writ in burnished rows of steel:
   "As ye deal with my contemners, so with you my grace shall deal;
   Let the Hero born of woman crush the serpent with his heel,
   Since God is marching on.

   [*to Chorus*]

4. He has sounded forth the trumpet that shall never call retreat;
   He is sifting out the hearts of men before His judgment seat:
   Oh, be swift, my soul, to answer Him! be jubilant, my feet!
   Our God is marching on.

   [*to Chorus*]

5. In the beauty of the lilies Christ was born across the sea,
   With a glory in his bosom that transfigures you and me;
   As he died to make men holy, let us die to make men free,
   While God is marching on.

   [*to Chorus*]


# Beautiful Dreamer

W & M: STEPHEN C. FOSTER (1864)

1. Beautiful dreamer, wake unto me,
   Starlight and dewdrops are waiting for thee.
   Sounds of the rude world heard in the day,
   Lulled by the moonlight have all passed away.

   Beautiful dreamer, queen of my song,
   List while I woo thee with soft melody.
   Gone are the cares of life's busy throng,
     Beautiful dreamer, awake unto me.
     Beautiful dreamer, awake unto me.

2. Beautiful dreamer, out on the sea,
   Mermaids are chanting the wild Lorelei.
   Over the streamlet vapors are borne,
   Waiting to fade at the bright coming morn.

   Beautiful dreamer, beam on my heart,
   E'en as the morn on the streamlet and sea.
   Then will all clouds of sorrow depart,
   Beautiful dreamer, awake unto me.
   Beautiful dreamer, awake unto me.

# Beautiful Isle of Somewhere

W: JESSIE B. POUNDS / M: J. S. FEARIS (1897)

1. Somewhere the sun is shining,
   Somewhere the songbirds dwell;
   Hush, then, thy sad repining,
   God lives, and all is well.

   Somewhere, somewhere,
   Beautiful Isle of Somewhere!
   Land of the true,
   Where we live anew,
   Beautiful Isle of Somewhere!

2. Somewhere the day is longer,
   Somewhere the task is done;
   Somewhere the heart is stronger,
   Somewhere the guerdon won.

   Somewhere, somewhere,
   Beautiful Isle of Somewhere!
   Land of the true,
   Where we live anew,
   Beautiful Isle of Somewhere!

3. Somewhere the load is lifted,
   Close by an open gate;
   Somewhere the clouds are rifted,
   Somewhere the angels wait.

   Somewhere, somewhere,
   Beautiful Isle of Somewhere!
   Land of the true,
   Where we live anew,
   Beautiful Isle of Somewhere!

# Beautiful Ohio

W: BALLARD MACDONALD / M: "MARY EARL" [Robert A. King] (1918)

Long, long ago,
Someone I know
Had a little red canoe,
In it room for only two;
Love found its start,
Then in my heart,
And like a flower grew.

*Chorus:*
Drifting with the current down a moonlit stream,
While above the heavens in their glory gleam,
    And the stars on high
    Twinkle in the sky;

Seeming in a paradise of love divine,
Dreaming of a pair of eyes that looked in mine,
Beautiful Ohio, in dreams again I see
Visions of what used to be.


# Because

W: EDWARD TESCHEMACHER
M: "GUY D'HARDELOT" [Helen Guy] (1902)

Because you come to me with naught save love
And hold my hand and lift mine eyes above,
A wider world of hope and joy I see
Because you come to me.

Because you speak to me in accents sweet,
I find the roses waking 'round my feet,
And I am led through tears and joy to thee
Because you speak to me.

Because God made thee mine I'll cherish thee
Through light and darkness, through all time to be,
And pray His love may make our love divine
Because God made thee mine.

# Believe Me, If All Those Endearing Young Charms
W: THOMAS MOORE (1808) / M: TRADITIONAL IRISH MELODY

1. Believe me, if all those endearing young charms,
    Which I gaze on so fondly today,
   Were to change by tomorrow and fleet in my arms
    Like fairy gifts fading away,
   Thou would'st still be ador'd as this moment thou art,
    Let thy loveliness fade as it will,
   And around the dear ruin each wish of my heart
    Would entwine itself verdantly still.

2. It is not while beauty and youth are thine own,
    And thy cheeks unprofaned by a tear,
   That the fervor and faith of a soul can be known,
    To which time will but make thee more dear!
   Oh! The heart that has truly loved never forgets,
    But as truly loves on to the close;
   As the sunflower turns on her God, when he sets,
    The same look which she turned when he rose.


# The Belle of Av'noo "A"
W & M: SAFFORD WATERS (1895)

1. I am de belle dey say ov Av'noo "A,"
   And if yer strollin' down dat way,
   Yer pretty sure ter see me on de street.

   'Cos I'm somethin' of a walker,
   And de fact I'm a "Corker,"
   Is de talk ov ev'ry Copper on de beat.

   Billy McNeil he is me steady,
   And yer'll allus find him ready
   For a scrappin' match or any sort of fight.

   He's de bouncer down at Clary's,
   And he says, of all de fairies
   I'm de only one he tinks is out o' sight!

      Git off de earth, and don't attempt to stay,
      'Cos I'm a Queen! De belle ov Av'noo "A."
      *Ta ra ra ra ra ra ra.*

*Chorus:*
I am de belle dey say ov Av'noo "A,"
And yez can bet yer stuff dat I'm up to snuff;
It fairly makes me smile to tink of my style,
'Cos I'm de belle dey say ov Av'noo "A."

Yez ought ter see me spiel wid Billy McNeil,
He is a bouncer, and he's loaded wid sand;
I may be gay, but, say! well, dat is my way,
'Cos I'm de belle ov Av'noo "A."

2. Billy McNeil he says ter me, he says,
   Y' are de stuff, sez he, he sez,
   Der aint no odder girl dats half so sweet.

   And if I marry you, sez he,
   I swear dat I'll be true, sez he,
   And we will make a pair dats hard to beat.

   'Cos if he really tries
   He'll take a feller twic'st his size,
   And he will tump him till he can't begin to see.

   While as sure as my name's Sadie,
   I can polish any lady
   What is anxious fer ter have a scrap wid me!

   Git off de earth and don't attempt to stay,
   'Cos I'm a Queen! De belle ov Av'noo "A."
   *Ta ra ra ra ra ra ra.*

   [*to Chorus*]


# The Bells of St. Mary's
W: DOUGLAS FURBER / M: A. EMMETT ADAMS (1917)

1. The bells of St. Mary's at sweet eventide,
   Shall call me, belovéd, to come to your side;
   And out in the valley, in sound of the sea,
   I know you'll be waiting, yes, waiting for me.

   *Chorus:*
   The Bells of St. Mary's, ah! hear, they are calling
   The young loves, the true loves, who come from the sea;
   And so, my belovéd, when red leaves are falling,
   The love-bells shall ring out, ring out, for you and me.

   *(repeat Chorus)*

**2.** At the porch of St. Mary's I'll wait there with/(for) you,
In your/(my) soft wedding dress with its ribbons of blue;
In the church of St. Mary's, sweet voices shall sing,
For you and me, dearest, the wedding bells ring.

[*to Chorus, repeated*]


# Be My Little Baby Bumblebee
W: STANLEY MURPHY / M: HENRY I. MARSHALL (1912)

Be my little baby bumblebee,
    (Buzz around, buzz around, keep around)
Bring home all the honey, love, to me,
    (Little bee, little bee, little bee).

Let me spend the happy hours
Roving with you 'mongst the flowers,
And when we get where no one else can see
    (Cuddle up, cuddle up, cuddle up).

Be my little baby bumblebee,
    (Buzz around, buzz around, keep around)
We'll be just as happy as can be,
    (You and me, you and me, you and me).

Honey, keep a-buzzin', please,
I've got a dozen cousin bees,
But I want you to be my baby bumblebee.


# The Big Rock Candy Mountain
AMERICAN FOLK SONG

On a summer day in the month of May,
A burly bum came hiking
Down a shady lane, through the sugar cane,
He was looking for his liking.

As he roamed along he sang a song
Of the land of milk and honey,
Where a bum can stay for many a day
And he won't need any money.

*Chorus:*
Oh! the buzzin' of the bees in the Cigarette Trees,
Near the Soda Water Fountain,
At the Lemonade Springs
Where the bluebird sings,
In the Big Rock Candy Mountain.

# Bill Bailey, Won't You Please Come Home?
W & M: HUGHIE CANNON (1902)

1. On one summer's day,
   Sun was shining fine;
   The lady love of old Bill Bailey
   Was hanging clothes on de line
     in her back yard
     and weeping hard.

   She married a B. and O. brakeman
   Dat took and throw'd her down,
   Bellering like a prune-fed calf,
   Wid a big gang hanging 'round;
     and to dat crowd,
     she yelled out loud:

   *Chorus:*
   "Won't you come home, Bill Bailey,
   Won't you come home?"
   She moans de whole day long.

   "I'll do de cooking, darling,
   I'll pay de rent;
   I knows I've done you wrong.

   "'Member dat rainy eve dat I drove you out,
   Wid nothing but a fine tooth comb?
   I knows I'se to blame; well, ain't dat a shame?
   Bill Bailey, won't you please come home?"

2. Bill drove by dat door
   In an automobile,
   A great big diamond, coach and footman;
   Hear dat big wench squeal:
     "He's all alone,"
     hear her groan.

36

She hollered thro' that door,
"Bill Bailey, is you sore?
Stop a minute, won't you listen to me?
Won't I see you no more?"
   Bill winked his eye
   as he heard her cry:

[*to Chorus*]


# Billy Boy
TRADITIONAL

1. Oh, where have you been, Billy Boy, Billy Boy?
   Oh, where have you been, charming Billy?
     *I have been to seek a wife, she's the joy of my life,*
     *She's a young thing and cannot leave her mother.*

2. Did she bid you to come in, Billy Boy, Billy Boy?
   Did she bid you to come in, charming Billy?
     *Yes, she bade me to come in, there's a dimple in her chin,*
     *She's a young thing and cannot leave her mother.*

3. Did she set for you a chair, Billy Boy, Billy Boy?
   Did she set for you a chair, charming Billy?
     *Yes, she set for me a chair, she has ringlets in her hair,*
     *She's a young thing and cannot leave her mother.*

4. Can she make a cherry pie, Billy Boy, Billy Boy?
   Can she make a cherry pie, charming Billy?
     *She can make a cherry pie, quick as a cat can wink her eye,*
     *She's a young thing and cannot leave her mother.*

5. How old is she, Billy Boy, Billy Boy?
   How old is she, charming Billy?
     *She's three-times six, four-times seven, twenty-eight and eleven,*
     *She's a young thing and cannot leave her mother.*

*(This conversation continues through many verses with numerous variants.)*

# A Bird in a Gilded Cage
W: ARTHUR J. LAMB / M: HARRY VON TILZER (1900)

1. The ballroom was filled with fashion's throng,
   It shone with a thousand lights,
   And there was a woman who passed along,
   The fairest of all the sights.

   A girl to her lover then softly sighed,
   There's riches at her command;
   But she married for wealth, not for love, he cried,
   Though she lives in a mansion grand.

   *Chorus:*
   She's only a bird in a gilded cage,
   A beautiful sight to see,
   You may think she's happy and free from care,
   She'd not, though she seems to be.

   'Tis sad when you think of her wasted life,
   For youth cannot mate with age,
   And her beauty was sold for an old man's gold,
   She's a bird in a gilded cage.

2. I stood in a churchyard just at eve',
   When sunset adorned the west,
   And looked at the people who'd come to grieve
   For loved ones now laid at rest.

   A tall marble monument marked the grave
   Of one who'd been fashion's queen,
   And I thought she is happier here at rest
   Than to have people say when seen:

   [*to Chorus*]


# Black Is the Color of My True Love's Hair
APPALACHIAN FOLK SONG

   Black, black, black,
   Is the color of my true love's hair.
   Those lips are like some rosy fair;
   The purest eyes and the neatest hands,
   I love the grass whereon she stands.

How I love my love
And well she knows,
I love the grass whereon she goes:
When she on earth no more I see,
My life will quickly over be.

# Blow the Man Down

HAULING CHANTY (possibly British) (19th c.)

1. Come all ya young fellers that follow the sea
   *With a yo ho, blow the man down*
   Now just pay attention and listen to me.
   *Give me some time to blow the man down*

2. Aboard the Black Baller I first served my time
   *With a yo ho, blow the man down*
   But on the Black Baller I wasted my time.
   *Give me some time to blow the man down*

3. We'd tinkers and tailors and sailors and all
   *With a yo ho, blow the man down*
   That sailed for good seamen aboard the Black Ball.
   *Give me some time to blow the man down*

4. 'Tis larboard and starboard, on deck you will crawl
   *With a yo ho, blow the man down*
   When kicking Jack Williams commands the Black Ball.
   *Give me some time to blow the man down*

5. Now when the Black Baller's preparin' for sea
   *With a yo ho, blow the man down*
   You'd bust your sides laughin' at sights that you see.
   *Give me some time to blow the man down*

6. But when the Black Baller is clear of the land
   *With a yo ho, blow the man down*
   Old kicking Jack Williams gives ev'ry command.
   *Give me some time to blow the man down*

# The Blue Bells of Scotland

W: ANNIE McVICAR GRANT (1799) / M: ANON.

1. Oh where, please tell me where is your highland laddie gone?
   Oh where, please tell me where is your highland laddie gone?
   He's gone with streaming banners where the noble deeds are done,
   And my sad heart will tremble until he comes safely home.

2. Oh where, please tell me where does your highland laddie dwell?
   Oh where, please tell me where does your highland laddie dwell?
   He dwells in merry Scotland at the sign of the blue bell,
   And my blessing went with him on the day he went away.

3. Oh what, please tell me what does your highland laddie wear?
   Oh what, please tell me what does your highland laddie wear?
   A bonnet with a proud plume, 'tis the gallant badge of war,
   And a plaid 'cross his bold breast will one day wear a star.

4. Suppose, oh supposing that your highland laddie should die,
   Suppose, oh supposing that your highland laddie should die,
   The bagpipes shall play o'er him and I'd lay me down and cry.
   But it's oh! in my heart that I do wish he may not die.


# The Boar's Head Carol

TRADITIONAL ENGLISH
*(version from Queen's College, Oxford)*

1. The boar's head in hand bear I,
   Bedecked with bays and rosemary;
   And I pray you, my masters, be merry,
   *Quot estis in convivio.*
       *Caput apri defero,*
       *Reddens laudes Domino.*

2. The boar's head, as I understand,
   Is the rarest dish in all this land,
   Which thus bedeck'd with a gay garland
   Let us *servire cantico.*
       *Caput apri defero,*
       *Reddens laudes Domino.*

3. Our steward hath provided this
   In honour of the King of bliss;
   Which on this day to be servéd is
   *In Reginensi atrio.*
       *Caput apri defero,*
       *Reddens laudes Domino.*

# Bobby Shaftoe

SCOTTISH FOLK SONG

> *Chorus:*
> Bobby Shaftoe's gone to sea,
> Silver buckles at his knee,
> He'll come back and marry me,
> Bonnie Bobby Shaftoe.

1. Bobby Shaftoe's bright and fair,
   Combing down his yellow hair;
   He's my ain for evermair,
   Bonnie Bobby Shaftoe.

2. Bobby Shaftoe's tall and slim,
   Always dressed so neat and trim,
   Lassies they all keek at him,
   Bonnie Bobby Shaftoe.

3. Bobby Shaftoe's getting a bairn,
   For to dangle on his airm;
   In his airm an' on his knee,
   Bonnie Bobby Shaftoe.

> *Chorus:*
> Bobby Shaftoe's gone to sea,
> Silver buckles at his knee,
> He'll come back and marry me,
> Bonnie Bobby Shaftoe.


# The Bowery

W: CHARLES H. HOYT / M: PERCY GAUNT
[from *A Trip to Chinatown,* 1890]

1. Oh! the night that I struck New York,
   I went out for a quiet walk;
   Folks who are "on to" the city say,
   Better by far that I took Broadway;

   But I was out to enjoy the sights,
   There was the Bow'ry a-blaze with lights;
   I had one of the devil's own nights!
   I'll never go there any more!

*Chorus:*
The Bow'ry, the Bow'ry!
They such things, and they do strange things
On the Bow'ry! the Bow'ry!
I'll never go there anymore!

2. I had walk'd but a block or two,
When up came a fellow and me he knew;
Then a policeman came walking by,
Chased him away, and I asked him why?

"Wasn't he pulling your leg," said he;
Said I, "He never laid hands on me!"
"Get off the Bow'ry, you Yep!" said he,
I'll never go there any more!

   [*to Chorus*]

3. I went into an auction store,
I never saw any thieves before;
First he sold me a pair of socks,
Then said he, "How much for the box?"

Someone said, "Two dollars!" I said "Three!"
He emptied the box and gave it to me,
"I sold you the box, not the socks," said he,
I'll never go there any more!

   [*to Chorus*]

4. I went into a concert hall,
I didn't have a good time at all;
Just the minute that I sat down
Girls began singing, "New Coon in Town."

I got up mad and spoke out free,
"Somebody put that man out," said she;
A man called a bouncer attended to me,
I'll never go there any more!

   [*to Chorus*]

5. I went into a barber shop,
He talk'd till I thought he would never stop;
I said, "Cut it short"; he misunderstood,
Clipp'd down my hair just as close as he could.

He shaved with a razor that scratch'd like a pin,
Took off my whiskers and most of my chin;
That was the worst scrape I ever got in,
I'll never go there any more!

[*to Chorus*]

**6.** I struck a place that they called a "dive,"
I was in luck to get out alive;
When the policeman heard my woes,
Saw my black eyes and my battered nose.

"You've been held up!" said the "copper" fly!
"No, sir! but I've been knock'd down," said I;
Then he laughed, tho' I couldn't see why!
I'll never go there any more!

[*to Chorus*]

# Brahms' Lullaby
## ("Wiegenlied")
GERMAN WORDS & ENGLISH TRANSLATION: ANON.
M: JOHANNES BRAHMS (No. 5 of *Fünf Lieder,* Op. 49 / 1868)

*Original text (first stanza)*
Guten Abend, gut' Nacht, mit Rosen bedacht,
Mit Näglein besteckt, schlupf unter die Deck.
Morgen früh, wenn Gott will, wirst du wieder geweckt,
Morgen früh, wenn Gott will, wirst du wieder geweckt.

*English text*
**1.** Lullaby and goodnight, with roses bedight,
With down overspread is baby's wee bed.
Lay thee down now and rest, may thy slumber be blest,
Lay thee down now and rest, may thy slumber be blest.

**2.** Lullaby and goodnight, thy mother's delight,
Bright angels beside my darling abide.
They will guard thee at rest, thou shalt wake on my breast,
They will guard thee at rest, thou shalt wake on my breast.

# Break Forth, O Beauteous, Heav'nly Light

CHRISTMAS SONG

*(anonymous English translation of words by Johann Rist, 17th c., set to a traditional melody)*

Break forth, O beauteous, heav'nly light,
And usher in the morning;
O shepherds, greet that glorious sight,
Our Lord a crib adorning.

This child, this little helpless boy,
Shall be our confidence and joy,
The power of Satan breaking,
Our peace eternal making.

# Bring a Torch, Jeannette, Isabella!

FRENCH NOEL
ENGLISH WORDS: EDWARD C. NUNN

1. Bring a torch, Jeannette, Isabella!
   Bring a torch, to the cradle run!
   It is Jesus, good folk of the village;
   Christ is born and Mary's calling:
   Ah! ah! beautiful is the mother!
   Ah! ah! beautiful is her son!

2. It is wrong when the child is sleeping,
   It is wrong to talk so loud;
   Silence, all, as you gather around,
   Lest your noise should waken Jesus:
   Hush! hush! see how fast he slumbers!
   Hush! hush! see how fast he sleeps!

3. Softly to the little stable,
   Softly for a moment come;
   Look and see how charming is Jesus,
   How he is white, his cheeks are rosy!
   Hush! hush! see how the child is sleeping;
   Hush! hush! see how he smiles in dreams.

# Bringing in the Sheaves

W: KNOWLES SHAW / M: GEORGE A. MINOR

1. Sowing in the morning, sowing seeds of kindness,
Sowing in the noontide and the dewy eve;
Waiting for the harvest and the time of reaping,
We shall come rejoicing, bringing in the sheaves.

   *Chorus:*
   Bringing in the sheaves, bringing in the sheaves,
   We shall come rejoicing, bringing in the sheaves;
   Bringing in the sheaves, bringing in the sheaves,
   We shall come rejoicing, bringing in the sheaves.

2. Sowing in the sunshine, sowing in the shadows,
Fearing neither clouds nor winter's chilling breeze;
By and by the harvest and the labor ended,
We shall come rejoicing, bringing in the sheaves.

   [*to Chorus*]

3. Going forth with weeping, sowing for the Master,
Tho' the loss sustained our spirit often grieves;
When our weeping's over He will bid us welcome,
We shall come rejoicing, bringing in the sheaves.

   [*to Chorus*]


# Brother, Come and Dance with Me

W: ORIGINAL GERMAN ("Brüderchen komm tanz mit mir")
     BY ADELHEID WETTE
M: ENGELBERT HUMPERDINCK
[from *Hansel and Gretel,* 1893]

Brother, come and dance with me,
Both my hands I offer thee,
Right foot first, left foot then,
Round-about and back again.

With your foot, you tap, tap, tap,
With your hand, you clap, clap, clap,
Right foot first, left foot then,
Round-about and back again.

With your head, you nick, nick, nick,
With your fingers you click, click, click,
Right foot first, left foot then,
Round-about and back again.

# Buffalo Gals

W & M: "COOL WHITE" [John Hodges]

1. As I was lumb'ring down the street,
   Down the street, down the street,
   A handsome gal I chanced to meet,
   Oh, she was fair to view.

   *Chorus:*
   Buffalo gals, won'cha come out tonight,
   Come out tonight, come out tonight,
   Buffalo gals, won'cha come out tonight
   And dance by the light of the moon.

2. I asked her if she'd have a talk,
   Have a talk, have a talk,
   Her feet took up the whole sidewalk
   As she stood close to me.

   [*to Chorus*]

3. I asked her, "Would you want to dance,
   Want to dance, want to dance?"
   I thought that I would have a chance
   To shake a foot with her.

   [*to Chorus*]

4. Oh, I danced with the gal with a hole in her stockin',
   And her hip kept a-rockin' and her toe kept a-knockin',
   I danced with the gal with a hole in her stockin',
   And we danced by the light of the moon.

   [*to Chorus*]

5. I wanna make that gal my wife,
   Gal my wife, gal my wife,
   Then I'd be happy all my life
   If I had her with me.

   [*to Chorus*]

# By the Beautiful Sea

W: HAROLD R. ATTERIDGE / M: HARRY CARROLL (1914)

1. Joe and Jane were always together,
   Said Joe to Jane, "I love summer weather,
   So let's go to that beautiful sea,
      Follow along
      Say you're with me!"

   Anything that Joe would suggest to her,
   Jane would always think it was best for her,
      So he'd get his Ford,
      Holler "All aboard.
      Gee! I want to be . . .

         *Chorus:*
         "By the sea, by the sea,
         By the beautiful sea,
         You and I, you and I,
         Oh! how happy we'll be.

         "When each wave comes a-rolling in,
         We will duck or swim,
         And we'll float and fool around the water.

         "Over and under
         And then up for air,
         Pa is rich, Ma is rich,
         So now what do we care?

         "I love to be beside your side,
         Beside the sea, beside the seaside,
         By the beautiful sea."

2. Joe was quite a sport on a Sunday,
   Though he would eat at Childs on a Monday,
   And Jane would lose her millionaire air,
      And go to work,
      Marcelling hair.

   Ev'ry Sunday he'd leave his wife at home,
   Say "It's business, honey, I've got to roam."
      Then he'd miss his train,
      Get his Ford and Jane,
      And say "Come with me . . .

      [*to Chorus*]

47

# By the Light of the Silvery Moon

W: ED MADDEN / M: GUS EDWARDS (1909)

1. Place park, scene dark,
    Silv'ry moon is shining thro' the trees;
    Cast two, me, you,
    Sound of kisses floating on the breeze.

    Act one, begun,
    Dialogue, "Where would you like to spoon?"
    My cue, with you,
    Underneath the silv'ry moon.

    > *Chorus:*
    > By the light of the silvery moon,
    > I want to spoon,
    > To my honey I'll croon love's tune.
    >
    > Honey moon, keep a shining in June,
    > Your silv'ry beams will bring love dreams,
    > We'll be cuddling soon,
    > By the silvery moon.

    > [*repeat Chorus*]

2. Act two, scene new,
    Roses blooming all around the place;
    Cast three, you, me,
    Preacher with a solemn looking face.

    Choir sings, bell rings,
    Preacher: "You are wed forevermore."
    Act two, all through,
    Ev'ry night the same encore.

    > [*to Chorus*]

# The Caissons Go Rolling Along

SONG OF THE UNITED STATES ARTILLERY
W & M: MAJOR EDMUND L. GRUBER (1907)
*(incorrectly credited to John Philip Sousa)*

1. Over hill, over dale, we have hit the dusty trail,
   *And those caissons go rolling along.*
   In and out, hear them shout: "Counter march and right about!"
   *And those caissons go rolling along.*

   *Chorus:*
   Then it's hi! hi! hee! in the field artillery,
   Sound off your numbers loud and strong.
   Where'er you go, you will always know
      *That those caissons are rolling along.*
   (Keep them rolling!)
      *And those caissons go rolling along.*

2. Through the storm, through the night, up to where the doughboys fight,
   *All our caissons go rolling along.*
   At zero we'll be there, answering every call and flare,
   *While our caissons go rolling along.*

   [*to Chorus*]

3. Cavalry, boot to boot, we will join in the pursuit,
   *While those caissons go rolling along.*
   Action front, at a trot; volley fire with shell and shot,
   *While those caissons go rolling along.*

   [*to Chorus*]

4. Should the foe penetrate, every gunner lies in wait,
   *And those caissons go rolling along.*
   Fire at will, lay 'em low, never stop for any foe,
   *While those caissons go rolling along.*

   [*to Chorus*]

5. But if fate me should call, and in action I should fall,
   *Keep those caissons a-rolling along.*
   Then in peace I'll abide when I take my final ride
   *On a caisson that's rolling along.*

   [*to Chorus*]

# The Campbells Are Comin'
TRADITIONAL SCOTTISH

> *Chorus:*
> The Campbells are comin', o-ho, o-ho;
> The Campbells are comin', o-ho, o-ho;
> The Campbells are comin' to bonnie Lochleven:
> The Campbells are comin', o-ho, o-ho.

1. Upon the Lomonds I lay, I lay,
   Upon the Lomonds I lay, I lay;
   I looked down to bonnie Lochlevan,*
   And saw three bonnie pipers play.

   [*to Chorus*]

2. Great Argyle goes before, before,
   He makes the cannons and gun to roar;
   Wi' sound o' trumpet, pipe and drum,
   The Campbells are comin' o-ho, o-ho.

   [*to Chorus*]

3. The Campbells they are a' in arms,
   Their royal faith and truth to show;
   Wi' banners rattlin' in the wind,
   The Campbells are comin', o-ho, o-ho.

   [*to Chorus*]

*The song was said to have been composed on the imprisonment of Mary Queen of Scots in Lochleven Castle in 1567.*


# Camptown Races
W & M: STEPHEN C. FOSTER (1850)

1. The Camptown ladies sing this song,
      *Doo-dah, doo-dah*
   The Camptown racetrack five miles long.
      *Oh doo-dah-day*

   I came there with my hat caved in,
      *Doo-dah, doo-dah*
   I go back home with a pocket full of tin.
      *Oh doo-dah-day*

*Chorus:*
Goin' to run all night,
Goin' to run all day,
I'll bet my money on the bobtail nag,
Somebody bet on the bay.

**2.** The long-tail filly and the big black horse,
   *Doo-dah, doo-dah*
   They fly the track and they both cut across.
   *Oh doo-dah-day*

   The blind horse stickin' in a big mud hole,
   *Doo-dah, doo-dah*
   Can't touch bottom with a ten-foot pole.
   *Oh doo-dah-day*

   [*to Chorus*]

**3.** Old muley cow come on the track,
   *Doo-dah, doo-dah*
   The bobtail fling her over his back.
   *Oh doo-dah-day*

   Then fly along like a railroad car,
   *Doo-dah, doo-dah*
   And runnin' a race with a shootin' star.
   *Oh doo-dah-day*

   [*to Chorus*]

**4.** See them a-flyin' on a ten-mile heat,
   *Doo-dah, doo-dah*
   Around the racetrack, then repeat.
   *Oh doo-dah-day*

   I win my money on the bobtail nag,
   *Doo-dah, doo-dah*
   I keep my money in an old tow bag.
   *Oh doo-dah-day*

   [*to Chorus*]

# Captain Jinks of the Horse Marines

W & M: WILLIAM HORACE LINGARD (1868)

*(An unspecified credit for "T. MacLagen" appears in some sources.)*

1. I'm Captain Jinks of the Horse Marines;
   I often live beyond my means;
   I sport young ladies in their teens,
       To cut a swell in the army.

   I teach young ladies how to dance,
   How to dance, how to dance,
   I teach young ladies how to dance,
       For I'm their pet in the army.

       [*spoken:* "Ha! ha! ha!"]

       *Chorus:*
   I'm Captain Jinks of the Horse Marines;
   I give my horses good corn and beans;
   Of course, 'tis quite beyond my means,
       Tho' a Captain in the army.

2. I joined my corps when twenty-one;
   Of course, I thought it was capital fun;
   When the enemy came, then off I ran;
       I wasn't cut out for the army.

   When I left home, Mama she cried,
   Mama she cried, Mama she cried,
   When I left home, Mama she cried,
       "He ain't cut out for the army."

       [*spoken:* "No; she tho't I was too young;
   but then I said, 'Ah! Mama'—"]

       [*to Chorus*]

3. The first day I went out to drill,
   The bugle-sound made me quite ill;
   At the balance-step, my hat it fell,
       And that wouldn't do for the army.

   The officers they all did shout;
   They all cried out, they all did shout;
   The officers they all did shout,
       "Oh, that's the cure for the army."

       [*spoken:* "Of course, my hat did fall off;
   but ah! nevertheless—"

       [*to Chorus*]

4. My tailor's bills came in so fast,
Forced me one day to leave at last;
And ladies too no more did cast
    Sheep's-eyes at me in the army.

My creditors at me did shout,
At me did shout, at me did shout,
My creditors at me did shout,
    "Why, kick him out of the army."

    [*spoken:* "I said, 'Ah! gentlemen;
    ah! kick me out of the army!
    Perhaps you are not aware that—'"]

    [*to Chorus*]


# Carolina in the Morning
W: GUS KAHN / M: WALTER DONALDSON (1922)

*Chorus:*
Nothing could be finer
than to be in Carolina
    in the morning.
No one could be sweeter
than my sweetie when I meet her
    in the morning.

    Where the morning glories
    Twine around the door,
    Whispering pretty stories
    I long to hear once more.

Strolling with my girlie
where the dew is pearly early
    in the morning.
Butterflies all flutter up
and kiss each little buttercup
    at dawning.

If I had Aladdin's lamp for only a day,
I'd make a wish, and here's what I'd say:
Nothing could be finer
than to be in Carolina
    in the morning.

*Verses:*

1. Wishing is good time wasted,
   Still it's a habit, they say.
   Wishing for sweets I've tasted,
   That's all I do all day.
   Maybe there's nothing in wishing,
   But speaking of wishing, I'll say:

   [*return to Chorus*]

2. Dreaming was meant for nighttime;
   I live in dreams all the day.
   I know it's not the right time,
   But still I dream away.
   What could be sweeter than dreaming,
   Just dreaming and drifting away?

   [*return to Chorus*]

# Carol of the Bells

UKRAINIAN CHRISTMAS CAROL
*(anonymous English version)*

Hark! to the bells, hark! to the bells,
Telling us all Jesus is King!
Strongly they chime, sound with a rhyme,
Christmas is here! Welcome the King!

Hark! to the bells, hark! to the bells,
This is the day, day of the King!
Peal out the news o'er hill and dale,
And 'round the town, telling the tale.

Hark! to the bells, hark! to the bells,
Telling us all Jesus is King!
Come, one and all, happily sing
Songs of good will, O, let them sing!

Ring, silv'ry bells,
Sing, joyous bells!

Strongly they chime, sound with a rhyme,
Christmas is here, welcome the King!
Hark! to the bells, hark! to the bells,
Telling us all Jesus is King!

Ring!
Ring!
Bells!

54

# Carry Me Back to Old Virginny

W & M: JAMES A. BLAND (1878)

1. Carry me back to old Virginny,
   That's where the cotton and the corn and 'taters grow.
   There's where the birds warble sweet in the springtime,
   There's where my old weary heart is long'd to go.

   There's where I labored so hard for my master,
   Day after day in the field of yellow corn.
   No place on earth do I love more sincerely
   Than old Virginny, she's the state where I was born.

2. Carry me back to old Virginny,
   There let me live until I wither and decay.
   Long by the old Dismal Swamp have I wandered,
   There's where my old weary life will pass away.

   Master and Mistress have long gone before me,
   Soon we will meet on the bright and golden shore.
   There we'll be happy and free from all sorrow,
   There's where we'll meet and will never part no more.


# Casey Jones

W: T. LAWRENCE SEIBERT / M: EDDIE NEWTON (1909)

1. Come all you rounders, for I want you to hear
   A story about a brave engineer.
   Casey Jones was the rounder's name,
   On a six eight wheeler, boys, he won his fame.

   The caller called Casey at a half-past four,
   Kissed his wife at the station door,
   Mounted to the cab with his orders in his hand,
   And he took his farewell trip to that promised land.

   *Chorus:*
   Casey Jones! mounted to the cabin,
   Casey Jones! with his orders in his hand;
   Casey Jones! mounted to the cabin
   And he took his farewell trip to that Promised Land.

2. "Put in your water and shovel in your coal,
   Put your head out the window, watch them drivers roll;
   I'll run her till she leaves the rail
   'Cause I'm eight hour late with that western mail."

55

He looked at his watch and his watch was slow,
He looked at the water and the water was low,
He turned to the fireman and he said,
"We're going to reach 'Frisco but we'll all be dead."

> *Chorus:*
> Casey Jones! going to reach 'Frisco,
> Casey Jones! but we'll all be dead;
> Casey Jones! going to reach 'Frisco,
> We're going to reach 'Frisco but we'll all be dead.

3. Casey pulled up that Reno hill,
He tooted for the crossing with an awful shrill;
The firemen knew by the engine's moan
That the man at the throttle was Casey Jones.

He pulled up within two miles of the place,
Number Four stared him right in the face;
Turned to the fireman said, "Boy, you'd better jump
'Cause there's two locomotives that's a-going to bump."

> *Chorus:*
> Casey Jones! two locomotives,
> Casey Jones! that's a-going to bump;
> Casey Jones! two locomotives,
> There's two locomotives that's a-going to bump.

4. Casey said just before he died,
"There's two more roads that I'd like to ride."
Fireman said, "What could that be?"
"The Southern Pacific and the Santa Fe."

Mrs. Jones sat on her bed a-sighing,
Just received a message that Casey was dying;
Said, "Go to bed, children, and hush your crying
'Cause you got another Papa on the Salt Lake line."

> *Chorus:*
> Mrs. Casey Jones! "Got another Papa,"
> Mrs. Casey Jones! "on that Salt Lake line";
> Mrs. Casey Jones! "Got another Papa,
> And you've got another Papa on that Salt Lake line."

# The Cavalry Song

SONG OF THE UNITED STATES CAVALRY
W & M: ANON.

1. Come, listen unto this my song,
   I'm happy as can be;
   I'm a masher and a dasher
   In the U. S. Cavalree.

   I stand up straight with legs apart,
   Bowed slightly at the knee,
   With folded arms across my breast;
   'Tis the pose of the Cavalree.

   *Chorus:*
   So fill your glasses to the brim,
   And brace your courage with sloe gin.
   I tell you all it is a sin
   To belong to the Infantry.

2. I'm a cavalryman so fierce and bold,
   I'm a soldier through and through;
   I ride a horse because, of course,
   It's the proper thing to do.

   I wear my spurs both day and night
   So that everyone may see
   Whatever else I might have been,
   I'm not the Infantry.

   [*to Chorus*]

3. We went to fight the Chino horde,
   With saber, horse and gun;
   We met him and we beat him,
   Just the way it should be done.

   But we left our horses, corn and hay
   Down on the ships in Taku Bay,
   And consequently had to stay
   While the doughboys hiked away.

   [*to Chorus*]

# Charlie Is My Darling

SCOTTISH FOLK SONG

*Chorus:*
Oh! Charlie is my darling,
My darling, my darling,
Oh! Charlie is my darling,
The young Chevalier.

1. 'Twas on a Monday morning,
   Right early in the year,
When Charlie came into our town,
   The young Chevalier.

   [*to Chorus*]

2. As he cam' marchin' up the street,
   The pipes play'd loud and clear;
And a' the folk cam' rinnin' out
   To meet the Chevalier.

   [*to Chorus*]

3. Wi' Hieland bonnets on their heads,
   And claymores bright and clear,
They cam' to fight for Scotland's right,
   And the young Chevalier.

   [*to Chorus*]

4. They've left their bonnie Hieland hills,
   Their wives and bairnies dear,
To draw the sword for Scotland's lord,
   The young Chevalier.

   [*to Chorus*]

5. Oh! there were mony beating hearts,
   And mony a hope and fear;
And mony were the prayers put up
   For the young Chevalier.

   [*to Chorus*]

# The Cherry Tree Carol

TRADITIONAL ENGLISH

Joseph was an old man,
An old man was he:
He married sweet Mary,
The Queen of Galilee.

As they went a-walking,
In the garden so gay,
Maid Mary spied cherries,
Hanging over yon tree.

Mary said to Joseph
With her sweet lips so mild,
"Pluck those cherries, Joseph,
For to give to my child."

"O then," replied Joseph
With words so unkind,
"I will pluck no cherries
For to give to thy child."

Mary said to cherry tree,
"Bow down to my knee,
That I may pluck cherries
By one, two and three."

The uppermost twig then
Bowed down to her knee:
"Thus you may see, Joseph,
These cherries are for me."

"O eat your cherries, Mary,
O eat your cherries now,
O eat your cherries, Mary,
That grow upon the bough."

As Joseph was a-walking
He heard angels sing,
"This night there shall be born
Our heavenly King.

"He neither shall be born
In house nor in hall,
Nor in the place of Paradise,
But in an ox-stall.

"He shall not be clothed
In purple nor pall;
But all in fair linen,
As wear babies all.

"He shall not be rocked
In silver nor gold,
But in a wooden cradle
That rocks on the mould.

"He neither shall be christened
In milk nor in wine,
But in pure spring-well water
Fresh sprung from Bethine."

Mary took her baby,
She dressed him so sweet,
She laid him in a manger
All there for to sleep.

As she stood over him
She heard angels sing,
"Oh! bless our dear Saviour,
Our heavenly King."


# A Child This Day Is Born
ENGLISH CAROL

1. A child this day is born,
   A child of high renown,
   Most worthy of a scepter,
   A scepter and a crown.

   > *Chorus:*
   > Nowell, Nowell, Nowell,
   > Nowell, sing all we may,
   > Because the King of all kings
   > Was born this blessed day.

2. These tidings shepherds heard,
   In field watching their fold,
   Were by an angel unto them
   That night revealed and told.

   > [*to Chorus*]

**3.** To whom the angel spoke,
Saying, "Be not afraid;
Be glad, poor silly shepherds—
Why are you so dismayed?"

  [*to Chorus*]

**4.** "For lo! I bring you tidings
Of gladness and of mirth,
Which cometh to all people by
This Holy Infant's birth."

  [*to Chorus*]

**5.** Then was there with the angel
An host incontinent
Of heavenly bright soldiers,
Which from the Highest was sent.

  [*to Chorus*]

**6.** Lauding the Lord of God,
And his celestial King;
"All glory be in Paradise,"
This heavenly host did sing.

  [*to Chorus*]

**7.** And as the angel told them,
So to them did appear;
They found the young Child, Jesus Christ,
With Mary, his mother dear.

  [*to Chorus*]

# China Boy
W & M: DICK WINFREE & PHIL BOUTELJE (1922)

**1.** Oriental moonbeams thru a willow tree,
Sprinkle light in silv'ry rays.
Almond eyes with baby, crooning song is she,
In her quaint Celestial way:

  *Chorus:*
  "China boy, go sleep,
  Close your eyes, don't peep,
  Sandman soon will come,
  While I softly hum.

61

"Buddha smiles on you,
Moonman loves you, too;
So, while their watch they keep,
China boy, go sleep."

2. Ev'ry day at twilight thru a golden fair,
Almond eyes will wend her way,
China boy she's holding, you can see him there,
And to him she'll softly say:

[*to Chorus*]


# Chinatown, My Chinatown
W: WILLIAM JEROME / M: JEAN SCHWARTZ (1910)

1. When the town is fast asleep,
And it's midnight in the sky,
That's the time the festive Chink
Starts to wink his other eye,
Starts to wink his dreamy eye,
Lazily you'll hear him sigh:

*Chorus:*
Chinatown, my Chinatown,
Where the lights are low,
Hearts that know no other land,
Drifting to and fro.

Dreamy, dreamy Chinatown,
Almond eyes of brown,
Hearts seem light and life seems bright
In dreamy Chinatown.

2. Strangers taking in the sights,
Pigtails flying here and there;
See that broken Wall Street sport
Still thinks he's a millionaire,
Still thinks he's a millionaire,
Pipe dreams banish ev'ry care.

[*to Chorus*]

# The Chisholm Trail

AMERICAN COWBOY SONG

1. Oh, come along boys, and listen to my tale,
   I'll tell you of my troubles on the old Chisholm trail.
   *Come-a ti ya yippy, yippy ya, yippy yeh,*
   *Come-a ti yi yippy, yippy yeh.*

2. I woke up one morning on the old Chisholm trail,
   A rope in my hand and a cow by the tail.
   *Come-a ti ya yippy, yippy ya, yippy yeh,*
   *Come-a ti yi yippy, yippy yeh.*

3. Oh, a ten dollar hoss and a forty dollar saddle,
   I'm going to punching Texas cattle.
   *Come-a ti ya yippy, yippy ya, yippy yeh,*
   *Come-a ti yi yippy, yippy yeh.*

4. Cloudy in the west and looking like rain,
   And my damned old slicker's in the wagon again.
   *Come-a ti ya yippy, yippy ya, yippy yeh,*
   *Come-a ti yi yippy, yippy yeh.*

5. No chaps, no slicker and it's pouring down rain,
   And I swear, by God, I'll never night-herd again.
   *Come-a ti ya yippy, yippy ya, yippy yeh,*
   *Come-a ti yi yippy, yippy yeh.*

6. Last night I was on guard and the cattle broke ranks,
   I hit my hoss along the shoulders and spurred him in the flanks.
   *Come-a ti ya yippy, yippy ya, yippy yeh,*
   *Come-a ti yi yippy, yippy yeh.*

7. The wind began to blow and the rain began to fall,
   And it looked, by God, like we was gonna lose 'em all.
   *Come-a ti ya yippy, yippy ya, yippy yeh,*
   *Come-a ti yi yippy, yippy yeh.*

8. I jumped in the saddle and I grabbed a-hold the horn,
   I'm the best damned cow puncher ever was born.
   *Come-a ti ya yippy, yippy ya, yippy yeh,*
   *Come-a ti yi yippy, yippy yeh.*

9. I herded and I hollered and I done very well,
   Till the boss said, "Boys, just let 'em go to hell."
   *Come-a ti ya yippy, yippy ya, yippy yeh,*
   *Come-a ti yi yippy, yippy yeh.*

**10.** I'm on my best hoss and I'm going at a run,
   I'm the quickest shooting cowboy that ever drawed a gun.
   *Come-a ti ya yippy, yippy ya, yippy yeh,*
   *Come-a ti yi yippy, yippy yeh.*


# Cielito Lindo

*(First published in Mexico, 1919, as a "popular song";*
*later credited to Quirino Mendoza y Cortez, 1929.)*

**1.** De la sierra morena,
   *cielito lindo*
   vienen bajando
   un par de ojitos negros
   *cielito lindo*
   de contrabando.

> *Chorus:*
> ¡Ay, ay, ay, ay!
> canta y no llores,
> porque cantando se alegran
> *cielito lindo*
> los corazones.

**2.** Una flecha en el aire
   *cielito lindo*
   lanzó Cupido
   y como fué jugando,
   *cielito lindo*
   yo fuí el herido.

> *[to Chorus]*

**3.** Pájaro que abandona
   *cielito lindo*
   su primer nido,
   vuelve y lo halla ocupado
   *cielito lindo*
   y muy merecido.

> *[to Chorus]*

**4.** Ese lunar que tienes
   *cielito lindo*
   junto a la boca,
   no se lo des a nadie
   *cielito lindo*
   que a mí me toca.

> *[to Chorus]*

5. Todas las ilusiones
   *cielito lindo*
   que el amor fragua,
   son como las espumas
   *cielito lindo*
   que forma el agua.

   > *Chorus:*
   > ¡Ay, ay, ay, ay!
   > suben y crecen
   > y con el mismo viento
   > *cielito lindo*
   > desaparecen.

# Clementine

W & M: PERCY MONTROSE (1884)

1. In a cavern, in a canyon,
   Excavating for a mine,
   Dwelt a miner, 'Forty-niner,
   And his daughter, Clementine.

   > *Chorus:*
   > Oh, my darling, oh, my darling,
   > Oh, my darling Clementine,
   > You are lost and gone forever,
   > Dreadful sorry, Clementine.

2. Light she was and like a fairy,
   And her shoes were number nine,
   Herring boxes without topses,
   Sandals were for Clementine.

   > [*to Chorus*]

3. Drove she ducklings to the water
   Ev'ry morning just at nine,
   Hit her foot against a splinter,
   Fell into the foaming brine.

   > [*to Chorus*]

4. Ruby lips above the water
   Blowing bubbles soft and fine,
   But alas, I was no swimmer,
   So I lost my Clementine.

   > [*to Chorus*]

5. In a churchyard near the canyon
   Where the myrtle doth entwine,
   There grow roses and the posies
   Fertilized by Clementine.

   *[to Chorus]*

6. Then the miner, 'Forty-niner,
   Soon began to peak and pine.
   Thought he ought-er join his daughter,
   Now he's with his Clementine.

   *[to Chorus]*

7. In my dreams she still doth haunt me,
   Robed in garments soaked in brine,
   Though in life I used to hug her,
   Now she's dead, I'll draw the line.

   *[to Chorus]*

8. How I missed her, how I missed her,
   How I missed my Clementine,
   Then I kissed her little sister
   And forgot my Clementine.

   *[to Chorus]*

# Columbia, the Gem of the Ocean
## (The Red, White and Blue)
W: DAVID T. SHAW / M: THOMAS A. BECKETT (1843)
*(This authorship is unclear, there being considerable controversy over the song's origin as American or English.)*

1. O, Columbia, the gem of the ocean,
   The home of the brave and the free,
   The shrine of each patriot's devotion,
   A world offers homage to thee.

   Thy mandates make heroes assemble,
   When Liberty's form stands in view;
   Thy banners make tyranny tremble,
   When borne by the red, white and blue,

   *Chorus:*
   When borne by the red, white and blue,
   When borne by the red, white and blue;
   Thy banners make tyranny tremble,
   When borne by the red, white and blue.

**2.** When war wing'd its wide desolation,
   And threatened the land to deform,
   The ark then of freedom's foundation,
   Columbia, rode safe thro' the storm;

   With the garlands of vic'try around her,
   When so proudly she bore her brave crew,
   With her flag proudly floating before her,
   The boast of the red, white and blue,

   *Chorus:*
   The boast of the red, white and blue,
   The boast of the red, white and blue;
   With her flag proudly floating before her,
   The boast of the red, white and blue.

**3.** The star-spangled banner bring hither,
   O'er Columbia's true sons let it wave,
   May the wreaths they have won never wither,
   Nor its stars cease to shine on the brave;

   May the service united ne'er sever,
   But hold to their colors so true;
   The Army and Navy forever,
   Three cheers for the red, white and blue,

   *Chorus:*
   Three cheers for the red, white and blue,
   Three cheers for the red, white and blue;
   The Army and Navy forever,
   Three cheers for the red, white and blue.

# Come Back to Erin

W & M: "CLARIBEL" [Charlotte Alington Barnard] (1866)

**1.** Come back to Erin, Mavourneen, Mavourneen,
   Come back, Aroon, to the land of thy birth.
   Come with the shamrocks and springtime, Mavourneen,
   And it's Killarney shall ring with our mirth.

   Sure, when we lent ye to beautiful England,
   Little we tho't of the lone winter days,
   Little we tho't of the hush of the starshine
   Over the mountain, the bluffs and the brays!
   Then—

   *Chorus:*
   Come back to Erin, Mavourneen, Mavourneen,
   Come back again to the land of thy birth,

Come back to Erin, Mavourneen, Mavourneen,
And it's Killarney shall ring with our mirth.

2. Over the green sea, Mavourneen, Mavourneen,
Long shone the white sail that bore ye away,
Riding the white waves that fair summer mornin',
Just like a Mayflow'r afloat on the bay.

Oh, but my heart sank when clouds came between us,
Like a gray curtain, the rain falling down,
Hid from my sad eyes the path o'er the ocean,
Far, far away, where the Colleen had flown.
Then—

   [to Chorus]

3. Oh, may the angels a-wakin' and sleepin'
Watch o'er my bird in the land far away,
And it's my pray'rs will consign to their keepin',
Care of my jewel by night and by day.

When by the fireside I watch the bright embers,
Then all my heart flies to England and thee,
Cravin' to know if my darlin' remembers,
Or if her tho'ts may be crossin' to me.
Then—

   [to Chorus]


# Come, Josephine, in My Flying Machine
## (Up She Goes!)
W: ALFRED BRYAN / M: FRED FISCHER [later, Fisher] (1910)

1. Oh, say! let us fly, dear.
Where, kid? to the sky, dear.
Oh, you flying machine!
Jump in, Miss Josephine.

Ship ahoy! Oh, joy! what a feeling.
Where, boy? In the ceiling.
Ho, high, hoopla!
We fly to the sky so high.

   *Chorus:*
   Come, Josephine, in my flying machine,
   Going up, she goes! up she goes!
   Balance yourself like a bird on a beam,
   In the air she goes, there she goes!

Up, up, a little bit higher.
Oh, my! the moon is on fire.
Come, Josephine, in my flying machine,
Going up, all on, "Good bye!"

[*repeat Chorus*]

2. One, two, now we're off, dear.
Say you, pretty soft, dear.
Whoa! dear, don't hit the moon.
No, dear, not yet but soon.

You for me, Oh, gee! you're a fly kid.
Not me, I'm a sky kid.
Gee! I'm up in the air
About you for fair.

[*to Chorus*]

# Come, Thou Almighty King
W: CHARLES WESLEY (18th c.) / M: FELICE GIARDINI

1. Come, Thou almighty King,
Help us Thy name to sing,
Help us to praise,
Father! all-glorious,
O'er all victorious,
Come and reign over us,
Ancient of days.

2. Come, Thou incarnate Word,
Gird on Thy mighty sword;
Our pray'r attend;
Come, and Thy people bless,
And give Thy word success,
Spirit of holiness!
On us descend.

3. Come, holy Comforter!
Thy sacred witness bear,
In this glad hour.
Thou who almighty art,
Now rule in ev'ry heart,
And ne'er from us depart,
Spirit of pow'r!

**4.** To the great One in Three,
   The highest praises be,
   Hence evermore!
   His sov'reign majesty
   May we in glory see,
   And to eternity
   Love and adore.

# Comin' Thro' the Rye

TRADITIONAL SCOTTISH
*(Although Robert Burns collected an early version of this text,
the authorship of both words and music is unclear.)*

**1.** Gin a body meet a body
   Comin' thro' the rye,
   Gin a body kiss a body,
   Need a body cry?

> *Chorus:*
> Every lassie has her laddie;
> Nane, they say, hae I;
> Yet a' the lads they smile at me
> When comin' thro' the rye.
>
> A-mang the train there is a swain
> I dearly lo'e my sel',
> But whaur his hame, or what his name,
> I dinna care to tell.

**2.** Gin a body meet a body
   Comin' frae the town,
   Gin a body greet a body,
   Need a body frown?

> *[to Chorus]*

**3.** Gin a body meet a body
   Comin' frae the well,
   Gin a body kiss a body—
   Need a body tell?

> *[to Chorus]*

**4.** Ilka Jenny has her Jocky,
   Ne'er ane ha'e I;
   But a' the lads they look at me—
   And what the whaur am I?

> *[to Chorus]*

70

# The Coventry Carol
## (Lully, Lulla)

W: ROBERT CROO (1534) / M: ANON.

**1.** *Lully, lulla, thou little tiny child,*
*By by, lully lullay.*

O sisters too, how may we do
For to preserve this day
This poor youngling,
For whom we do sing,
By by, lully lullay?

> *Lully, lulla, thou little tiny child,*
> *By by, lully lullay.*

**2.** *Lully, lulla, thou little tiny child,*
*By by, lully lullay.*

Herod, the king, in his raging,
Chargéd he hath this day
His men of might,
In his own sight,
All young children to slay.

> *Lully, lulla, thou little tiny child,*
> *By by, lully lullay.*

**3.** *Lully, lulla, thou little tiny child,*
*By by, lully lullay.*

That woe is me, poor child, for thee!
And every morn and day,
For thy parting
Neither say nor sing
By by, lully lullay!

> *Lully, lulla, thou little tiny child,*
> *By by, lully lullay.*

# La Cucaracha

MEXICAN FOLK SONG

1. Cuando uno quiere a una
   Y esta una no lo quiere,
   Es lo mismo que si un calvo
   En la calle encuentr' un peine.

   *Chorus:*
   La cucaracha, la cucaracha,
   Ya no quiere caminar,
   Porque no tiene,
   Porque le falta,
   Marihuana que fumar.

2. Las muchachas son de oro;
   Las casadas son de plata;
   Las viudas son de cobre,
   Y las viejas hoja de lata.

   [*to Chorus*]

3. Mi vecina de enfrente
   Se llamaba Doña Clara,
   Y sí no había muerto
   Es probable se llamara.

   [*to Chorus*]

4. Las muchachas de Las Vegas
   Son muy altas y delgaditas,
   Pero son más pedigüeñas
   Que las animas benditas.

   [*to Chorus*]

5. Mas muchachas de la villa
   No saben ni dar un beso,
   Cuando las de Albuquerque
   Hasta estiran el pescuezo.

   [*to Chorus*]

# Cuddle Up a Little Closer, Lovey Mine

W: "O. A. HAUERBACH" [Otto Harbach] / M: KARL HOSCHNA
[from *Three Twins*, 1908]

1. On the Summer shore
   Where the breakers roar,
     Lovers sat on the glist'ning sand.
   And they talked of love
   While the moon above
     And the stars seemed to understand.

   Then she grew more cold,
   And he grew more bold,
     Till she tho't that they had better go.

   But altho' he heard,
   He not even stirred,
     Only murmured in tones soft and low:

     *Chorus:*
     Cuddle up a little closer, Lovey mine,
     Cuddle up and be my little clinging vine.
       Like to feel your cheek so rosy,
       Like to make you comfy, cozy,
       'Cause I love from head to toesie
     Lovey mine.

2. Then she deigned to rest
   On his manly chest
     Her dear head with its flowing curls.
   And she said, "I'd stay
   On this lap for aye,
     How I envy the Lapland* girls.

   For Miss Esquimaux,
   'Mid the ice and snow,
     Has no steam heat when he comes to call.

   Not a single glim,
   So it's up to him
     To whisper in summer or fall:

     [*to Chorus*]

*spelled* Capland *in the original sheet music*

# Daddy Wouldn't Buy Me a Bow-Wow!

W & M: JOSEPH TABRAR (1892)

1. I love my little cat, I do,
     with soft black silky hair;
   It comes each day with me to school,
     and sits upon the chair.

   When teacher says, "Why do you bring
     that little pet of yours?"
   I tell her that I bring my cat
     along with me because . . .

   *Chorus:*
   Daddy wouldn't buy me a bow-wow!
   Daddy wouldn't buy me a bow-wow!
   Bow-wow, I've got a little cat
   And I'm very fond of that,
   But I'd rather have a bow-wow,
       wow, wow, wow, wow.

2. We used to have two tiny dogs,
     such pretty little dears!
   But Daddy sold 'em 'cos they used
     to bite each other's ears.

   I cried all day, at eight each night,
     Papa sent me to bed;
   When Ma came home and wiped my eyes,
     I cried again and said . . .

   [*to Chorus*]

3. I'll be so glad when I get old,
     to do just as I "likes";
   I'll keep a parrot, and at least
     a half a dozen tykes;

   And when I've got a tiny pet,
     I'll kiss the little thing,
   Then put it in its little cot,
     and unto it I'll sing . . .

   [*to Chorus*]

# Daisy Bell
## (A Bicycle Built for Two)
W & M: HARRY DACRE (1892)

1. There is a flower within my heart,
   Daisy, Daisy!
   Planted one day by a glancing dart,
   Planted by Daisy Bell!

   Whether she loves me or loves me not,
   Sometimes it's hard to tell;
   Yet I am longing to share the lot
   Of beautiful Daisy Bell!

   > *Chorus:*
   > Daisy, Daisy,
   > Give me your answer, do!
   > I'm half crazy
   > All for the love of you!
   >
   > It won't be a stylish marriage,
   > I can't afford a carriage,
   > But you'll look sweet on the seat
   > Of a bicycle built for two!

2. We will go "tandem" as man and wife,
   Daisy, Daisy!
   "Ped'ling" away down the road of life,
   I and my Daisy Bell!

   When the road's dark, we can both despise
   P'licemen and "lamps" as well;
   There are "bright lights" in the dazzling eyes
   Of beautiful Daisy Bell!

   *[to Chorus]*

3. I will stand by you in "wheel" or woe,
   Daisy, Daisy!
   You'll be the bell(e) which I'll ring, you know!
   Sweet little Daisy Bell!

   You'll take the "lead" in each "trip" we take,
   Then if I don't do well
   I will permit you to use the brake,
   My beautiful Daisy Bell!

   *[to Chorus]*

# Danny Boy

W: FREDERICK E. WEATHERLY (1855)

M: "THE LONDONDERRY AIR"

*( The first known printing of this melody, 1855, appeared without a title. It apparently acquired its name as a result of a note indicating that the music was originally collected by a Miss J. Ross of the county of Londonderry, Ireland, from the unpublished melodies of that country.)*

1. Oh, Danny Boy, the pipes, the pipes are calling
   From glen to glen, and down the mountainside;
   The summer's gone, and all the roses falling,
   It's you, it's you must go and I must bide.

   But come ye back when summer's in the meadow,
   Or when the valley's hush'd and white with snow;
   It's I'll be there in sunshine or in shadow,
   Oh, Danny Boy, oh, Danny Boy, I love you so!

2. But when ye come, and all the flow'rs are dying,
   If I am dead, as dead I well may be,
   Ye'll come and find the place where I am lying,
   And kneel and say an Ave there for me;

   And I shall hear, though soft you tread above me,
   And all my grave will warmer, sweeter be,
   For you will bend and tell me that you love me,
   And I shall sleep in peace until you come to me!


# Dardanella

W: FRED FISHER / M: FELIX BERNARD & JOHNNY S. BLACK (1919)

1. Down beside the Dardanella Bay,
   Where Oriental breezes play,
   There lives a lonesome maid Armenian.

   By the Dardanelles with glowing eyes,
   She looks across the seas and sighs,
   And weaves her love spell so sirenian.

   > Soon I shall return to Turkistan,
   > I will ask for her heart and hand.

   > *Chorus:*
   > Oh, sweet Dardanella,
   > I love your harem eyes.
   > I'm a lucky fellow
   > To capture such a prize.

Oh, Allah knows my love for you,
And he tells you to be true,
Dardanella, oh, hear my sigh,
    My Oriental.

Oh, sweet Dardanella,
Prepare the wedding wine,
There'll be one girl in my harem
When you're mine.

We'll build a tent
Just like the children of the Orient.
Oh, sweet Dardanella,
    My star of love divine.

**2.** When the Turkish sultan saw her eyes,
Oh, he was taken by surprise!
He said, "I'll buy her for my harem."

I just told the sultan to be nice,
She can't be bought for any price,
She said to me she couldn't bear him.

    So beneath the Oriental moon,
    I'll be wooing my love real soon.

[*to Chorus*]


# The Darktown Strutters' Ball

W & M: SHELTON BROOKS (1917)

**1.** I've got some good news, Honey,
    An invitation to the Darktown Ball,
    It's a very swell affair,
    All the "high-browns" will be there.

I'll wear my high silk hat, and a frock tail coat,
You wear your Paris gown, and your new silk shawl;
There ain't no doubt about it, babe,
We'll be the best dressed in the hall.

    *Chorus:*
    I'll be down to get you in a taxi, Honey,
    You better be ready about half past eight,
    Now, dearie, don't be late,
    I want to be there when the band starts playing.

    Remember when we get there, Honey,
    The two steps I'm goin' to have 'em all;

Goin' to dance out both my shoes
When they play the "Jelly Roll Blues"
Tomorrow night, at the Darktown Strutters' Ball.

2. We'll meet our high-toned neighbors,
   An exhibition of the "Baby Dolls,"
   And each one will do their best
   Just to outclass all the rest.

   And there'll be dancers from ev'ry foreign land,
   The classic, buck and wing, and the wooden clog;
   We'll win that fifty dollar prize,
   When we step out and "Walk the Dog."

   [*to Chorus*]


# The Daughter of Rosie O'Grady

W: MONTY C. BRICE / M: WALTER DONALDSON (1918)

1. Yesterday while out a-walkin',
   I met a dear little girl,
   Somehow we started a-talkin',
   My brain was all in a whirl.

   She said she came from old Killarney,
   So I started in to quiz;
   I got a surprise that opened my eyes,
   For who do you think she is?

   *Chorus:*
   She's the daughter of Rosie O'Grady,
   A regular old-fashioned girl;
   She isn't crazy for diamond rings,
   Silkens and satins and fancy things.

   She's just a sweet little lady,
   And when you meet her you'll see
   Why I'm glad I caught her,
   The daughter of Rosie O'Grady!

2. I'm goin' to ask her to marry,
   I wonder what she will say;
   I know that if I should tarry,
   Someone will steal her away.

   I've got the ring to fit her finger,
   And if she will name the day,
   Imagine my pride when she is my bride
   And I hear the neighbors say:

   [*to Chorus*]

# Deck the Halls

W & M: THOMAS OLIPHANT (19th c.)

1. Deck the halls with boughs of holly,
   *Fa la la la la, la la la la*
   'Tis the season to be jolly.
   *Fa la la la la, la la la la*

   Fill the mead cup, raise the wassail,
   *Fa la la, fa la la, la la la*
   Sing the ancient Christmas carol.
   *Fa la la la la, la la la la*

2. See the flowing bowl before us,
   *Fa la la la la, la la la la*
   Strike the harp and join the chorus.
   *Fa la la la la, la la la la*

   Follow me in merry measure,
   *Fa la la, fa la la, la la la*
   While I sing of mirth and pleasure.
   *Fa la la la la, la la la la*

3. Fast away the old year passes,
   *Fa la la la la, la la la la*
   Hail the new, ye lads and lasses.
   *Fa la la la la, la la la la*

   Singing gaily all together,
   *Fa la la, fa la la, la la la*
   Heedless of the wind and weather.
   *Fa la la la la, la la la la*


# Deep River

SPIRITUAL

Deep river, my home is over Jordan,
Deep river, Lord, I want to cross over into campground.

Oh, don't you want to go over to that gospel feast,
That promised land where all is peace?

Oh, deep river, my home is over Jordan,
Deep river, Lord, I want to cross over into campground.

# Dixie
## (Dixie's Land)

W: TRADITIONAL / M: DANIEL EMMET (ca. 1859)

1. I wish I was in de land ob cotton,
   Old times dar am not forgotten,
   *Look away! Look away!*
   *Look away, Dixie Land.*

   In Dixie Land whar I was born in
   Early on one frosty mornin',
   *Look away! Look away!*
   *Look away, Dixie Land.*

   > *Chorus:*
   > Den I wish I was in Dixie,
   > Hooray! Hooray!
   > In Dixie Land I'll take my stand,
   > To lib and die in Dixie!
   >
   > Away, away,
   > Away down South in Dixie!
   > Away, away,
   > Away down South in Dixie!

2. Old Missus marry . . . Will de weaber,
   Willium was a gay deceaber,
   *Look away! Look away!*
   *Look away, Dixie Land.*

   But when he put his arm around 'er,
   He smil'd as fierce as a forty pounder,
   *Look away! Look away!*
   *Look away, Dixie Land.*

   [*to Chorus*]

3. His face was a sharp as a butcher's cleaber,
   But dat did not seem to greab 'er,
   *Look away! Look away!*
   *Look away, Dixie Land.*

   Old Missus acted the foolish part,
   And died for a man dat broke her heart,
   *Look away! Look away!*
   *Look away, Dixie Land.*

   [*to Chorus*]

**4.** Now here's a health to the next old Missus,
And all de gals dat want to kiss us,
  *Look away! Look away!*
  *Look away, Dixie Land.*

But if you want to drive 'way sorrow,
Come and hear dis song to-morrow,
  *Look away! Look away!*
  *Look away, Dixie Land.*

  [*to Chorus*]

**5.** Dar's buckwheat cakes an' Ingen batter,
Makes you fat or a little fatter,
  *Look away! Look away!*
  *Look away, Dixie Land.*

Den hoe it down an' scratch your grabble,
To Dixie's land I'm bound to trabble,
  *Look away! Look away!*
  *Look away, Dixie Land.*

  [*to Chorus*]


# Dona Nobis Pacem
THREE-PART LATIN ROUND

*First Part*
  Dona nobis pacem, pacem,
  Dona nobis pacem.

*Second Part*
  Dona nobis pacem,
  Dona nobis pacem.

*Third Part*
  Dona nobis pacem,
  Dona nobis pacem.

81

# Down Among the Sheltering Palms

W: JAMES BROCKMAN / M: ABE OLMAN (1915)

1. I'm way down east, down east,
   And my heart is pining, pining for you;
   You're way out west, out west,
   And my soul is craving, craving for you.

   I love you so,
   Just you, I know,
   It takes six days to go there with a train,
   Just one week more, and I'll be with you again.
       I long to be . . .

> *Chorus:*
> Down among the sheltering palms,
> O honey, wait for me, O honey, wait for me;
> Meet me down by the old Golden Gate,
> Out where the sun goes down about eight.
>
> How my love is burning, burning, burning,
> How my heart is yearning, yearning, yearning,
> To be down among the sheltering palms,
> O honey, wait for me!

2. When I was south, down south,
   There I saw some pretty, pretty places;
   When I was north, way north,
   I saw many, many pretty faces;

   Not one so fair,
   None could compare,
   There's only one place way out in the west,
   And you are there, where with you I long to rest.
       I long to be . . .

   [*to Chorus*]

# Down by the Old Mill Stream

W & M: TELL TAYLOR (1910)

1. My darling, I am dreaming of the days gone by,
   When you and I were sweethearts, beneath the summer sky;
   Your hair has turned to silver, the gold has faded too;
   But still I will remember where I first met you.

   *Chorus:*
   Down by the old mill stream,
   Where I first met you,
   With your eyes so blue,
   Dressed in gingham, too.

   It was there I knew
   That you loved me true.
   You were sixteen,
   My village queen,
   Down by the old mill stream.

2. The old mill wheel is silent, and has fallen down;
   The old oak tree has withered, and lies there on the ground;
   While you and I are sweethearts, the same as days of yore,
   Although we've been together forty years and more.

   [*to Chorus*]


# Down by the Riverside

SPIRITUAL

1. Gonna lay down my sword and shield,
   *Down by the riverside,*
   *Down by the riverside,*
   *Down by the riverside,*
   Gonna lay down my sword and shield,
   *Down by the riverside,*
   And study war no more.

   *Chorus:*
   Ain't gonna study war no more,
   Ain't gonna study war no more,
   Ain't gonna study war no more.

2. Gonna put on my long white robe,
   *Down by the riverside,*
   *Down by the riverside,*
   *Down by the riverside,*

83

Gonna put on my long white robe,
*Down by the riverside,*
And study war no more.

[*to Chorus*]

3. Gonna talk with the Prince of Peace,
   *Down by the riverside,*
   *Down by the riverside,*
   *Down by the riverside,*
   Gonna talk with the Prince of Peace,
   *Down by the riverside,*
   And study war no more.

   [*to Chorus*]

4. Gonna join hands with ev'ryone,
   *Down by the riverside,*
   *Down by the riverside,*
   *Down by the riverside,*
   Gonna join hands with ev'ryone,
   *Down by the riverside,*
   And study war no more.

   [*to Chorus*]


# Down in Alabam'
## (Ain't I Glad I Got Out de Wilderness)
TRADITIONAL

*(Several songs share the same tune but contain lyrics that range from
slight to significant variants: "Down in Alabam'"... "Get out of the
wilderness".... "Ain't I glad I got out de wilderness"... "Old blind horse
come from Jerusalem"... "Old grey hoss come a-tearin' out o' the
wilderness," and so on. An 1858 publication credits music and words of
"Down in Alabam'" to J. Warner.)*

1. My old massa he's got the dropser, um,
      He's got the dropser, um,
      He's got the dropser, um;
   He am sure to die 'kase he's got no doctor, um,
      Down in Alabam'.

   *Chorus:*
   Ain't I glad I got out de wilderness,
   Got out de wilderness, got out de wilderness;
   Ain't I glad I got out de wilderness,
   Down in Alabam'.

2. Old blind horse come from Jerusalum,
   Come from Jerusalum,
   Come from Jerusalum;
   He kicks so high dey put him in de museum,
   Down in Alabam'.

   [*to Chorus*]

3. Dis am a holiday, we hab assembled, um,
   We hab assembled, um,
   We hab assembled, um,
   To dance and sing for de ladies and gentleum,
   Down in Alabam'.

   [*to Chorus*]

4. Far you well to de wild goose nation,
   Wild goose nation,
   Wild goose nation,
   I neber will leab de old plantation,
   Down in Alabam'.

   [*to Chorus*]


# Down in My Heart

SPIRITUAL

1. I've got that joy, joy, joy, joy,
   *Down in my heart, down in my heart,*
   I've got that joy, joy, joy, joy,
   *Down in my heart, down in my heart today.*

2. I've got that love of Jesus
   *Down in my heart, down in my heart,*
   I've got that love of Jesus
   *Down in my heart, down in my heart today.*

3. I've got that peace that passeth understanding
   *Down in my heart, down in my heart,*
   I've got that peace that passeth understanding
   *Down in my heart, down in my heart today.*

# Down in the Valley

AMERICAN FOLK SONG

1. Down in the valley, the valley so low,
   Hang your head over, hear the wind blow.
   Hear the wind blow, dear, hear the wind blow,
   Hang your head over, hear the wind blow.

2. Bird in a cage, dear, bird in a cage,
   Dying for freedom, ever a slave.
   Ever a slave, dear, ever a slave,
   Dying for freedom, ever a slave.

3. If you don't love me, love whom you please,
   Throw your arms 'round me, give my heart ease.
   Give my heart ease, dear, give my heart ease,
   Throw your arms 'round me, give my heart ease.

4. Write me a letter, send it by mail,
   Send it in care of Birmingham jail.
   Birmingham jail, dear, Birmingham jail,
   Send it in care of Birmingham jail.

5. Writing this letter containing three lines,
   Answer my question: "Will you be mine?"
   "Will you be mine, dear, will you be mine?"
   Answer my question: "Will you be mine?"

6. Roses love sunshine, vi'lets love dew,
   Angels in heaven know I love you.
   Know I love you, dear, know I love you,
   Angels in heaven know I love you.


# Down Where the Wurzburger Flows

W: VINCENT P. BRYAN / M: HARRY VON TILZER (1902)

1. Now poets may sing of the dear Fatherland
   And the soft flowing, dreamy, old Rhine;
   Beside the Blue Danube in fancy they stand
   And they rave of its beauties divine.

   But there is a spot where the sun never shines,
   Where mirth and good fellowship reign;
   For dear old Bohemia my lonely heart pines,
   And I long to be there once again.

*Chorus:*
Take me down, down, down where the Wurzburger
   flows, flows, flows;
It will drown, drown, drown all your troubles and
   cares and woes.

Just order two seidels of lager, or three,
If I don't want to drink it, please force it on me;
The Rhine may be fine but a cold stein for mine,
Down where the Wurzburger flows.

2. The Rhine by moonlight's a beautiful sight
   When the wind whispers low thro' the vines;
   But give me some good old Rathskeller at night,
   Where the brilliant electric light shines.

   The poets may think it's delightful to hear
   The nightingale piping his lay;
   Give me a piano, a cold stein of beer,
   And a fellow who knows how to play.

   [*to Chorus*]


# Drill, Ye Tarriers, Drill!
W & M: THOMAS CASEY (?) (1888)

1. Oh! ev'ry morn' at seven o'clock
   There are twenty tarriers on the rock;
   The boss came along and says "Be still
   And put all your power in the cast-steel drill!"

   *Chorus:*
   Then drill, ye tarriers, drill,
   Drill, ye tarriers, drill!
   Oh, it's work all day without sugar in your tay
   When ye work beyant on the railway,
   And drill, ye tarriers, drill!

2. The boss was a fine man all around
   But he married a great, big, fat fardown;
   She baked good bread and baked it well,
   And baked it hard as the hobs of H—l.

   [*to Chorus*]

3. The new foreman is Dan McCann,
   I'll tell you sure he's a blame mean man;
   Last week a premature blast went off,
   And a mile in the air went big Jim Goff.

   [*to Chorus*]

4. When pay day next it came around,
   Poor Jim's pay a dollar short he found;
   "What for?" says he, then came this reply,
   "You are docked for the time you were up in the sky."

   [*to Chorus*]


# Drink to Me Only with Thine Eyes
W: BEN JONSON (17th c.) / M: ANON.

1. Drink to me only with thine eyes,
   And I will pledge with mine;
   Or leave a kiss but in the cup
   And I'll not look for wine.

   The thirst that from the soul doth rise
   Doth ask a drink divine,
   But might I of Jove's nectar sip,
   I would not change for thine.

2. I sent thee later a rosy wreath,
   Not so much hon'ring thee,
   As giving it a hope, that there
   It could not wither'd be.

   But thou thereon didst only breathe
   And sent'st it back to me,
   Since when it grows and smells, I swear,
   Not of itself but thee!

# Dry Bones

SPIRITUAL

*Ezekiel cried, "Them dry bones!"*
*Ezekiel cried, "Them dry bones!*
*Oh, hear the word of the Lord!"*

The foot bone connected to the leg bone,
The leg bone connected to the knee bone,
The knee bone connected to the thigh bone,
    "Oh, hear the word of the Lord!

*"Them bones, them bones, them dry bones,*
*Them bones, them bones, them dry bones,*
*Them bones, them bones, them dry bones,*
*Oh, hear the word of the Lord!"*

The thigh bone connected to the back bone,
The back bone connected to the neck bone,
The neck bone connected to the head bone,
    "Oh, hear the word of the Lord!

*"Them bones, them bones, gonna walk aroun',*
*Them bones, them bones, gonna walk aroun',*
*Them bones, them bones, gonna walk aroun',*
*Oh, hear the word of the Lord!"*

The head bone connected to the neck bone,
The neck bone connected to the back bone,
The back bone connected to the thigh bone,
    "Oh, hear the word of the Lord!

*"Them bones, them bones, them dry bones,*
*Them bones, them bones, them dry bones,*
*Them bones, them bones, them dry bones,*
*Oh, hear the word of the Lord!"*

The thigh bone connected to the knee bone,
The knee bone connected to the leg bone,
The leg bone connected to the foot bone,
    "Oh, hear the word of the Lord!

*"Them bones, them bones, gonna walk aroun',*
*Them bones, them bones, gonna walk aroun',*
*Them bones, them bones, gonna walk aroun',*
*Oh, hear the word of the Lord!"*

# East Side, West Side
## (The Sidewalks of New York)
W & M: CHARLES B. LAWLOR & JAMES W. BLAKE (1894)

1. Down in front of Casey's
   Old brown wooden stoop,
   On a summer's evening,
   We formed a merry group.

   Boys and girls together,
   We would sing and waltz
   While Tony played the organ
   On the sidewalks of New York.

   > *Chorus:*
   > East side, west side,
   > All around the town,
   > The tots sang "Ring-a-rosie,"
   > "London bridge is falling down."
   >
   > Boys and girls together,
   > Me and Mamie O'Rourke
   > Tripped the light fantastic
   > On the sidewalks of New York.

2. That's where Johnny Casey,
   Little Jimmy Crowe,
   Jakey Krause, the baker,
   Who always had the dough,

   Pretty Nellie Shannon (with a)
   Dud as light as cork,
   She first picked up the waltz step
   On the sidewalks of New York.

   > [*to Chorus*]

3. Things have changed since those times,
   Some are up in "G,"
   Others, they are wand'rers
   But they all feel just like me.

   They'd part with all they've got,
   Could they once more walk
   With their best girl and have a twirl
   On the sidewalks of New York.

   > [*to Chorus*]

# Eency Weency Spider
CHILDREN'S FINGER-PLAY SONG

Eency weency spider went up the water spout,
Down came the rain and washed the spider out,
Out came the sun and dried up all the rain,
Now eency weency spider went up the spout again.

# The Erie Canal
AMERICAN WORK SONG

1. I've got a mule, her name is Sal,
Fifteen miles on the Erie Canal;
She's a good old worker and a good old pal,
Fifteen miles on the Erie Canal.

We've haul'd some barges in our day,
Fill'd with lumber, coal and hay,
And we know ev'ry inch of the way
From Albany to Buffalo.

*Chorus:*
Low bridge, ev'rybody down!
Low bridge, for we're going through a town,
And you'll always know your neighbor,
You'll always know your pal,
If you ever navigated on the Erie Canal.

2. We better get along on our way, old gal,
Fifteen miles on the Erie Canal,
'Cause you bet your life I'd never part with Sal,
Fifteen miles on the Erie Canal.

Git up there, mule, here comes a lock,
We'll make Rome 'bout six o'clock;
One more trip and back we'll go
Right back home to Buffalo.

[*to Chorus*]

# Every Day Is Ladies' Day with Me

W: HENRY BLOSSOM / M: VICTOR HERBERT

[from *The Red Mill,* 1906]

1. I should like, without undue reiteration of the ego,
   To explain how very hard I find it to make my pay go
   'Round among my vulgar creditors, I'm fearfully in debt
   For I always have afforded anything that I could get!

   But I must say I've enjoyed the best of what there is in life;
   I've been lucky in my love affairs, I've never had a wife!
   I can summon little int'rest in the dry affairs of state,
   And the bus'nessmen who call on me are coldly left to wait!

   *Chorus*:
   For every day is ladies' day with me,
   I'm quite at their disposal all the while!
      And my pleasure it is double
      if they come to me in trouble,
   For I always find a way to make them smile,
      the little darlings!

   I've no doubt I should have married long ago!
   It's the proper thing to do, you'll all agree!
      But I never could find any fun
      in wasting all my time on one,
   So ev'ry day is ladies' day with me!

2. It's a frightful thing to think of all the hearts I have broken,
   Altho' each one fell in love with me without the slightest token;
   That my fatal gift of beauty had inflamed her little heart,
   But I found that some small favor always seemed to ease the smart:

   A position for a cousin or a loan to dear papa,
   Just a dainty diamond necklace or a pretty motor car.
   But I don't begrudge the collarets and necklaces or pearls,
   All the money that I ever saved is what I've spent on girls!

   [*to Chorus*]

# Everything Is Peaches Down in Georgia

W: GRANT CLARKE / M: MILTON AGER & GEORGE W. MEYER (1918)

1. Down in Georgia there are peaches,
   Waiting for you, yes, and each is
   Sweet as any peach
   That you could reach for on a tree.

   Southern beauties they are famous,
   Georgia's where they grow.
   My folks write me, they invite me,
   Don't you want to go?

   *Chorus:*
   Ev'rything is peaches down in Georgia,
   What a peach of a clime,
   For a peach of a time,
     Believe me,

   Paradise is waiting down there for you,
   I've got a peach of a Pa,
   Peach of a Ma,
   Oh! what a peach of a couple they are!

   There's a preacher preaches down in Georgia,
   Always ready to say: "Will you love and obey?"
     I bet you'll pick yourself a peach of a wife,
     Settle down to a peach of a life,
   Ev'rything is peaches down in Georgia.

2. All of Georgia's full of peaches,
   They're all gorgeous, each one reaches
   Right into your heart
   And makes you part of Georgia, too.

   Clingstone peaches cling right to you,
   Peaches haunt your dream,
   Think of getting, always getting
   Peaches in your cream.

   [*to Chorus*]

# Ezekiel Saw the Wheel

SPIRITUAL

> *Chorus:*
> Ezekiel saw the wheel,
> *'Way up in the middle of the air*
> Ezekiel saw the wheel
> *'Way up in the middle of the air.*
>
> The big wheel runs by faith,
> Little wheel runs by the grace of God,
> A wheel in a wheel
> *'Way in the middle of the air.*

1. I'll tell you what a hypocrite'll do,
   *'Way in the middle of the air*
   He'll talk about me and he'll talk about you.
   *'Way in the middle of the air.*

   [*to Chorus*]

2. Ezekiel saw the wheel of time,
   *'Way in the middle of the air*
   And ev'ry spoke was humankind,
   *'Way in the middle of the air.*

   [*to Chorus*]


# Far Above Cayuga's Waters

W: ARCHIBALD C. WEEKS & WILMOT. M. SMITH (1872)
M: H. S. THOMPSON (1858)
*(Thompson's original song appeared as "Annie Lisle." His melody was used for the Alma Maters of Cornell University and other colleges.)*

1. Far above Cayuga's waters,
   With its waves of blue,
   Stands our noble Alma Mater,
   Glorious to view.

   > Raise the chorus, speed it onward,
   > Loud her praises tell;
   > Hail to thee, our Alma Mater!
   > Hail! All hail! Cornell!

2. Far above the busy humming
   Of the bustling town,
   Reared against the arch of heaven
   Looks she proudly down.

94

Raise the chorus, speed it onward,
Loud her praises tell;
Hail to thee, our Alma Mater!
Hail! All hail! Cornell!

# The Farmer in the Dell

NURSERY SONG

1. The farmer in the dell,
   The farmer in the dell,
   Heigh ho, the derry-o!
   The farmer in the dell.

2. The farmer takes a wife,
   The farmer takes a wife,
   Heigh ho, the derry-o!
   The farmer takes a wife.

3. The wife takes a child,
   *(etc.)*

4. The child takes the nurse,
   *(etc.)*

5. The nurse takes the dog,
   *(etc.)*

6. The dog takes the cat,
   *(etc.)*

7. The cat takes the rat,
   *(etc.)*

8. The rat takes the cheese,
   *(etc.)*

9. The cheese stands alone,
   *(etc.)*

# The First Nowell

ENGLISH CHRISTMAS CAROL

1. The first Nowell the angel did say
   Was to certain poor shepherds in field as they lay;
   In field where they lay, keeping their sheep,
   On a cold winter's night that was so deep.
   *Nowell, Nowell,*
   *Nowell, Nowell,*
   *Born is the King of Israel!*

2. They lookéd up and saw a star,
   Shining in the east beyond them far;
   And to the earth it gave great light,
   And so continued both day and night.
   *Nowell, Nowell,*
   *Nowell, Nowell,*
   *Born is the King of Israel!*

3. And by the light of that same star,
   Three Wise Men came from country far;
   To seek for a king was their intent,
   And to follow the star wheresoever it went.
   *Nowell, Nowell,*
   *Nowell, Nowell,*
   *Born is the King of Israel!*

4. This star drew nigh to the northwest;
   O'er Bethlehem it took its rest,
   And there did both stop and stay
   Right over the place where Jesus lay.
   *Nowell, Nowell,*
   *Nowell, Nowell,*
   *Born is the King of Israel!*

5. Then did they know assuredly
   Within that house the King did lie:
   One entered in then for to see,
   And found the Babe in poverty.
   *Nowell, Nowell,*
   *Nowell, Nowell,*
   *Born is the King of Israel!*

6. Then entered in those Wise Men three,
   Fell reverently upon their knee,
   And offered there in His presence
   Both gold and myrrh and frankincense.
   *Nowell, Nowell,*
   *Nowell, Nowell,*
   *Born is the King of Israel!*

7. Between an ox-stall and an ass
   This Child truly there born He was;
   For want of clothing they did Him lay
   All in the manger, among the hay.
   *Nowell, Nowell,*
   *Nowell, Nowell,*
   *Born is the King of Israel!*

8. Then let us all with one accord
   Sing praises to our heavenly Lord,
   That hath made heav'n and earth of naught,
   And with His blood mankind hath bought.
   *Nowell, Nowell,*
   *Nowell, Nowell,*
   *Born is the King of Israel!*

9. If we in our time shall do well,
   We shall be free from death and hell;
   For God hath prepared for us all
   A resting place in general.
   *Nowell, Nowell,*
   *Nowell, Nowell,*
   *Born is the King of Israel!*

# The Flowers That Bloom in the Spring
W: W. S. GILBERT / M: SIR ARTHUR SULLIVAN
[from *The Mikado*, 1885]

1. The flowers that bloom in the spring, *tra la,*
   Breathe promise of merry sunshine.
   As we merrily dance and we sing, *tra la,*
   We welcome the hope that they bring, *tra la,*
   Of a summer of roses and wine,
   Of a summer of roses and wine.

   And that's what we mean when we say that a thing
   Is welcome as flowers that bloom in the spring,
   *Tra la la la la*
   *Tra la la la la*

The flowers that bloom in the spring.
*Tra la la la la*
*Tra la la la la*
*Tra la la la la la*

2. The flowers that bloom in the spring, *tra la,*
   Have nothing to do with the case.
   I've got to take under my wing, *tra la,*
   A most unattractive old thing, *tra la,*
       With a caricature of a face,
       With a caricature of a face.

   And that's what I mean when I say, or I sing
   "O, bother the flowers that bloom in the spring,"
       *Tra la la la la*
       *Tra la la la la*
   "O, bother the flowers of spring."
       *Tra la la la la*
       *Tra la la la la*
       *Tra la la la la la*

# Flow Gently, Sweet Afton

W: ROBERT BURNS (before 1818) / M: J. E. SPILMAN (1838)

1. Flow gently, sweet Afton, among thy green braes!
   Flow gently, I'll sing thee a song in thy praise!
   My Mary's asleep by thy murmuring stream—
   Flow gently, sweet Afton, disturb not her dream!

2. Thou stock dove whose echo resounds thro' the glen,
   Ye wild whistling blackbirds in yon thorny den,
   Thou green-crested lapwing, thy screaming forbear—
   I charge you, disturb not my slumbering fair!

3. How lofty, sweet Afton, thy neighboring hills,
   Far mark'd with the courses of clear, winding rills!
   There daily I wander, as noon rises high,
   My flocks and my Mary's sweet cot in my eye.

4. How pleasant thy banks and green valleys below,
   Where wild in the woodlands the primroses blow.
   There oft, as mild Ev'ning weeps over the lea,
   The sweet-scented birk shades my Mary and me.

5. Thy crystal stream, Afton, how lovely it glides,
   And winds by the cot where my Mary resides!
   How wanton thy waters her snowy feet lave,
   As, gathering sweet flowerets, she stems thy clear wave!

6. Flow gently, sweet Afton, among thy green braes!
   Flow gently, sweet river, the theme of my lays!
   My Mary's asleep by thy murmuring stream—
   Flow gently, sweet Afton, disturb not her dream!

# The Foggy, Foggy Dew
ENGLISH FOLK SONG

1. When I was a bach'lor I lived all alone,
   I worked at the weaver's trade,
   And the only, only thing I did that was wrong
   Was to woo a fair young maid.

   I wooed her in the winter time
   And in the summer, too,
   And the only, only thing I did that was wrong
   Was to keep her from the foggy, foggy dew.

2. One night she knelt near me, so close to my side,
   When I was so fast asleep.
   Then she threw her lovely, lovely arms 'round my neck
   And she then began to weep.

   She wept, she cried, she tore her hair,
   Ah me, what could I do?
   So I held her in my arms, all night in my arms,
   Just to keep her from the foggy, foggy dew.

3. Again I'm a bach'lor and live with my son,
   We work at the weaver's trade,
   And now ev'ry, ev'ry time I look in his eyes,
   I can see the fair young maid.

   Reminds me of the winter time
   And of the summer, too,
   And the many, many times I held her in my arms
   Just to keep her from the foggy, foggy dew.

# For He's a Jolly Good Fellow

TRADITIONAL

*(same melody as "The Bear Went Over the Mountain" as well as*
*"Malbrouck s'en Va-t-en Guerre")*

> For he's a jolly good fellow,
> > For he's a jolly good fellow,
> > > For he's a jolly good fellow,
> > > > Which nobody can deny,
> > > > Which nobody can deny,
> > > > Which nobody can deny,
> For he's a jolly good fellow,
> > For he's a jolly good fellow,
> > > For he's a jolly good fellow,
> > > > Which nobody can deny.

# For Me and My Gal

W: EDGAR LESLIE & E. RAY GOETZ / M: GEORGE W. MEYER (1917)

1. What a beautiful day
   For a wedding in May,
   See the people all stare
   At the lovable pair.

   She's a vision of joy,
   He's the luckiest boy,
   In his wedding array,
   Hear him smilingly say:

   > *Chorus:*
   > The bells are ringing for me and my gal,
   > The birds are singing for me and my gal;
   > > Ev'rybody's been knowing
   > > To a wedding they're going,
   > > And for weeks they've been sewing
   > > Ev'ry Susie and Sal.

   > They're congregating for me and my gal,
   > The Parson's waiting for me and my gal;
   > > And sometime, I'm goin' to build a little home for two
   > > For three or four, or more,
   > > In Loveland
   > > For me and my gal.

2. See the relatives there,
   Looking over the pair,
   They can tell at a glance,
   It's a loving romance.

   It's a wonderful sight,
   As the fam'lies unite,
   Gee! it makes the boy proud
   As he says to the crowd:

   [*to Chorus*]


# Forty-five Minutes from Broadway

W & M: GEORGE M. COHAN
[from the musical play of the same name, 1905]

1. The West, so they say, is the home of the jay,
   And Missouri's the state that can grind them.
   This may all be, but just take it from me,
   You don't have to go out West to find them.

   If you want to see the real jay delegation,
   The place where the real rubens dwell,
   Just hop on a train at the Grand Central Station,
   Get off when they shout "New Rochelle."

   > *Chorus:*
   > Only forty-five minutes from Broadway,
   > Think of the changes it brings;
   > For the short time it takes, what a difference it makes
   > In the ways of the people and things.
   >
   > Oh! what a fine bunch of rubens,
   > Oh! what a jay atmosphere;
   > They have whiskers like hay, and imagine Broadway
   > Only forty-five minutes from here.

2. When the bunco men hear that their game is so near,
   They'll be swarming here thicker than bees are;
   In Barnum's best days, why he never saw jays
   That were easier to get to than these are.

   You tell them old jokes and they laugh till they sicken;
   There's giggles and grins here to let.
   I told them that one about "Why does a chicken . . ."
   The rubens are all laughing yet.

101

*Chorus:*
Only forty-five minutes from Broadway,
Not a café in the town;
Oh! the place is a bird, no one here ever heard
Of Delmonico, Rector or Browne.

With a ten dollar bill you're a spendthrift;
If you open a bottle of beer
You're a sport, so they say, and imagine Broadway
Only forty-five minutes from here.


# Forty-nine Bottles
TRADITIONAL DRINKING SONG

Forty-nine bottles of beer on the wall,
Forty-nine bottles of beer on the wall;
Take one away from them all,
Forty-eight bottles of beer on the wall.

Forty-eight bottles of beer on the wall,
Forty-eight bottles of beer on the wall;
Take one away from them all,
Forty-seven bottles of beer on the wall.

Forty-seven bottles, *etc., etc.*


# Frankie and Johnny
*(Folk song of the American West, thought to date back to the 1840s;*
*first printing, 1904, under the title "He Done Me Wrong," by Hughie Cannon,*
*with a variant of the familiar melody. The text below is one of numerous versions.)*

1. Frankie and Johnny were lovers, O lordy how they could love.
   Swore to be true to each other, true as the stars above;
   He was her man but he done her wrong, so wrong.

2. Johnny's mother told him, and she was mighty wise,
   Don't spend Frankie's money on that parlor Ann Eliz;
   You're Frankie's man, and you're doin' her wrong, so wrong.

3. Frankie and Johnny went walking, Johnny in his bran' new suit,
   "O good Lawd," says Frankie, "Don't my Johnny look cute?"
   He was her man but he done her wrong, so wrong.

4. Frankie went down to the corner, to buy a glass of beer;
   She says to the fat bartender, "Has my lovinest man been here?
   He was my man but he's done me wrong, so wrong."

5. Frankie went down to the pawn shop, she bought herself a little forty-four,
   She aimed it at the ceiling, shot a big hole in the floor;
   "Where is my man? He's doin' me wrong, so wrong."

6. Frankie went back to the hotel, she didn't go there for fun,
   'Cause under her long red kimono she toted a forty-four gun.
   He was her man but he done her wrong, so wrong.

7. Frankie went down to the hotel, looked in the window so high,
   There she saw her lovin' Johnny a-lovin' up Alice Bly;
   He was her man but he done her wrong, so wrong.

8. Frankie went down to the hotel, she rang that hotel bell,
   "Stand back, all of you floozies, or I'll blow you all to hell,
   I want my man, he's doin' me wrong, so wrong."


# Frère Jacques
FRENCH CHILDREN'S ROUND

Frère Jacques, frère Jacques,
Dormez-vous, dormez-vous?
Sonnez les matines, sonnez les matines,
Din dan don! Din dan don!


# Froggie Went a-Courtin'
ENGLISH FOLK SONG

1. Froggie went a-courtin' and he did ride,
   *Uh-huh, uh-huh*
   Froggie went a-courtin' and he did ride,
   A sword and pistol by his side.
   *Uh-huh, uh-huh*

2. Well, he rode down to Miss Mouse's door,
   *Uh-huh, uh-huh*
   Well, he rode down to Miss Mouse's door,
   Where he had often been before.
   *Uh-huh, uh huh*

103

3. He took Miss Mousie on his knee,
   *Uh-huh, uh-huh*
   He took Miss Mousie on his knee,
   Said, "Miss Mousie, will you marry me?"
   *Uh-huh, uh-huh*

4. "I'll have to ask my Uncle Rat,"
   *(etc.)*
   "See what he will say to that."
   *(etc.)*

*(Verses 5 through 17 continue in the same pattern.)*

5. "Without my Uncle Rat's consent,
   I would not marry the President."

6. Well, Uncle Rat laughed and shook his fat sides,
   To think his niece would be a bride.

7. Well, Uncle Rat rode off to town
   To buy his niece a wedding gown.

8. "Where will the wedding supper be?"
   "'Way down yonder in a hollow tree."

9. "Who's going to make the wedding gown?"
   "Old Miss Toad from the lily pond."

10. "What will the wedding supper be?"
    "A fried mosquito and a roasted flea."

11. First to come in were two little ants,
    Fixing around to have a dance.

12. Next to come in was a bumblebee,
    Bouncing a fiddle on his knee.

13. Next to come in was a fat sassy lad,
    Thinks himself as big as his dad.

14. Thinks himself a man, indeed,
    Because he chews the tobacco weed.

15. And next to come in was a big tomcat;
    He swallowed the frog and the mouse and the rat.

16. Next to come in was a big old snake;
    He chased the party into the lake.

17. If you want this song again to ring,
    Make it up yourself and start to sing.

# Funiculì, Funiculà

ORIGINAL ITALIAN LYRICS: G. TURCO
ENGLISH VERSION: EDWARD OXENFORD
M: LUIGI DENZA (ca. 1880)

1. Some think the world is made for fun and frolic,
   And so do I! And so do I!
   Some think it well to be all melancholic,
   To pine and sigh, to pine and sigh.

   But I, I love to spend my time in singing
   Some joyous song, some joyous song;
   To set the air with music bravely ringing
   Is far from wrong! Is far from wrong!

   *Chorus:*
   Listen! Listen! Echoes sound afar!
   Listen! Listen! Echoes sound afar!
   *Tra la la la, tra la la la,*
   *Tra la la la, tra la la la!*
   Echoes sound afar!
   *Tra la la la, tra la la la!*
   Oh! *[omit for repeat]* . . .

   *[repeat Chorus]*

2. Some think it wrong to set the feet a-dancing,
   But not so I! But not so I!
   Some think that eyes should keep from coyly glancing
   Upon the sly! Upon the sly!

   But oh! to me the mazy dance is charming,
   Divinely sweet, divinely sweet!
   And surely there is naught that is alarming
   In nimble feet? In nimble feet?

   *Chorus:*
   Listen! Listen! Music sounds afar!
   Listen! Listen! Music sounds afar!
   *Tra la la la, tra la la la,*
   *Tra la la la, tra la la la!*
   Music sounds afar!
   *Tra la la la, tra la la la!*
   Oh! . . .

   *[repeat Chorus]*

3. Ah, me! 'tis strange that some should take to sighing,
   And like it well! And like it well!
   For me, I have not thought it worth the trying,
   So cannot tell! So cannot tell!

With laugh and dance and song the day soon passes,
Full soon is gone, full soon is gone;
For mirth was made for joyous lads and lassies
To call their own! To call their own!

> *Chorus:*
> Listen! Listen! Hark, the soft guitar!
> Listen! Listen! Hark, the soft guitar!
> *Tra la la la, tra la la la,*
> *Tra la la la, tra la la la!*
> Hark, the soft guitar!
> *Tra la la la, tra la la la!*
> Oh! . . .

*[repeat Chorus]*


# Get on Board, Little Children
SPIRITUAL

> *Chorus:*
> Get on board, little children,
> Get on board, little children,
> Get on board, little children,
> There's room for many-a more.

1. The gospel train's a-coming,
   I hear it just at hand,
   I hear the car wheels rumbling
   And rolling through the land.

   *[to Chorus]*

2. I hear the train a-coming,
   A-coming 'round the curve,
   She loosened all her steam and brakes,
   She's straining every nerve.

   *[to Chorus]*

3. The fare is cheap and all can go,
   The rich and poor are there,
   No second class aboard this train,
   No diff'rence in the fare.

   *[to Chorus]*

# Gimme That Old-Time Religion

SPIRITUAL

1. Gimme that old-time religion,
   Gimme that old-time religion,
   Gimme that old-time religion,
   It's good enough for me.

2. Makes me love ev'rybody,
   Makes me love ev'rybody,
   Makes me love ev'rybody,
   It's good enough for me.

3. It was good for our mothers,
   *(etc.)*

4. It has saved our fathers,
   *(etc.)*

5. It was good for the Prophet Daniel,
   *(etc.)*

6. It was good for the Hebrew children,
   *(etc.)*

7. It was tried in the fiery furnace,
   *(etc.)*

8. It was good for Paul and Silas,
   *(etc.)*

9. It will do when I'm dying,
   *(etc.)*

10. It will take us all to heaven,
    *(etc.)*

# The Girl I Left Behind Me

IRISH BALLAD

*(Another version is a ballad of the American West.)*

1. The dames of France are fond and free,
   And Flemish lips are willing,
   And soft the maids of Italy,
   And Spanish eyes are thrilling;

   Still, though I bask beneath their smile,
   Their charms fail to bind me,
   And my heart falls back to Erin's Isle,
   To the girl I left behind me.

2. For she's as fair as Shannon's side,
   And purer than its water,
   But she refused to be my bride,
   Though many a year I sought her;

   Yet, since to France I sailed away,
   Her letters oft remind me,
   That I promised never to gainsay
   The girl I left behind me.

3. She says, "My own dear love, come home,
   My friends are rich and many,
   Or else, abroad with you I'll roam,
   A soldier stout as any.

   "If you'll not come, nor let me go,
   I'll think you have resigned me,"
   My heart nigh broke when I answered "No,"
   To the girl I left behind me.

4. For never shall my true love brave
   A life of war and toiling,
   And never as a skulking slave
   I'll tread my native soil on;

   But were it free or to be freed,
   The battle's close would find me
   To Ireland bound, nor message need
   From the girl I left behind me.

# Git Along Home, Cindy

AMERICAN FOLK SONG

1. Oh, have you seen my Cindy,
   She comes from 'way down south,
   And she's so sweet, the honey bees
   Just swarm around her mouth.

   *Chorus:*
   Git along home, Cindy, Cindy,
   Git along home, Cindy, Cindy,
   Git along home, Cindy, Cindy,
   I'll marry you some day.

2. I wish I was an apple
   A-hangin' in a tree,
   And ev'ry time my sweetheart passed,
   She'd take a bite of me.

   [*to Chorus*]

3. She told me that she loved me,
   She called me Sugar Plum,
   She throwed 'er arms around me,
   I thought my time had come.

   [*to Chorus*]

4. She took me to the parlor,
   She cooled me with her fan,
   She swore I was the purtiest thing
   In the shape of mortal man.

   [*to Chorus*]

5. I wish I had a needle,
   As fine as I could sew;
   I'd sew the girl to my coat tail,
   And down the road I'd go.

   [*to Chorus*]

# Give My Regards to Broadway

W & M: GEORGE M. COHAN
[from *Little Johnny Jones,* 1904]

1. Did you ever see two Yankees
   Part upon a foreign shore,
   When the good ship's just about to start
   For old New York once more?

   With a tear-dimmed eye they say goodbye,
   They're friends without a doubt,
   When the man on the pier up and shouts "Let them clear"
   As the ship strikes out.

   *Chorus:*
   Give my regards to Broadway,
   Remember me to Herald Square.
   Tell all the gang at Forty-second Street
   That I will soon be there.

   Whisper of how I'm yearning
   To mingle with the old-time throng.
   Give my regards to old Broadway
   And say that I'll be there e'er long.

2. Say hello to dear old Coney Isle
   If there you chance to be.
   When you're at the Waldorf, have a smile,
   And charge it up to me.

   Mention my name ev'ry place you go
   As 'round the town you roam.
   Wish you'd call on my gal, now remember, old pal,
   When you get back home.

   [*to Chorus*]


# The Glow-Worm
## ("Glühwürmchen")

ENGLISH WORDS: LILLA CAYLEY / M: PAUL LINCKE
[Originally from *Lysistrata,* 1902; English version from *The Girl Behind the Counter,* 1907]

1. When the night falls silently,
     The night falls silently on forests dreaming,
       Lovers wander forth to see,
     They wander forth to see the bright stars gleaming;

       And lest they should lose their way,
     Lest they should lose their way, the glow-worms nightly

110

Light their tiny lanterns gay,
Their tiny lanterns gay and twinkle brightly.

Here and there and ev'rywhere,
From mossy dell and hollow,
Floating, gliding through the air,
They call on us to follow!

*Chorus:*
Shine, little glow-worm, glimmer,
Shine, little glow-worm, glimmer!
  Lead us, lest too far we wander,
  Love's sweet voice is calling yonder!
Shine, little glow-worm, glimmer,
Shine, little glow-worm, glimmer!
  Light the path below, above,
  And lead us on to Love!

2. "Little glow-worm, tell me, pray,
   Oh, glow-worm, tell me, pray, how did you kindle
   Lamps that by the break of day,
   That by the break of day must fade and dwindle?"

   "Ah, this secret, by your leave,
   This secret, by your leave, is worth the learning!
   When true lovers come at eve,
   True lovers come at eve, their hearts are burning!

   "Glowing cheeks and lips betray
   How sweet the kisses tasted!
   Till we steal the fire away,
   For fear lest it be wasted!"

   [*to Chorus*]


# God of Our Fathers
W: GEORGE W. WARREN / M: DANIEL C. ROBERTS

1. God of our fathers, whose almighty hand
   Leads forth in beauty all the starry band;
   Of shining worlds in splendor through the sky,
   Our grateful songs before Thy throne arise.

2. Thy love divine hath led us in the past,
   In this free land by Thee our lot is cast;
   Be Thou our Ruler, Guardian, Guide and Stay,
   Thy word our law, Thy paths our chosen way.

**3.** Refresh Thy people on their toilsome way,
Lead us from night to never-ending day;
Fill all our lives with love and grace divine,
And glory, laud and praise be ever Thine.

# Go Down, Moses
## (Let My People Go) (Down in Egypt Land)
SPIRITUAL

**1.** When Israel was in Egypt's land,
*Let my people go,*
Oppressed so hard they could not stand.
*Let my people go.*
*Go down, Moses, 'way down in Egypt land,*
*Tell ol' Pharaoh, let my people go.*

**2.** Thus spoke the Lord, bold Moses said,
*Let my people go,*
If not, I'll smite your first-born dead.
*Let my people go.*
*Go down, Moses, 'way down in Egypt land,*
*Tell ol' Pharaoh, let my people go.*

**3.** No more shall they in bondage toil,
*Let my people go,*
Let them come out with Egypt's spoil.
*Let my people go.*
*Go down, Moses, 'way down in Egypt land,*
*Tell ol' Pharaoh, let my people go.*

*(Verses 4–11 continue in the same pattern.)*

**4.** The Lord told Moses what to do
To lead his people right on through.

**5.** 'Twas on a dark and dismal night
When Moses led the Israelites.

**6.** Oh, Moses, clouds will cleave the way,
A fire by night, a shade by day.

**7.** When Israel reached the water side,
Commanded God, "It shall divide."

**8.** "Come, Moses, you will not get lost."
"Stretch out your rod and come across."

**9.** When they had reached the other shore,
 They sang a song of triumph o'er.

**10.** Now Pharaoh said he'd go across,
 But Pharaoh and his host were lost.

**11.** Oh, take your shoes from off your feet
 And walk into the golden street.

# God Rest Ye Merry, Gentlemen
ENGLISH CAROL

**1.** God rest ye merry, gentlemen,
 Let nothing you dismay;
 Remember Christ, our Saviour,
 Was born on Christmas Day,
 To save us all from Satan's pow'r
 When we were gone a-stray:
   *O tidings of comfort and joy, comfort and joy;*
   *O tidings of comfort and joy.*

**2.** In Bethlehem in Jewry
 This blessed Babe was born,
 And laid within a manger
 Upon this blessed morn;
 The which His mother, Mary,
 Did nothing take in scorn:
   *O tidings of comfort and joy, comfort and joy;*
   *O tidings of comfort and joy.*

**3.** From God, our heav'nly Father,
 A blessed angel came,
 And unto certain shepherds
 Brought tidings of the same,
 How that in Bethlehem was born
 The Son of God by name:
   *O tidings of comfort and joy, comfort and joy;*
   *O tidings of comfort and joy.*

**4.** "Fear not," then said the angel,
 "Let nothing you affright,
 This day is born a Saviour,
 Of virtue, pow'r and might;
 So frequently to vanquish all
 The friends of Satan quite":
   *O tidings of comfort and joy, comfort and joy;*
   *O tidings of comfort and joy.*

113

5. The shepherds at those tidings
   Rejoicéd much in mind,
   And left their flocks a-feeding,
   In tempest, storm and wind,
   And went to Bethlehem straightway
   This blessed Babe to find:
     *O tidings of comfort and joy, comfort and joy;*
     *O tidings of comfort and joy.*

6. But when to Bethlehem they came,
   Whereat this Infant lay,
   They found Him in a manger,
   Where oxen feed on hay;
   His mother, Mary, kneeling,
   Unto the Lord did pray:
     *O tidings of comfort and joy, comfort and joy;*
     *O tidings of comfort and joy.*

7. Now to the Lord sing praises,
   All you within this place,
   And with true love and brotherhood
   Each other now embrace;
   This holy tide of Christmas
   All others doth deface:
     *O tidings of comfort and joy, comfort and joy;*
     *O tidings of comfort and joy.*


# God Save the King/(Queen)

TRADITIONAL ENGLISH ANTHEM
*(same melody as "America")*

God save our gracious King/(Queen),
Long live our noble King /(Queen),
God save the King/(Queen).

Send him/(her) victorious,
Happy and glorious,
Long to reign over us,
God save the King/(Queen).

# Goober Peas

TRADITIONAL AMERICAN

*( This extremely popular Confederate camp song honored the old-fashioned peanut—a diet stable in times of lean rations. A first edition, 1866, facetiously credited authorship to "P. Nutt" and "A. Pindar"—* pinda *is the Deep South's label for the peanut. One standard reference work soberly lists author of words and music as "Johnny Reb— erroneously credited to A. Pindar, Esq." "Johnny Reb" is, of course, the Confederate soldier's equivalent of "G. I. Joe.")*

1. Sitting by the roadside on a summer day,
   Chatting with my messmates, passing time away,
   Lying in the shadow underneath the trees,
   Goodness, how delicious, eating goober peas!

   *Chorus:*
   Peas! Peas! Peas! Peas!
   Eating goober peas!
   Goodness, how delicious,
   Eating goober peas!

2. When a horseman passes, the soldiers have a rule,
   To cry out at their loudest, "Mister, here's your mule,"
   But another pleasure enchantinger than these
   Is wearing out your grinders eating goober peas!

   *[to Chorus]*

3. Just before the battle, the General hears a row,
   He says, "The Yanks are coming, I hear their rifles now";
   He turns around in wonder, and what do you think he sees,
   The Georgia Militia, eating goober peas!

   *[to Chorus]*

4. I think my song has lasted almost long enough,
   The subject's interesting, but rhymes are mighty rough;
   I wish this war was over when free from rags and fleas,
   We'd kiss our wives and sweethearts and gobble goober peas!

   *[to Chorus]*

# Good-Bye!

W: C. J. WHYTE-MELVILLE / M: F. PAOLO TOSTI (1881)

Falling leaf and fading tree,
Lines of white in a sullen sea,
Shadows rising on you and me,
Shadows rising on you and me.

The swallows are making them ready to fly,
Wheeling out on a windy sky . . .
 Good-bye, Summer!
 Good-bye! Good-bye!
 Good-bye, Summer!
 Good-bye! Good-bye!

Hush! A voice from the far-away!
"Listen and learn," it seems to say,
"All the tomorrows shall be as today,
All the tomorrows shall be as today."

The cord is frayed, the crust is dry,
The link must break, and the lamp must die . . .
 Good-bye to Hope!
 Good-bye! Good-bye!
 Good-bye to Hope!
 Good-bye! Good-bye!

What are we waiting for? Oh! my heart!
Kiss me straight on the brows! and part!
Again! Again! my heart! my heart!
Again! Again! my heart! my heart!

What are we waiting for, you and I?
A pleading look, a stifled cry;
 Good-bye forever!
 Good-bye forever!
 Good-bye! Good-bye!
 Good-bye!

# Goodbye, Broadway! Hello, France!

W: C. FRANCIS REISNER & BENNY DAVIS

M: BILLY BASKETTE (1917)

1. Goodbye, New York town, Goodbye, Miss Liberty,
   Your light of freedom will guide us across the sea;
   Ev'ry soldier's sweetheart bidding goodbye,
   Ev'ry soldier's mother drying her eye.
   > Cheer up, we'll soon be there,
   > Singing this Yankee air:

   > *Chorus:*
   > Goodbye, Broadway! Hello, France,
   > We're ten million strong;
   > Goodbye, sweethearts, wives and mothers,
   > It won't take us long.

   Don't you worry while we're there,
   It's for you we're fighting too,
   (*2nd time, ad lib.:* It's you we're fighting for,)
   So goodbye, Broadway, Hello, France,
   We're going to square our debt to you.
   (*2nd time:* We're going to help you win this war.)

2. "Vive Pershing" is the cry across the sea,
   We're united in this fight for liberty;
   France sent us a soldier, brave Lafayette,
   Whose deeds and fame we cannot forget.
   > Now that we have the chance,
   > We'll pay our debt to France:

   [*to Chorus*]


# Good Bye, My Lady Love

W & M: JOSEPH E. HOWARD (1904)

1. So you're going away
   Because your heart has gone astray,
   And you promised me
   That you would always faithful be.

   Go to him you love,
   And be as true as stars above;
   But your heart will yearn,
   And then some day you will return.

117

*Chorus:*
Good bye, my lady love,
Farewell, my turtle-dove,
  You are the idol and darling of my heart;
  But some day
You will come back to me,
And love me tenderly,
  So good bye, my lady love, good bye.

2. When the dewdrops fall,
  'Tis then your heart, I know, will call.
  So beware, my dove,
  Don't trust your life to some false love.

But if you must go,
Remember, dear, I love you so,
Sure as stars do shine,
You'll think of when I called you mine.

  [*to Chorus*]


# Goodbye, Old Paint
AMERICAN COWBOY SONG

1. Goodbye, old Paint, I'm a-leaving Cheyenne,
  Goodbye, old Paint, I'm a-leaving Cheyenne.

2. I'm a-leaving Cheyenne, I'm off for Montan',
  Goodbye, old Paint, I'm a-leaving Cheyenne.

3. Old Paint's a good pony, he paces when he can,
  Goodbye, old Paint, I'm a-leaving Cheyenne.

4. Go hitch up your hosses and give them some hay,
  And seat yourself by me so long as you stay.

5. My hosses ain't hungry, they won't eat your hay,
  My wagon is loaded and rolling away.

6. My foot's in the stirrup, my bridle's in my hand,
  Good morning, young lady, my hosses won't stand.

7. Goodbye, old Paint, I'm a-leaving Cheyenne,
  Goodbye, old Paint, I'm a-leaving Cheyenne.

# Good King Wenceslas

W: REV. JOHN MASON NEALE (1853) / M: ANON.

1. Good King Wenceslas looked out,
   On the Feast of Stephen,
   When the snow lay 'round about,
   Deep and crisp and even.

   Brightly shone the moon that night,
   Though the frost was cruel,
   When a poor man came in sight,
   Gath'ring winter fuel.

2. "Hither, page, and stand by me,
   If thou know'st it, telling:
   Yonder peasant, who is he?
   Where and what his dwelling?"

   "Sire, he lives a good league hence,
   Underneath the mountain,
   Right against the forest fence,
   By Saint Agnes' fountain."

3. "Bring me flesh and bring me wine,
   Bring me pine-logs hither:
   Thou and I shall see him dine,
   When we bear him thither."

   Page and monarch, forth they went,
   Forth they went together;
   Through the rude wind's wild lament
   And the bitter weather.

4. "Sire, the night is darker now,
   And the wind blows stronger;
   Fails my heart, I know not how;
   I can go no longer."

   "Mark my footsteps, good my page;
   Tread thou in them boldly:
   Thou shalt find the winter's rage
   Freeze thy blood less coldly."

5. In his master's step he trod,
   Where the snow lay dinted;
   Heat was in the very sod
   Which the Saint had printed.

   Therefore, Christian men, be sure,
   Wealth or rank possessing;
   Ye, who now will bless the poor,
   Shall yourself find blessing.

# Goodnight, Ladies

W & M: E. P. CHRISTY (1847)
*(originally, "Farewell Ladies")*

1. Goodnight, ladies!
   Goodnight, ladies!
   Goodnight, ladies!
   We're going to leave you now.

   > *Chorus:*
   > Merrily we roll along,
   > Roll along, roll along,
   > Merrily we roll along,
   > O'er the dark blue sea.

   *[repeat Chorus, softly]*

2. Farewell, ladies!
   Farewell, ladies!
   Farewell, ladies!
   We're going to leave you now.

   > *[to Chorus, repeated]*

3. Sweet dreams, ladies!
   Sweet dreams, ladies!
   Sweet dreams, ladies!
   We're going to leave you now!

   > *[to Chorus, repeated]*


# Go Tell Aunt Rhody

AMERICAN FOLK SONG

1. Go tell Aunt Rhody,
   Go tell Aunt Rhody,
   Go tell Aunt Rhody
   The old grey goose is dead.

2. The one she was saving,
   The one she was saving,
   The one she was saving
   To make a feather bed.

3. The gander is weeping
   *(etc.)*
   Because his wife is dead.

4. The gosling are crying
     (*etc.*)
   Because their mama's dead.

5. She died in the water
     (*etc.*)
   With her heels above her head.

---

# Go, Tell It on the Mountain
SPIRITUAL

1. While shepherds kept their watching
   O'er silent flocks by night,
   Behold throughout the heavens,
   There shone a holy light.

     *Chorus:*
     Go, tell it on the mountain,
     Over the hills and ev'rywhere;
     Go, tell it on the mountain
     That Jesus Christ is born.

2. The shepherds feared and trembled
   When lo! above the earth
   Rang out the angel chorus
   That hailed our Saviour's birth.

     [*to Chorus*]

3. Down in a lowly manger
   Our humble Christ was born,
   And God sent us salvation
   That blessed Christmas morn.

     [*to Chorus*]

4. When I was a seeker,
   I sought both night and day;
   I sought the Lord to help me,
   And He showed me the way.

     [*to Chorus*]

5. He made me a watchman
   Upon the city wall,
   And if I am a Christian,
   I am the least of all.

     [*to Chorus*]

# Go 'Way f'om Mah Window
LAMENT FROM THE OZARKS

1. Go 'way f'om mah window,
   Go 'way f'om mah doh,
   Go 'way f'om mah bedside,
   Don' you tease me no mo'.

2. Go 'way in de springtime,
   Come back in de fall,
   Bring you back mo' money
   Dan we bofe can haul.


# Grandfather's Clock
W & M: HENRY CLAY WORK (1876)

1. My grandfather's clock was too large for the shelf,
   So it stood ninety years on the floor;
   It was taller by half than the old man himself,
   Though it weighed not a pennyweight more.

   It was bought on the morn of the day he was born,
   And was always his treasure and pride;
   But it stopp'd short—never to run again—
   When the old man died.

   *Chorus:*
   Ninety years, without slumbering
      (tick, tick, tick, tick),
   His life-seconds numbering
      (tick, tick, tick, tick),
   It stopp'd short—never to run again—
   When the old man died.

2. In watching its pendulum swing to and fro,
   Many hours had he spent while a boy;
   And in childhood and manhood the clock seemed to know,
   And to share both his grief and his joy.

   For it struck twenty-four when he entered the door,
   With a blooming and beautiful bride;
   But it stopp'd short—never to run again—
   When the old man died.

   [*to Chorus*]

**3.** My grandfather said that of those he could hire,
Not a servant so faithful, he found;
For it wasted no time, and had but one desire,
At the close of each week to be wound.

And it kept in its place—not a frown upon its face,
And its hands never hung by its side;
But it stopp'd short—never to run again—
When the old man died.

[*to Chorus*]

**4.** It rang an alarm in the dead of the night,
An alarm that for years had been dumb;
And we knew that his spirit was pluming for flight,
That his hour of departure had come.

Still the clock kept the time, with a soft and muffled chime,
As we silently stood by his side.
But it stopp'd short—never to run again—
When the old man died.

[*to Chorus*]


# Greensleeves
W: RICHARD JONES? (1580) / M: ANON. (before 1652)

**1.** Alas, my love, you will do me wrong
If you cast me off so discourteously,
And I have loved you so very long
And delighting in your winning company.

*Chorus:*
Greensleeves, you were all my joy,
And you know, Greensleeves, you were my delight.
Greensleeves, you're my heart of gold,
No one else but my dear Lady Greensleeves.

**2.** I have been ready and at your hand
For to grant whatever your heart would crave,
And I have waged both my life and land
Your dear love and your good will to hold and have.

[*to Chorus*]

**3.** I bought thee kerchers to 'dorn thy head
That were wrought so fine and so gallantly.
I kept thee well both at board and bed,
Which did cost my own purse so well favoredly.

*[to Chorus]*

4. I bought thee petticoats of the best
   With a cloth so fine and soft as might be.
   I gave thee jewels for thine own chest,
   And yet all of this cost I did spend on thee.

   *[to Chorus]*

5. Well I will pray to our God on high
   So that thou my constancy mayest see,
   And that yet once more before I die
   Thou so surely wilt vouchsafe to love me.

   *[to Chorus]*

6. Greensleeves, now farewell, adieu, adieu.
   For to God I pray Him to prosper thee,
   For I am still thy one lover true,
   Come to me once again and do love me.

   *[to Chorus]*


# Gypsy Love Song
## (Slumber On, My Little Gypsy Sweetheart)
W: HARRY B. SMITH / M: VICTOR HERBERT
[from *The Fortune Teller,* 1898]

1. The birds of the forest are calling for thee,
   And the shades and the glades are lonely;
   Summer is there with her blossoms fair,
   And you are absent only.

   No bird that nests in the greenwood tree
   But sighs to greet you and kiss you,
   All the violets yearn, yearn for your safe return,
   But most of all I miss you.

   *Chorus:*
   Slumber on, my little gypsy sweetheart,
   Dream of the field and the grove;
   Can you hear me, hear me in that dreamland
   Where your fancies rove?

   Slumber on, my little gypsy sweetheart,
   Wild little woodland dove;
   Can you hear the song that tells you
   All my heart's true love?

**2.** The fawn that you tamed has a look in its eyes
   That doth say "We are too long parted";
   Songs that are trolled by our comrades old
   Are not now as they were light-hearted.

The wild rose fades in the leafy shades,
Its ghost will find you and haunt you,
All the friends say "Come, come to your woodland home,"
And most of all I want you.

   [*to Chorus*]


# Hail Columbia

W: JOSEPH HOPKINSON / M: PHILIP FAYLES (ca. 1790)

**1.** Hail Columbia, happy land,
   Hail ye heroes, heav'n-born band
   Who fought and bled in freedom's cause,
   Who fought and bled in freedom's cause,
      And when the storm of war was gone,
      Enjoyed the peace your valor won.

Let independence be your boast,
Ever mindful what it cost,
Ever grateful for the prize,
Let its altar reach the skies.

   *Chorus:*
   Firm, united let us stand,
   Rallying 'round our liberty
   As a band of brothers joined,
   Peace and safety we shall find.


**2.** Immortal patriots, rise once more,
   Defend your rights, defend your shore.
   Let no rude foe with impious hand,
   Let no rude foe with impious hand
      Invade the shrine where sacred lies,
      Of toil and blood, the well-earned prize.

While off'ring peace, sincere and just,
In heav'n we place a manly trust
That truth and justice may prevail
And ev'ry scheme of bondage fail.

   [*to Chorus*]

3. Sound, sound the trumpet of fame,
   Let Washington's great name
   Ring through the world with loud applause,
   Ring through the world with loud applause.
   Let ev'ry chime to freedom dear
   Listen with a joyful ear.

   With equal skill, with steady pow'r,
   He governs in the fearful hour
   Of horrid war, or guides with ease
   The happier time of honest peace.

   [*to Chorus*]

4. Behold the chief who now commands.
   Once more to serve his country stands
   The rock on which the storm will beat,
   The rock on which the storm will beat.
   But armed in virtue, firm and true,
   His hopes are fixed on heav'n and you.

   When hope was sinking in dismay,
   When gloom obscured Columbia's day,
   His steady mind, from changes free,
   Resolved on death or liberty.

   [*to Chorus*]

# Hail! Hail! The Gang's All Here!

W: "D. A. ESROM"

M: THEODORE MORSE (?) & SIR ARTHUR SULLIVAN
*(Origin of the lyrics is in doubt, although Theodora Morse—called Dolly,
pen name "D. A. Esrom"—has been credited as author. The melody originally was known as "Come, Friends, Who Plough the Sea," from Gilbert
and Sullivan's* The Pirates of Penzance, *1879.)*

1. A gang of good fellows are we (are we),
   With never a worry you see (you see),
   We laugh and joke, we sing and smoke,
   And live life merrily;
      No matter the weather
      when we get together
      we have just a jubilee.

   *Chorus:*
   Hail! Hail! The gang's all here,
   What the (deuce) do we care,
   What the (deuce) do we care,

Hail! We're full of cheer,
What the (deuce) do we care, Bill!

[*repeat Chorus*]

2. We love one another we do (we do),
   With brotherly love and it's true (it's true),
   It's one for all, the big and small,
   It's always me for you;
       No matter the weather
       when we get together
       we drink a toast or two.

   [*to Chorus*]

3. When out for a good time we go (we go),
   There's nothing we do that is slow (is slow),
   Of joy we get our share you bet,
   The gang will tell you so;
       No matter the weather
       when we get together
       we sing this song you know.

   [*to Chorus*]

# Hallelujah Chorus

W: COMPILED & ADAPTED BY CHARLES JENNENS
M: GEORGE FRIDERIC HANDEL
[from *Messiah*, 1742]

*Hallelujah!*
*Hallelujah!*
*Hallelujah! Hallelujah!*
*Hallelujah!*

   [*repeats*]

For the Lord God Omnipotent reigneth!
*Hallelujah! Hallelujah! Hallelujah! Hallelujah!*

   [*repeats*]

The kingdom of this world
is become the kingdom of our Lord,
and of His Christ, and of His Christ;

And He shall reign forever and ever,
King of kings . . .
   *Forever and ever,*
   *Hallelujah! Hallelujah!*

and Lord of lords,
*Forever and ever,*
*Hallelujah! Hallelujah!*
King of kings, and Lord of lords!

And He shall reign forever and ever,
King of kings, and Lord of lords,
*Forever and ever,*
*Hallelujah! Hallelujah!*

[*repeats freely*]

Hallelujah!


# Hand Me Down My Walking Cane

SPIRITUAL
*(Some sources name James A. Bland as composer.)*

Hand me down my walking cane,
Hand me down my walking cane,
Oh, hand me down my walking cane,
I'm a-goin' to leave on that midnight train,
'Cause all of my sins are taken away.

Hand me down my bottle of corn,
Hand me down my bottle of corn,
Oh, hand me down my bottle of corn,
I'm a-goin' to leave drunk as sure as you're born,
'Cause all of my sins are taken away.


# Hark! The Herald Angels Sing

W: CHARLES WESLEY (1739)
M: FELIX MENDELSSOHN (ca. 1840)

1. Hark! the herald angels sing,
   "Glory to the new-born King!
   Peace on earth, and mercy mild,
   God and sinners reconciled."

   Joyful, all ye nations rise,
   Join the triumph of the skies;
   With th' angelic host proclaim,
   "Christ is born in Bethlehem."
   *Hark! the herald angels sing,*
   *"Glory to the new-born King!"*

128

2. Christ, by highest heav'n adored;
   Christ, the everlasting Lord;
   Late in time behold Him come,
   Offspring of the favored One.

   Veil'd in flesh, the Godhead see;
   Hail th' incarnate Deity:
   Pleased, as man, with men to dwell,
   Jesus, our Immanuel!
       *Hark! the herald angels sing,*
       *"Glory to the new-born King!"*

3. Hail! the heav'n-born Prince of Peace!
   Hail! the Son of Righteousness!
   Light and life to all He brings,
   Risen with healing in His wings.

   Mild He lays His glory by,
   Born that man no more may die:
   Born to raise the sons of earth,
   Born to give them second birth.
       *Hark! the herald angels sing,*
       *"Glory to the new-born King!"*

# The Harp That Once Thro' Tara's Halls
W: THOMAS MOORE (ca. 1810) / M: ANON.

1. The harp that once thro' Tara's halls
   The soul of music shed,
   Now hangs as mute on Tara's walls
   As if that soul were fled;

   So sleeps the pride of former days,
   So glory's thrill is o'er;
   And hearts that once beat high for praise,
   Now feel that pulse no more.

2. No more to chiefs and ladies bright
   The harp of Tara swells;
   The chord alone, that breaks at night,
   Its tale of ruin tells;

   Thus Freedom now so seldom wakes,
   The only throb she gives
   Is when some heart indignant breaks
   To show that she still lives!

# Harrigan

W & M: GEORGE M. COHAN
[from *Fifty Miles from Boston*, 1907]

1. Who is the man who will spend or will even lend?
   Harrigan, that's me!
   Who is your friend when you find that you need a friend?
   Harrigan, that's me!

   I'm just as proud of my name, you see,
   As an Emperor, Czar or a King could be:
   Who is the man helps a man ev'ry time he can?
   Harrigan, that's me!

   > *Chorus:*
   > H - A - double R - I -
   > G-A-N spells Harrigan,
   > Proud of all the Irish blood that's in me;
   > Divil a man can say a word agin me.
   >
   > H - A - double R - I -
   > G-A-N, you see,
   > Is a name that a shame never has been connected with,
   > Harrigan, that's me!

2. Who is the man never stood for a gadabout?
   Harrigan, that's me!
   Who is the man that the town's simply mad about?
   Harrigan, that's me!

   The ladies and babies are fond of me,
   I'm fond of them, too, in return, you see:
   Who is the gent that's deserving a monument?
   Harrigan, that's me!

   > [*to Chorus*]


# Has Anybody Here Seen Kelly?

W & M: C. W. MURPHY & WILL LETTERS
*( Originally an English music-hall song called "Kelly from the Isle of Man," the American version was part of William J. McKenna's* The Jolly Bachelors, *1909.)*

1. Michael Kelly with his sweetheart came from County Cork,
       And bent upon a holiday, they landed in New York.
   They strolled around to see the sights, alas, it's sad to say,
       Poor Kelly lost his little girl upon the Great White Way.
   She walked uptown from Herald Square to Forty-Second Street,
       The traffic stopped as she cried to the copper on the beat:

Has anybody here seen Kelly?
K. E. double-L. Y,
Has anybody here seen Kelly?
Have you seen him smile?

Sure, his hair is red, his eyes are blue,
And he's Irish through and through,
Has anybody here seen Kelly?
Kelly from the Emerald Isle.

2. Over on Fifth Avenue, a band began to play,
   Ten thousand men were marching, for it was Saint Patrick's Day.
   "The Wearing of the Green" rang out upon the morning air,
   'Twas Kelly's fav'rite song, so Mary said, "I'll find him there."
   She climbed upon the grandstand in hopes her Mike she'd see,
   Five hundred Kellys left the ranks in answer to her plea.

   [*to Chorus*]


# Havah Nagilah
ISRAELI DANCE-SONG

Havah nagilah, havah nagilah,
Havah nagilah vay nism'chayh!
Havah nagilah, havah ṅagilah,
Havah nagilah vay nism'chayh!

Havah n'ranenah, havah n'ranenah,
Havah n'ranenah vay nism'chayh!
Havah n'ranenah, havah n'ranenah,
Havah n'ranenah vay nism'chayh!

Uru, uru, achim,
Uru achim, b'lev sameach,
Uru achim, b'lev sameach,
Uru achim, b'lev sameach,
Uru achim, b'lev sameach,
Uru achim!
Uru achim!
B'lev sameach!

# Hello Central, Give Me Heaven

W & M: CHARLES K. HARRIS (1901)

1. "Papa, I'm so sad and lonely,"
   Sobbed a tearful little child.
   "Since dear mama's gone to heaven,
   Papa darling, you've not smiled.

   "I will speak to her and tell her
   That we want her to come home;
   Just you listen and I'll call her
   Through the telephone:

   > *Chorus:*
   > "Hello Central, give me heaven,
   > For my mama's there;
   > You can find her with the angels
   > On the golden stair.
   >
   > "She'll be glad it's me who's speaking;
   > Call her, won't you please;
   > For I want to surely tell her
   > We're so lonely here."

2. When the girl received this message,
   Coming o'er the telephone,
   How her heart thrilled in that moment,
   And the wires seemed to moan:

   "I will answer just to please her,
   Yes, dear heart, I'll soon come home."
   "Kiss me, mama, kiss your darling
   Through the telephone:

   > [*to Chorus*]

# Hello! Ma Baby

W & M: JOSEPH E. HOWARD & IDA EMERSON (1899)

1. I'se got a little baby, but she's out of sight,
   I talk to her across the telephone;
   I'se never seen my honey but she's mine, all right;
   So take my tip, an' leave this gal alone.

   Ev'ry single morning, you will hear me yell,
   "Hey Central! fix me up along the line."
   He connects me with ma honey, then I rings the bell,
   And so each day I shout along the line:

*Chorus:*
"Hello! ma baby, Hello! ma honey,
Hello! ma ragtime gal,
Send me a kiss by wire,
Baby, my heart's on fire!

"If you refuse me, honey, you'll lose me,
Then you'll be left alone; oh, baby,
Telephone and tell me I'se your own.
    (Hello! hello! hello there!)

2. This morning, thro' the 'phone, she said her name was Bess,
And now I kind of know where I am at;
I'se satisfied because I'se got my babe's address,
Here pasted in the lining of my hat.

I am mighty scared, 'cause if the wires get crossed
'Twill separate me from ma baby mine,
Then some other coon will win her, and my game is lost,
And so each day I shout along the line:

    [*to Chorus*]


# He's Got the Whole World in His Hand
SPIRITUAL

*Chorus:*
He's got the whole world in His hand,
He's got the whole wide world in His hand,
He's got the whole world in His hand,
He's got the whole world in His hand.

1. He's got the mountains and the rivers in His hand,
He's got the mountains and the rivers in His hand,
He's got the mountains and the rivers in His hand,
He's got the whole world in His hand.

    [*to Chorus*]

2. He's got the tiny bitsy baby in His hand,
He's got the tiny bitsy baby in His hand,
He's got the tiny bitsy baby in His hand,
He's got the whole world in His hand.

    [*to Chorus*]

**3.** He's got the mighty and the humble in His hand,
He's got the mighty and the humble in His hand,
He's got the mighty and the humble in His hand,
He's got the whole world in His hand.

[*to Chorus*]

**4.** He's got the kingdom up in Heaven in His hand,
He's got the kingdom up in Heaven in His hand,
He's got the kingdom up in Heaven in His hand,
He's got the whole world in His hand.

[*to Chorus*]


# Hiawatha
## (His Song to Minnehaha)
W: JAMES O'DEA / M: NEIL MORET (1903)

**1.** Oh the moon is all a-gleam
on the stream
where I dream here of you, my pretty Indian maid,
while the rustling leaves are singing high above us overhead.

In the glory of the bright
summer night,
in the light and the shadows of the forest glade,
I am waiting here to kiss your lips so red.

There's a flood of melodies
on the breeze
from the trees and of you they breathe so tenderly
while the woodlands all around are resounding your name.

Oh my, all in life is you, only you,
fond and true
and your own forever I'll be.
Hear then the song I sing with lips a-flame:

*Chorus:*
I am your own dear Hiawatha brave,
My heart is yours, you know; Dear one, I love you so.
Oh Minnehaha, gentle maid, decide,
Decide and say you'll be my Indian bride.

**2.** In the tresses of your hair
lies a snare
and its there where my heart a willing captive is;
oh my woodland queen, I pray you'll hold it ever in your care.

In my little birch canoe,
  love, with you,
  just we two down the stream of life in wedded bliss
  I would drift, sweetheart, with you my lot to share.

When the birds upon the wing
  in the spring
  gaily sing of the green and golden summertime,
  when the snows of early winter robe the woodlands in white,

Then your Hiawatha free
  I will be
  and to thee ev'ry thought of mine will e'er incline.
  Heed then the vows I pledge to thee this night:

  [*to Chorus*]


# Hindustan
W & M: OLIVER G. WALLACE & HAROLD WEEKS (1918)

1. Camel trappings jingle,
   Harp-strings sweetly tingle,
   With a sweet voice mingle underneath the stars;

   Singing,
   Memories are bringing,
   Temple bells are ringing, calling me afar.

   *Chorus:*
   Hindustan,
     where we stopped to rest our tired caravan;
   Hindustan,
     where the painted peacock proudly spreads his fan;
   Hindustan,
     where the purple sun-bird flashed across the sand,
   Hindustan,
     where I met her and the world began.

2. Shades of night are falling,
   Nightingales are calling,
   Ev'ry heart enthralling underneath the stars;

   Sighing,
   Like the night wind dying,
   Soft my heart is crying for my love afar.

   [*to Chorus*]

# Hinky Dinky Parlay-Voo
## (Mademoiselle from Armentières)
TRADITIONAL WORLD WAR I SONG

1. Mademoiselle from Armentières, parlay-voo,
   Mademoiselle from Armentières, parlay-voo,
   Mademoiselle from Armentières,
   She hasn't been kissed in forty years.
   *Hinky dinky parlay-voo*

2. Farmer, have you a daughter fair, parlay-voo,
   Farmer, have you a daughter fair, parlay-voo,
   Farmer, have you a daughter fair
   To wash a poor soldier's underwear?
   *Hinky dinky parlay-voo*

3. Mademoiselle from Armentières, parlay-voo,
   Mademoiselle from Armentières, parlay-voo,
   Mademoiselle from Armentières,
   She never did hear of underwear.
   *Hinky dinky parlay-voo*

4. Officers came across the Rhine, parlay-voo,
   Officers came across the Rhine, parlay-voo,
   Officers came across the Rhine
   To kiss all the girls and drink the wine.
   *Hinky dinky parlay-voo*

5. Officers eat up all the steak, parlay-voo,
   Officers eat up all the steak, parlay-voo,
   Officers eat up all the steak,
   And all we can get's a bellyache.
   *Hinky dinky parlay-voo*

6. One night I had some "beaucoup" Jack, parlay-voo,
   One night I had some "beaucoup" Jack, parlay-voo,
   One night I had some "beaucoup" Jack
   Till mademoiselle got on my track.
   *Hinky dinky parlay-voo*

7. You may forget the gas and shells, parlay-voo,
   You may forget the gas and shells, parlay-voo,
   You may forget the gas and shells,
   You'll never forget the mademoiselles.
   *Hinky dinky parlay-voo*

**8.** Captain is carrying the pack, parlay-voo,
  Captain is carrying the pack, parlay-voo,
  Captain is carrying the pack,
  I'm hoping it breaks his darling back.
    *Hinky dinky parlay-voo*

**9.** Mademoiselle heard cannon roar, parlay-voo,
  Mademoiselle heard cannon roar, parlay-voo,
  Mademoiselle heard cannon roar,
  But all that we heard was "je t'adore."
    *Hinky dinky parlay-voo*

# The Holly and the Ivy
ENGLISH CAROL

**1.** The holly and the ivy,
  When they are both full grown,
  Of all the trees that are in the wood,
  The holly bears the crown.

> *Chorus*:
> The rising of the sun
> And the running of the deer,
> The playing of the merry organ,
> Sweet singing of the choir.

**2.** The holly bears the blossom,
  As white as the lily flower,
  And Mary bore sweet Jesus Christ
  To be our sweet Saviour.

> [*to Chorus*]

**3.** The holly bears a berry,
  As red as any blood,
  And Mary bore sweet Jesus Christ
  To do poor sinners good.

> [*to Chorus*]

**4.** The holly bears a prickle,
  As sharp as any thorn,
  And Mary bore sweet Jesus Christ
  On Christmas day in the morn.

> [*to Chorus*]

**5.** The holly bears a bark,
As bitter as any gall,
And Mary bore sweet Jesus Christ
For to redeem us all.

[*to Chorus*]


# Holy, Holy, Holy! Lord God Almighty!
W: REGINALD HEBER / M: JOHN B. DYKES

**1.** Holy, Holy, Holy!
Lord God Almighty!
Early in the morning
our song shall rise to Thee;

Holy, Holy, Holy!
Merciful and Mighty!
God in three Persons,
blessed Trinity!

**2.** Holy, Holy, Holy!
all the saints adore Thee,
Casting down their golden crowns
around the glassy sea;

Cherubim and Seraphim
falling down before Thee,
Which wert and art,
and evermore shall be.

**3.** Holy, Holy, Holy!
tho' the darkness hide Thee,
Tho' the eye of sinful man
Thy glory may not see;

Only Thou art Holy,
there is none beside Thee,
Perfect in pow'r,
in love, and purity.

**4.** Holy, Holy, Holy!
Lord God Almighty!
All Thy works shall praise Thy name
in earth, and sky, and sea;

Holy, Holy, Holy!
Merciful and Mighty!
God in three Persons,
blessed Trinity!

# Home on the Range
W: DR. BREWSTER M. HIGLEY / M: DANIEL E. KELLEY (ca. 1872)

1. Oh, give me a home where the buffalo roam,
   Where the deer and the antelope play,
   Where seldom is heard a discouraging word
   And the skies are not cloudy all day.

   *Chorus:*
   Home, home on the range,
   Where the deer and the antelope play,
   Where seldom is heard a discouraging word
   And the skies are not cloudy all day.

2. Where air is so pure and the zephyrs so free
   And the breezes so balmy and light,
   I would not exchange my own home on the range,
   Not for all of the cities so bright.

   [*to Chorus*]

3. How often a night when the heavens are bright
   With the light of the glittering stars,
   I stood there amazed and I asked as I gazed
   If their glory exceeds that of ours.

   [*to Chorus*]

4. I love the wild flow'rs in this dear land of ours,
   And the curlew I love to hear scream,
   I love the white rocks and the antelope flocks
   That are grazing on mountain tops green.

   [*to Chorus*]


# Home! Sweet Home!
W: JOHN HOWARD PAYNE / M: HENRY R. BISHOP
[from *Clari, the Maid of Milan,* 1823]

1. 'Mid pleasures and palaces, though we may roam,
   Be it ever so humble, there's no place like home;
   A charm from the skies seems to hallow us there,
   Which, seek thro' the world, is ne'er met with elsewhere.
   *Home, home, sweet, sweet home,*
   *Be it ever so humble, there's no place like home.*

139

**2.** I gaze on the moon, as I trace the drear wild,
And feel that my parent now thinks of her child;
She looks on that moon from our own cottage door,
Through woodbines whose fragrance shall cheer me no more.
*Home, home, sweet, sweet home,*
*Be it ever so humble, there's no place like home.*

**3.** An exile from home, splendor dazzles in vain;
Oh! give me my lowly thatched cottage again;
The birds sing so gaily, that come at my call:
Give me sweet peace of mine, dearer than all.
*Home, home, sweet, sweet home,*
*Be it ever so humble, there's no place like home.*

**4.** If I return home, overburdened with care,
The heart's dearest solace I'm sure to meet there;
The bliss I experience whenever I come,
Makes no other place seem like that of sweet home.
*Home, home, sweet, sweet home,*
*Be it ever so humble, there's no place like home.*

**5.** Farewell, peaceful cottage! farewell, happy home!
Forever I'm doomed a poor exile to roam;
This poor, aching heart must be laid in the tomb,
Ere it cease to regret the endearments of home.
*Home, home, sweet, sweet home,*
*Be it ever so humble, there's no place like home.*

# A Hot Time in the Old Town
W: JOE HAYDEN / M: THEODORE A. METZ (1896)

**1.** Come along, get ready, wear your bran', bran' new gown,
For dere's gwine to be a meeting in that good, good old town,
Where you knowded ev'rybody, and dey all knowded you,
And you've got a rabbit's foot to keep away de hoodo;

When you hear that the preaching does begin,
Bend down low for to drive away your sin,
And when you gets religion, you want to shout and sing,
There'll be a hot time in the old town tonight, my baby.

*Chorus:*
When you hear dem-a bells go ding, ling ling,
All join 'round and sweetly you must sing,
And when the verse am through, in the chorus all join in,
There'll be a hot time in the old town tonight.

140

**2.** There'll be girls for ev'rybody in that good, good old town,
For dere's Miss Consola Davis and dere's Miss Gondolia Brown;
And dere's Miss Johanna Beasly, she am dressed all in red,
I just hugged her and I kissed her and to me then she said:

"Please, oh, please, oh, do not let me fall,
You're all mine and I love you best of all,
And you must be my man, or I'll have no man at all,
There'll be a hot time in the old town tonight, my baby."

[*to Chorus*]

# How' Ya Gonna Keep 'Em Down on the Farm
## (After They've Seen Paree?)
W: SAM M. LEWIS & JOE YOUNG / M: WALTER DONALDSON (1919)

**1.** "Reuben, Reuben, I've been thinking,"
Said his wifey dear;
"Now that all is peaceful and calm,
The boys will soon be back on the farm."

Mister Reuben started winking,
And slowly rubbed his chin;
He pulled his chair up close to mother,
And he asked her with a grin:

*Chorus:*
"How' ya gonna keep 'em down on the farm,
After they've seen Paree?
How' ya gonna keep 'em away from Broadway,
Jazzin' aroun' and paintin' the town?

"How' ya gonna keep 'em away from harm?
That's a mystery;
They'll never want to see a rake or plow,
    (*2nd time:* Imagine Reuben when he meets his pa,)
And who the deuce can parley-vous a cow?
    (*2nd time:* He'll kiss his cheek and holler 'oo-la-la!')

"How' ya gonna keep 'em down on the farm,
After they've seen Paree?"

**2.** "Reuben, Reuben, you're mistaken,"
Said his wifey dear;
"Once a farmer, always a jay,
And farmers always stick to the hay."

"Mother Reuben, I'm not fakin';
Tho' you may think it strange;
But wine and women play the mischief
With a boy who's loose with change":

[*to Chorus*]

141

# Hush, Little Baby

AMERICAN LULLABY

1. Hush, little baby, don't say a word,
   Daddy's gonna buy you a mockingbird;
   And if that mockingbird won't sing,
   Daddy's gonna buy you a diamond ring.

2. And if that diamond ring turns to brass,
   Daddy's gonna buy you a looking glass;
   And if that looking glass gets broke,
   Daddy's gonna buy you a billy goat.

3. And if that billy goat won't pull,
   Daddy's gonna buy you a cart and bull;
   And if that cart and bull turn over,
   Daddy's gonna buy you a dog named Rover.

4. And if that dog named Rover won't bark,
   Daddy's gonna buy you a horse and cart;
   And if that horse and cart fall down,
   You'll still be the sweetest little baby in town.


# I Ain't Got Nobody
## (And Nobody Cares for Me)

W: DAVID YOUNG / M: CHARLES WARFIELD (1914)

1. I had a sweetheart once I loved,
   And I was happy as could be;
   But now he's gone and left me here
   For someone else, you see.

   Some of these days he'll look for me,
   And I'll be far away,
   And no more will I have to pine
   For the love I thought was mine.
   'Cause—

   *Chorus:*
   I ain't got nobody,
   And nobody cares for me,
   (*I want a little lovin' now and then*)
   That's why I'm sad and lonely,
   Say, won't you just take a chance with me?

   'Cause I'll sing sweet songs all the time,
   If you will be a pal of mine,

142

'Cause I ain't got nobody,
And nobody cares for me.

2. Say, did you ever feel lonesome,
Just as lonesome as could be,
About someone that you just knew
Had really mistreated you.

And you had that sad feeling that
Just made you awful blue,
And you could not get right somehow?
That's the way I'm feeling now.
'Cause—

   [*to Chorus*]


# I Am the Captain of the Pinafore

W: W. S. GILBERT / M: SIR ARTHUR SULLIVAN
[Captain and Chorus from *H. M. S. Pinafore*, 1878]

1. I am the Captain of the "Pinafore,"
   *And a right good captain, too!*
   You're very, very good and be it understood,
   I command a right good crew.
   *We're very, very good and be it understood,*
   *He commands a right good crew.*

   Tho' related to a peer, I can hand a beef and steer,
   Or ship a selvagee;
   I am never known to quail at the fury of the gale,
   And I'm never, never sick at sea!
   *What never?*
   No, never,
   *What never?*
   Hardly ever!
   *He's hardly ever sick at sea.*

   *Then give three cheers and one cheer more*
   *For the hardy Captain of the "Pinafore,"*
   *Then give three cheers and one cheer more*
   *For the Captain of the "Pinafore."*

2. I do my best to satisfy you all,
   *And with you we're quite content!*
   You're exceedingly polite, and I think it only right,
   To return the compliment.
   *We're exceedingly polite, and he thinks it only right,*
   *To return the compliment.*

Bad language or abuse, I never, never use,
Whatever the emergency;
Though "bother it" I may occasionally say,
I never use a big, big D!
*What never?*
No, never,
*What never?*
Hardly ever!
*Hardly ever swear a big, big D!*

*Then give three cheers and one cheer more*
*For the hardy Captain of the "Pinafore,"*
*Then give three cheers and one cheer more*
*For the Captain of the "Pinafore."*

# I Am the Very Model of a Modern Major General

W: W. S. GILBERT / M: SIR ARTHUR SULLIVAN
[General and Chorus from *The Pirates of Penzance*, 1879]

1. I am the very model of a modern major general,
   I've information vegetable, animal, and mineral;
   I know the kings of England and I quote the fights historical,
   From Marathon to Waterloo, in order categorical;

   I'm very well acquainted, too, with matters mathematical,
   I understand equations, both the simple and quadratical,
   About binomial theorem I'm teeming with a lot of news,
   With many cheerful facts about the square of the hypotenuse.
   *With many cheerful facts about the square of the hypotenuse,*
   *With many cheerful facts about the square of the hypotenuse,*
   *With many cheerful facts about the square of the hypotenuse.*

   I'm very good at integral and differential calculus,
   I know the scientific names of beings animalculous.
   In short, in matters vegetable, animal, and mineral,
   I am the very model of a modern major general.
   *In short, in matters vegetable, animal, and mineral,*
   *He is the very model of a modern major general.*
   *In short, in matters vegetable, animal, and mineral,*
   *He is the very model of a modern major general.*

2. I know our mythic history, King Arthur's and King Caradoc's,
   I answer hard acrostics, I've a pretty taste for paradox;
   I quote, in elegiacs, all the crimes of Heliogabalus,
   In Conics I can floor peculiarities parabolous;

   I can tell undoubted Raphaels from Gerard Dows and Zoffanies;
   I know the Croaking Chorus from "The Frogs" of Aristophanes!

Then I can hum a fugue of which I've heard the music's din afore,
And whistle all the airs from that infernal nonsense "Pinafore."
*And whistle all the airs from that infernal nonsense "Pinafore,"*
*And whistle all the airs from that infernal nonsense "Pinafore,"*
*And whistle all the airs from that infernal nonsense "Pinafore."*

Then I can write a washing bill in Babylonic cuneiform,
And tell you ev'ry detail of Caractacus's uniform.
In short, in matters vegetable, animal, and mineral,
I am the very model of a modern major general.
*In short, in matters vegetable, animal, and mineral,*
*He is the very model of a modern major general.*
*In short, in matters vegetable, animal, and mineral,*
*He is the very model of a modern major general.*


# Ida! Sweet as Apple Cider
W: EDDIE LEONARD / M: EDDIE MUNSON (1903)

1. In the region where the roses always bloom,
   Breathing out upon the air their sweet perfume,
   Lives a dusky maid I long to call my own,
   For I know my love for her will never die;

   When the sun am sinkin' in dat golden West,
   Little Robin Red Breast gone to seek their nests,
   Then I sneak down to dat place I love the best,
   Ev'ry ev'ning there alone I sigh.

   *Chorus:*
   Ida! sweet as apple cider,
   Sweeter than all I know,
   Come out! in the silv'ry moonlight,
   Of love we'll whisper, so soft and low!

   Seems tho' can't live without you,
   Listen, oh! Honey, do!
   Ida! I idolize yer,
   I love you, Ida, 'deed I do.

2. When the moon comes stealing up behind the hill,
   Ev'rything around me seems so calm and still,
   Save the gentle calling of the whippoorwill,
   Then I long to hold her little hand in mine;

   Thro' the trees the winds are sighing soft and low,
   Seem to come and whisper that your love is true,
   Come and be my own, sweetheart, do! oh do!
   Then my life will seem almost divine.

   *[to Chorus]*

145

# I Didn't Raise My Boy to Be a Soldier

W: ALFRED BRYAN / M: AL. PIANTADOSI (1915)

1. Ten million soldiers to the war have gone,
   Who may never return again.
   Ten million mothers' hearts must break
   For the ones who died in vain.

   Head bowed down in sorrow
   In her lonely years,
   I remember a mother murmur thro' her tears:

   *Chorus:*
   "I didn't raise my boy to be a soldier,
   I brought him up to be my pride and joy;
   Who dares to place a musket on his shoulder,
   To shoot some other mother's darling boy?"

   Let nations arbitrate their future troubles,
   It's time to lay the sword and gun away,
   There'd be no war today,
   If mothers all would say,
   'I didn't raise my boy to be a soldier.'"

2. What victory can cheer a mother's heart,
   When she looks at her blighted home?
   What victory can bring her back
   All she cared to call her own?

   Let each mother answer
   In the years to be,
   "Remember that my boy belongs to me!"

   [*to Chorus*]


# I'd Leave Ma Happy Home for You

W: WILL A. HEELAN / M: HARRY VON TILZER (1899)

1. A gal I knew, a nice gal, too,
       'Till someone told her she knew how to act;
   Then that baby blew ev'ry solitary sou,
       Chasin' roun' to cheap theatres, that's a fact.

   At last she got acquainted with an actor who was painted
   Like a darky in de show,
   And she followed him aroun' till the night they quit de town,
   Then she said, "Please take me with you when you go.
       For . . .

146

*Chorus:*
"I'd leave ma happy home for you,
 oo, oo, oo, oo,
You're de nicest man I ever knew,
 oo, oo, oo, oo;
If you take me,
and just break me in de bus'ness too, oo,
I'd leave ma happy home for you,
 oo, oo, oo, oo."

**2.** He said he'd shake de show and take
 That lady with a comp'ny of his own;
But he packed his grip and he took a trip,
 And he left that little baby all alone.

He tried his best to skip her, but she used to buy de Clipper,
 What de actors' news was in;
When she found out where he went, ev'ryday a note she sent,
 This is just how ev'ry letter would begin:
 "Well . . .

[*to Chorus*]

# I Don't Care

W: JEAN LENOX / M: HARRY O. SUTTON (1905)

**1.** They say I'm crazy, got no sense,
 But I don't care;
They may or may not mean offense,
 But I don't care.

You see I'm sort of independent,
Of a clever race descendant,
My star is on the ascendant,
That's why I don't care.

 *Chorus:*
 I don't care, I don't care,
 What they may think of me;
 I'm happy-go-lucky, men say I am plucky,
 So jolly and carefree.

 I don't care, I don't care,
 If I do get the mean and stony stare,
 If I'm never successful, it won't be distressful,
 'Cos I don't care.

**2.** Some people say I think I'm it,
   But I don't care;
   They say they don't like me a bit,
   But I don't care.

'Cos my good nature effervescing,
Is one, there is no distressing,
My spirit there is no oppressing,
Just 'cos I don't care.

   *Chorus:*
   I don't care, I don't care,
   If people don't like me;
   I'll try to outlive it, I know I'll forgive it,
   And live contentedly.

   I don't care, I don't care,
   If people do not try to treat me fair;
   There is naught can amaze me, dislike can not daze me,
   'Cos I don't care.

# I Don't Want to Play in Your Yard
W: PHILIP WINGATE / M: H. W. PETRIE (1894)

**1.** Once there lived, side by side, two little maids;
   Used to dress alike, hair down in braids,
   Blue ging'am pinafores, stockings of red,
   Little sunbonnets tied on each pretty head.

When school was over, secrets they'd tell,
Whispering arm in arm, down by the well.
One day a quarrel came, hot tears were shed:
"You can't play in our yard," but the other said:

   *Chorus:*
   "I don't want to play in your yard,
   I don't like you any more;
   You'll be sorry when you see me
   Sliding down our cellar door.

   "You can't holler down our rain-barrel,
   You can't climb our apple tree;
   I don't want to play in your yard
   If you won't be good to me."

**2.** Next day, two little maids each other miss,
   Quarrels are soon made up, sealed with a kiss;
   Then hand in hand again, happy they go,
   Friends all thro' life to be, they love each other so.

Soon school days pass away sorrows and bliss,
But love remembers yet, quarrels and kiss;
In sweet dreams of childhood, we hear the cry,
"You can't play in our yard," And the old reply:

[*to Chorus*]

# If I Had My Way
W: LOU KLEIN / M: JAMES KENDIS (1913)

1. I'd like to make your golden dreams come true, dear,
   If I only had my way;
   A paradise this world would seem to you,
   If I only had my way.

   *Chorus:*
   If I had my way, dear, forever there'd be
   A garden of roses for you and for me;
   A thousand and one things, dear, I would do,
   Just for you, just for you.

   If I had my way, we would never grow old,
   And sunshine I'd bring ev'ry day;
   You would reign all alone
   Like a queen on a throne,
   If I had my way.

2. You'd never know a care, a pain, or sorrow,
   If I only had my way;
   I'd fill your cup of happiness tomorrow,
   If I only had my way.

   [*to Chorus*]

# If You'll Be M-I-N-E Mine
AMERICAN TRADITIONAL

If you'll be M-I-N-E mine,
I'll be T-H-I-N-E thine,
And I'll L-O-V-E love you
All the T-I-M-E time.

You are the B-E-S-T best
Of all the R-E-S-T rest,
And I'll L-O-V-E love you
All the T-I-M-E time.

Wrap 'em up,
Stack 'em up,
Any old time.

# If You're Happy
## (And You Know It)
CHILDREN'S PLAY SONG

1. If you're happy and you know it, clap your hands,
   If you're happy and you know it, clap your hands,
   If you're happy and you know it,
   Then your face will surely show it,
   If you're happy and you know it, clap your hands.

2. If you're happy and you know it, stamp your foot,
   If you're happy and you know it, stamp your foot,
   If you're happy and you know it,
   Then your face will surely show it,
   If you're happy and you know it, stamp your foot.

3. If you're happy and you know it, nod your head . . .
   (*etc.*)

4. If you're happy and you know it, turn around . . .
   (*etc.*)

5. If you're happy and you know it, touch your nose . . .
   (*etc.*)


# I Gave My Love a Cherry
## (The Riddle)
ENGLISH BALLAD

1. I gave my love a cherry that has no stone,
   I gave my love a chicken that has no bone,
   I gave my love a ring that has no end,
   I gave my love a baby with no cry-in'.

2. How can there be a cherry that has no stone?
   How can there be a chicken that has no bone?
   How can there be a ring that has no end?
   How can there be a baby with no cry-in'?

3. A cherry when it's bloomin' it has no stone.
   A chicken in an eggshell it has no bone.
   A ring when it is rollin' it has no end.
   A baby when it's sleepin' has no cry-in'.

# I Heard the Bells on Christmas Day
W: HENRY WADSWORTH LONGFELLOW (1864) / M: ANON.

1. I heard the bells on Christmas Day
   Their old familiar carols play,
   And wild and sweet the words repeat
   Of peace on earth, good will to men.

2. I thought how, as the day had come,
   The belfries of all Christendom
   Had rolled along th' unbroken song
   Of peace on earth, good will to men.

3. And in despair I bowed my head;
   "There is no peace on earth," I said,
   "For hate is strong and mocks the song
   Of peace on earth, good will to men."

4. Then pealed the bells more loud and deep:
   "God is not dead, nor doth he sleep;
   The wrong shall fail, the right prevail,
   With peace on earth, good will to men."

5. Till ringing, singing on its way,
   The world revolved from night to day,
   A voice, a chime, a chant sublime,
   Of peace on earth, good will to men!


# I Hear You Calling Me
W: HAROLD HARFORD / M: CHARLES MARSHALL (1908)

I hear you calling me.
You called me when the moon had veiled her light,
Before I went from you into the night;
I came—do you remember?—back to you
For one last kiss beneath the kind stars' light.

I hear you calling me.
And oh, the ringing gladness of your voice!
The words that made my longing heart rejoice
You spoke—do you remember?—and my heart
Still hears the distant music of your voice.

I hear you calling me.
Though years have stretched their weary length between,
And on your grave the mossy grass is green;
I stand—do you behold me?—listening here,
Hearing your voice through all the years between.

151

# I'll Fly Away
SPIRITUAL

1. Some bright morning when this life is over,
   I'll fly away:
   To a land on God's celestial shore
   I'll fly away.

   *Chorus:*
   I'll fly away, O, Lordy,
   I'll fly away,
   When I die, hallelujah, by and by,
   I'll fly away.

2. When dark shadows of this life are nigh,
   I'll fly away:
   Like a bird, far from these prison walls,
   I'll fly away.

   [*to Chorus*]

3. Just a few more weary days and then
   I'll fly away:
   To a land where joys will never end,
   I'll fly away.

   [*to Chorus*]

# I'll Say She Does
W & M: BUD DE SYLVA, GUS KAHN & AL JOLSON (1918)

1. I've got a brand new sweetie,
   Better than the one before;
   Oh! she's got ev'rything
   And a little bit more.

   I don't know much about her
   And yet I know a lot,
   'Cause what it takes to make me love her
   I want to tell you she's got.

   *Chorus:*
   Does she make ev'rybody stare?
   I'll say she does.
   Does she give 'em that "I don't care"?
   I'll say she does.

   But is she nicer to me,
   And does she sit on my knee?
   Does she?
   I'll say she does.

152

And does she crave a wedding 'n' ev'rything?
I'll say she does.
Was she happy to get the ring?
You best she was.

And can she dance, can she twist,
Does she do a lot of things I can't resist?
Does she?
I'll say she does.

2. It was so hard to get her,
   She can never get away
   Because I'm watching her
   All the night and all the day.

   I've always had her picture,
   I had it in my mind;
   I always knew what kind I wanted
   And she's exactly the kind.

   [*to Chorus*]


# I'll See You in C-U-B-A
W & M: IRVING BERLIN (1920)

1. Not so far from here,
   There's a very lively atmosphere;
   Ev'rybody's going there this year,
       And there's a reason
       the season
   Opened last July;
   Ever since the U. S. A. went dry,
   Ev'rybody's going there,
       And I'm going, too.
       I'm on my way to . . .

   *Chorus:*
   Cuba, there's where I'm going,
   Cuba, there's where I'll stay,
   Cuba, where wine is flowing,
   And where dark-eyed Stellas
   Light their feller's panatellas.

   Cuba, where all is happy,
   Cuba, where all is gay,
   Why don't you plan a
   Wonderful trip to Havana?
       Hop on a ship
       And I'll see you in C-U-B-A.

153

2. Take a friend's advice,
   Drinking in a cellar isn't nice;
   Anybody who has got the price
       Should be a Cuban;
       Have you been
   Longing for the smile
   That you haven't had for quite awhile,
   If you have, then follow me
       and I'll show the way.
       Come on along to . . .

   [*to Chorus*]


# I'll Take You Home Again, Kathleen

W & M: THOMAS P. WESTENDORF (1876)

1. I'll take you home again, Kathleen,
   Across the ocean, wild and wide,
   To where your heart has ever been
   Since first you were my bonny bride.

   The roses all have left your cheek,
   I've watched them fade away and die.
   Your voice is sad whene'er you speak,
   And tears bedim your loving eye.

       *Chorus:*
       I will take you back, Kathleen,
       To where your heart will feel no pain,
       And when the fields are fresh and green,
       I'll take you to your home again.

2. I know you love me, Kathleen dear,
   Your heart was ever fond and true.
   I always feel, when you are near,
   That life holds nothing, dear, but you.

   The smiles that once you gave to me,
   I scarcely ever see them now,
   Though many, many times I see
   A dark'ning shadow on your brow.

       [*to Chorus*]

**3.** To that dear home beyond the sea
My Kathleen shall again return,
And when thy old friends welcome thee,
Thy loving heart will cease to yearn.

Where laughs the little silver stream
Besides your mother's humble cot
And brightest rays of sunshine gleam,
There all your grief will be forgot.

[*to Chorus*]

# I Love You So
## (Merry Widow Waltz)
ENGLISH WORDS: ADRIAN ROSS / M: FRANZ LEHÁR (1907)
[Originally from *Die lustige Witwe,* 1905: w: Victor Léon & Leo Smith]

Golden glowing lamps are throwing
    Light above,
While the swaying tune is saying,
    Love, love, love!

And the feet of dancers
    Sound it as they go,
Don't you hear them say, "My dear,
    I love you so!"

    And with the music's chime,
    My heart is beating time,
    As if to give a sign that it would cry,
    Be mine, be mine!

    Though our lips may say no word,
    Yet in the heart a voice is heard,
    That seems to whisper soft and low,
    I love you so!

Love that hovers over lovers
    Speaks in song,
In the finger's clasp that lingers
    Close and long;

And the music answers,
    Swaying to and fro,
Telling you, it's true, it's true,
    I love you so!

155

# I Love You Truly

W & M: CARRIE JACOBS-BOND (1907)

1. I love you truly, truly, dear,
   Life with its sorrow, life with its tear
   Fades into dreams when I feel you are near,
   For I love you truly, truly, dear.

2. Ah, love, 'tis something to feel your kind hand.
   Ah, yes, 'tis something by your side to stand.
   Gone is the sorrow, gone doubt and fear,
   For you love me truly, truly, dear.


# I'm Afraid to Come Home in the Dark

W: HARRY WILLIAMS / M: EGBERT VAN ALSTYNE (1907)

1. "Jonesie" married Mabel, a wise old owl was he,
   He told his wife he never drank a stronger thing than tea;
   But after honeymooning, at night he stayed away,
   And for a week he never got home 'till the break of day.
   At last poor Mabel asked the reason why,
   Said Jones, "I'm goin' to tell the truth or die."

   *Chorus:*
   "Baby dear, *(shh)* listen here,
   I'm afraid to come home in the dark.
   Ev'ry day the papers say a Robbery in the Park.
   So I sat alone in the Y.M.C.A., singing just like a lark,
   There's no place like home,
   But I couldn't come home in the dark."

2. That night after dinner, he bade his wife adieu,
   Said she, "Oh no, it's dark and so I'm goin' to go with you."
   But somehow Jonesie shook her for he was smooth as silk,
   He got home just in time to meet the man that brought the milk.
   His wife stood waiting for him on the stair,
   While Jonesie and the milkman sang this air:

   [*to Chorus*]

3. She kissed him good morning, to see him she was glad,
   And when she tucked him up in bed, says Jones, "I guess I'm bad."
   Next day, the same old story, he came home just at dawn,
   But he got sober right away when he found she was gone.
   At noon he heard her slam the garden gate,
   Said she to Jonesie, "Is my hat on straight?"

*Chorus:*
"Baby dear, *(shh)* listen here,
I'm afraid to come home in the dark.
Ev'ry day the papers say a Robbery in the Park.
So I sat alone in the C.A.F.E., singing just like a lark,
There's no place like home,
But I couldn't come home in the dark."

# I'm Always Chasing Rainbows

W: JOSEPH McCARTHY / M: HARRY CARROLL
[from *Oh Look!*, 1918 / melody based on Chopin's *Fantaisie-Impromptu*]

At the end of the rainbow there's happiness,
And to find it, how often I've tried,
But my life is a race,
Just a wild goose chase,
And my dreams have all been denied.

Why have I always been a failure,
What can the reason be?
I wonder if the world's to blame,
I wonder if it could be me?

*Chorus:*
I'm always chasing rainbows,
Watching clouds drifting by.
My schemes are just like all my dreams,
Ending in the sky.

Some fellows look and find the sunshine,
I always look and find the rain.
Some fellows make a winning sometime,
I never even make a gain,
Believe me,

I'm always chasing rainbows,
Waiting to find a little bluebird in vain.

# I'm Called Little Buttercup

W: W. S. GILBERT / M: SIR ARTHUR SULLIVAN
[from *H.M.S. Pinafore*, 1878]

I'm called little Buttercup,
  Dear little Buttercup,
Though I could never tell why;
  But still I'm called Buttercup,
Poor little Buttercup,
  Sweet little Buttercup I.

I've snuff and tobaccy,
  And excellent Jacky,
I've scissors and watches, and knives;
  I've ribbons and laces
To set off the faces
  Of pretty young sweethearts and wives.

I've treacle and toffee,
  I've tea and I've coffee,
Soft tommy and succulent chops;
  I've chickens and conies,
And pretty polonies,
  And excellent peppermint drops.

Then buy of your Buttercup,
  Dear little Buttercup,
Sailors should never be shy;
  So buy of your Buttercup,
Poor little Buttercup,
  Come! Of your Buttercup buy.


# I'm Falling in Love with Some One

W: RIDA JOHNSON YOUNG / M: VICTOR HERBERT
[from *Naughty Marietta*, 1910]

1. I've a very strange feeling I ne'er felt before,
   'Tis a kind of a grind of depression;
   My heart's acting strangely, it feels rather sore,
   At least it gives me that impression.

   My pulses leap madly without any cause,
   Believe me, I'm telling you truly;
   I'm gay without pause, then sad without cause,
   My spirits are truly unruly.

*Chorus:*
For I'm falling in love with some one,
Some one girl;
I'm falling in love with some one,
Head a-whirl;

Yes! I'm falling in love with some one,
Plain to see;
I'm sure I could love some one madly,
If some one would only love me!

2. Now, I don't mind confessing that I used to scoff
At this sort of a sport of flirtation;
I used to believe that I'd never be caught
In this foolish but fond complication.

I'm losing all relish for things that were dear,
I'm looking for trouble and know it;
When some one is near, I'm feeling quite queer,
But I heartily hope I don't show it.

[*to Chorus*]


# I'm Forever Blowing Bubbles

W & M: "JAAN KENBROVIN" & "JOHN W. KELLETTE" (1919)
*(pen names for James Kendis, James Brockman and Nat Vincent)*

1. I'm dreaming dreams,
I'm scheming schemes,
   I'm building castles high.
They're born anew,
Their days are few,
   Just like a sweet butterfly.

And as the daylight is dawning,
They come again on the morning.

   *Chorus:*
   I'm forever blowing bubbles,
   Pretty bubbles in the air;
   They fly so high,
   Nearly reach the sky,
   Then, like my dreams, they fade and die.

   Fortune's always hiding,
   I've looked ev'rywhere,
   I'm forever blowing bubbles,
   Pretty bubbles in the air.

**2.** When shadows creep,
   When I'm asleep,
      To lands of hope I stray;
   Then at daybreak,
   When I awake,
      My bluebird flutters away.

"Happiness, you seem so near me,
Happiness, come forth and cheer me."

   [*to Chorus*]


# I Might Be Your "Once-in-a-While"
W: ROBERT B. SMITH / M: VICTOR HERBERT
[from *Angel Face,* 1919]

**1.** It's hard to be true to one
   When I'm not built that way;
   I may promise, but it's two to one
   Before the week is out I'll stray.

   But frankness is due to one
   Who craves my ev'ry kiss;
   So I make it plain in my refrain
   That the best I can do is this:

      *Chorus:*
      I might be your "once-in-a-while,"
      I might see you once-in-a-while;
         But I can't be true to you or you or you.

      I can't be your "all-of-the-time,"
      Your "ever and ever,"
         But maybe your "once-in-a-while" will do.

**2.** My heart beats neutrality,
   But still some say I've none;
   Think of that when in reality
   I have a heart for ev'ryone.

   I fear its locality
   May change from day to day;
   It is ev'rywhere, now here, now there,
   That is why I'm obliged to say:

      [*to Chorus*]

# Indiana
W: BALLARD MACDONALD / M: JAMES F. HANLEY (1917)

1. I have always been a wand'rer,
   Over land and sea.
   Yet a moonbeam on the water
   Casts a spell o'er me;
       A vision fair I see,
       Again I seem to be . . .

   *Chorus:*
   Back home again
   In Indiana,
   And it seems that I can see
       The gleaming candle light
       still shining bright
   Thru the sycamores for me.

   The new-mown hay
   Sends all its fragrance
   From the fields I used to roam,
       When I dream about
       the moonlight on the Wabash,*
   Then I long for my Indiana home.

2. Fancy paints on mem'ry's canvas
   Scenes that we hold dear,
   We recall them in days after,
   Clearly they appear;
       And often time, I see
       A scene that's dear to me . . .

   [*to Chorus*]

*For this strain and picturesque references in his lyrics, Macdonald acknowledged his debt to
Paul Dresser's "On the Banks of the Wabash, Far Away" (1897) [see page 270].

# In My Merry Oldsmobile
W: VINCENT BRYAN / M: GUS EDWARDS (1905)

1. Young Johnny Steele has an Oldsmobile,
   He loves a dear little girl.
   She is the queen of his gas machine,
   She has his heart in a whirl.

   Now when they go for a spin, you know,
   She tries to learn the auto, so
   He lets her steer while he gets her ear
   And whispers soft and low:

161

*Chorus:*
"Come away with me, Lucile,
In my merry Oldsmobile.
Down the road of life we'll fly,
Automobubbling, you and I.

"To the church we'll swiftly steal,
Then our wedding bells will peal.
You can go as far as you like with me
In my merry Oldsmobile."

2. They love to spark in the dark old park
As they go flying along.
She says she knows why the motor goes,
The sparker's awfully strong.

Each day they spoon to the engine's tune,
Their honeymoon will happen soon.
He'll win Lucile with his Oldsmobile
And then he'll fondly croon:

[*to Chorus*]

# In the Bleak Midwinter

W: CHRISTINA ROSSETTI (1872) / M: ANON.

In the bleak midwinter, frosty wind made moan,
Earth stood hard as iron, water like a stone;
Snow had fallen, snow on snow, snow on snow,
In the bleak midwinter, long ago.

Our God, heaven cannot hold him, nor earth sustain;
Heav'n and earth shall flee away when he comes to reign:
In the bleak midwinter, a stable-place sufficed
The Lord God incarnate, Jesus Christ.

Angels and archangels may have gathered there,
Cherubim and seraphim throngéd in the air;
But his mother only, in her maiden bliss,
Worshipped the belovéd with a kiss.

What can I give him, poor as I am?
If I were a shepherd, I would bring a lamb;
If I were a wise man, I would do my part;
Yet what I can I give him, give him my heart.

# In the Gloaming
W: META ORRED / M: ANNE F. HARRISON (1877)

1. In the gloaming, oh, my darling!
   When the lights are dim and low,
   And the quiet shadows falling,
   Softly come and softly go;

   When the winds are sobbing faintly
   With a gentle unknown woe,
   Will you think of me, and love me,
   As you did once long ago?

2. In the gloaming, oh, my darling!
   Think not bitterly of me!
   Tho' I passed away in silence
   Left you lonely, set you free;

   For my heart was crush'd with longing,
   What had been could never be;
   It was best to leave you thus, dear,
   Best for you, and best for me.
      *It was best to leave you thus, dear,*
      *Best for you, and best for me.*


# In the Good Old Summertime
W: REN SHIELDS / M: GEORGE EVANS (1902)

1. There's a time in each year that we always hold dear,
   Good old summertime,
   With the birds and the trees-es and sweet scented breezes,
   Good old summertime.

   When your day's work is over, then you are in clover
   And life is one beautiful rhyme.
   No trouble annoying, each one is enjoying
   The good old summertime.

      *Chorus:*
      In the good old summertime, in the good old summertime,
      Strolling through the shady lanes with your baby mine.
      You hold her hand and she holds yours and that's a very good sign
      That she's your tootsey wootsey in the good old summertime.

163

**2.** Oh, to swim in the pool you'd play hooky from school,
Good old summertime.
You would play "ring-a-rosie" with Jim, Kate and Josie,
Good old summertime.

Those are days full of pleasure we now fondly treasure
When we never thought it a crime
To go stealing cherries with face brown as berries
In good old summertime.

[*to Chorus*]

# In the Shade of the Old Apple Tree
W: HARRY H. WILLIAMS / M: EGBERT VAN ALSTYNE (1905)

**1.** The oriole with joy was sweetly singing,
The little brook was bab'ling its tune,
The village bells at noon were gaily ringing,
The world seem'd brighter than a harvest moon;

For there within my arms I gently pressed you,
And blushing red, you slowly turned away,
I can't forget the way I once caressed you;
I only pray we'll meet another day.

> *Chorus:*
> In the shade of the old apple tree,
> Where the love in your eyes I could see,
> When the voice that I hear,
> Like the song of the bird,
> Seem'd to whisper sweet music to me;
>
> I could hear the dull buzz of the bee,
> In the blossom as you said to me,
> With a heart that is true,
> I'll be waiting for you,
> In the shade of the old apple tree.

**2.** I've really come a long way from the city,
And though my heart is breaking I'll be brave,
I've brought this bunch of flowers, I think they're pretty
To place upon a freshly moulded grave;

If you will show me, father, where's she's lying,
Or if it's far just point it out to me,
Said he, "She told us all when she was dying,
To bury her beneath the apple tree."

[*to Chorus*]

# In the Sweet Bye and Bye

W: S. F. BENNETT / M: J. P. WEBSTER (1868)

1. There's a land that is fairer than day,
   And by faith we can see it afar;
   For the Father waits over the way
   To prepare us a dwelling place there.

   *Chorus:*
   In the sweet bye and bye,
   We shall meet on that beautiful shore;
   In the sweet bye and bye,
   We shall meet on that beautiful shore.

2. We shall sing on that beautiful shore
   The melodious songs of the blest;
   And our spirits shall sorrow no more,
   Not a sigh for the blessing of rest.

   [*to Chorus*]

3. To our bountiful Father above,
   We will offer the tribute of praise
   For the glorious gift of His love
   And the blessings that hallow our days.

   [*to Chorus*]

# I Ride An Old Paint

AMERICAN COWBOY SONG

1. I ride an old Paint, I lead an old Dan,
   I'm goin' to Montan' for to throw the hooligan.
   They feed in the coulees, they water in the draw,
   Their tails are all matted, their backs are all raw.

   *Chorus:*
   Ride around, little dogies,
   Ride around them slow,
   For the fiery and snuffy are a-rarin' to go.

2. Old Bill Jones had two daughters and a song,
   One went to Denver and the other went wrong.
   His wife she died in a poolroom fight,
   Still he sings from mornin' till night:

   [*to Chorus*]

165

**3.** Oh, when I die, take my saddle from the wall,
Put it on my pony, lead him out of his stall.
Tie my bones to his back, turn our faces to the West,
And we'll ride the prairie that we love best.

   [*to Chorus*]


# I Saw Three Ships

ENGLISH CAROL

**1.** I saw three ships come sailing in,
   *On Christmas Day, on Christmas Day;*
I saw three ships come sailing in,
   *On Christmas Day in the morning.*

**2.** And what was in those ships all three,
   *On Christmas Day, on Christmas Day;*
And what was in those ships all three,
   *On Christmas Day in the morning?*

**3.** Our Saviour, Christ, and his lady,
   *On Christmas Day, on Christmas Day;*
Our Saviour, Christ, and his lady,
   *On Christmas Day in the morning.*

**4.** Pray, whither sailed those ships all three,
   *On Christmas Day, on Christmas Day;*
Pray, whither sailed those ships all three,
   *On Christmas Day in the morning?*

**5.** O, they sailed into Bethlehem,
   *On Christmas Day, on Christmas Day;*
O, they sailed into Bethlehem,
   *On Christmas Day in the morning.*

**6.** And all the bells on earth shall ring,
   *On Christmas Day, on Christmas Day;*
And all the bells on earth shall ring,
   *On Christmas Day in the morning.*

**7.** And all the angels in heaven shall sing,
   *On Christmas Day, on Christmas Day;*
And all the angels in heaven shall sing,
   *On Christmas Day in the morning.*

**8.** And all the souls on earth shall sing,
 *On Christmas Day, on Christmas Day;*
And all the souls on earth shall sing,
 *On Christmas Day in the morning.*

**9.** Then let us all rejoice and sing,
 *On Christmas Day, on Christmas Day;*
Then let us all rejoice and sing,
 *On Christmas Day in the morning.*


# Italian Street Song
## (Zing, Zing)
W: RIDA JOHNSON YOUNG / M: VICTOR HERBERT
[from *Naughty Marietta*, 1910]

Ah! my heart is back in Napoli,
Dear Napoli, dear Napoli,
And I seem to hear again in dreams
Her revelry, her sweet revelry.

The mandolina's playing sweet,
The pleasant fall of dancing feet,
Oh! could I return, oh! joy complete,
Napoli, Napoli, Napoli!

*Chorus:*
Zing, Zing, zizzy, zizzy, zing, zing,
Boom, boom, aye,
Zing, Zing, zizzy, zizzy, zing, zing,
Mandolinas gay.
Zing, Zing, zizzy, zizzy, zing, zing,
Boom, boom, aye.

La, la, la,
Ha, ha, ha,
Zing, boom, aye,
La, la, la, la, ha, ha, ha,
Zing, boom, aye.

[*repeat Chorus*]


167

# It Came Upon the Midnight Clear

W: EDWIN H. SEARS / M: RICHARD S. WILLIS (19th c.)

1. It came upon the midnight clear,
   That glorious song of old,
   From angels bending near the earth,
   To touch their harps of gold:

   "Peace to the earth, good will to men,
   From heaven's all-gracious King";
   The world in solemn stillness lay,
   To hear the angels sing!

2. Still through the cloven skies they come,
   With peaceful wings unfurled;
   And still their heavenly music floats
   O'er all the weary world;

   Above its sad and lowly plains
   They bend on hovering wing,
   And ever o'er its Babel sounds
   The blessed angels sing!

3. And ye beneath life's crushing load
   Whose forms are bending low,
   Who toil along the climbing way
   With painful steps and slow,

   Look now! for glad and golden hours
   Come swiftly on the wing;
   Oh, rest beside the weary road,
   And hear the angels sing!

4. For lo! the days are hast'ning on
   By prophet bards foretold,
   When with the ever-circling years
   Comes round the age of gold;

   When peace shall over all the earth
   Its ancient splendors fling,
   And all the world give back the song
   Which now the angels sing!

# It's a Long, Long Way to Tipperary
W & M: JACK JUDGE & HARRY WILLIAMS (1912)

**1.** Up to mighty London came an Irishman one day,
As the streets are paved with gold, sure ev'ryone was gay;
Singing songs of Piccadilly, Strand and Leicester Square,
Till Paddy got excited, then he shouted to them there:

*Chorus:*
"It's a long way to Tipperary,
It's a long way to go;
It's a long way to Tipperary,
To the sweetest girl I know!

Goodbye, Piccadilly,
Farewell, Leicester Square;
It's a long, long way to Tipperary,
But my heart's right there.

**2.** Paddy wrote a letter to his Irish Molly O',
Saying, "Should you not receive it, write and let me know!
If I make mistakes in spelling, Molly dear," said he,
"Remember it's the pen that's bad, don't lay the blame on me."

[*to Chorus*]

**3.** Molly wrote a neat reply to Irish Paddy O',
Saying, "Mike Maloney wants to marry me, and so
Leave the Strand and Piccadilly, or you'll be to blame,
For love has fairly drove me silly—hopping you're the same!"

[*to Chorus*]


# I've Been Working on the Railroad
AMERICAN FOLK SONG
*(same melody as "The Eyes of Texas," by John Lang Sinclair, 1903)*

I've been working on the railroad
All the livelong day,
I've been working on the railroad
To pass the time away.

Don't you hear the whistle blowing,
Rise up so early in the morn;
Don't you hear the captain shouting,
Dinah blow your horn.

169

Dinah, won't you blow, Dinah, won't you blow,
Dinah, won't you blow your horn, your horn?
Dinah, won't you blow, Dinah, won't you blow,
Dinah, won't you blow your horn?

Someone's in the kitchen with Dinah,
Someone's in the kitchen I know,
Someone's in the kitchen with Dinah
Strummin' on the old banjo . . . singing . . .

Fee fie fiddle-ee-i-o
Fee fie fiddle-ee-i-o-o-o-o
Fee fie fiddle-ee-i-o,
Strummin' on the old banjo.


# I've Got a Little List

W: W. S. GILBERT / M: SIR ARTHUR SULLIVAN
[from *The Mikado*, 1885]

As some day it may happen that a victim must be found,
    I've got a little list—I've got a little list
Of society offenders who might well be underground,
    And who never would be missed—who never would be missed!

There's the pestilential nuisances who write for autographs—
All people who have flabby hands and irritating laughs—
All children who are up in dates, and floor you with 'em flat—
All persons who in shaking hands, shake hands with you like *that*—
And all third persons who on spoiling *tête-à-têtes* insist—
    They'd none of 'em be missed—they'd none of 'em be missed!

There's the banjo serenader, and the others of his race,
    And the piano-organist—I've got *him* on the list!
And the people who eat peppermint and puff it in your face,
    They never would be missed—they never would be missed!

Then the idiot who praises, with enthusiastic tone,
All centuries but this, and every country but his own;
And the lady from the provinces, who dresses like a guy,
And who "doesn't think she waltzes, but would rather like to try";
And that singular anomaly, the lady novelist—
    I don't think she'd be missed—I'm *sure* she'd not be missed!

And that *Nisi Prius* nuisance, who just now is rather rife,
    The Judicial humorist—I've got *him* on the list!
All funny fellows, comic men, and clowns of private life—
    They'd none of 'em be missed—they'd none of 'em be missed.

And apologetic statesmen of a compromising kind,
Such as—What d'ye call him—Thing'em-bob, and likewise—Never-mind,
And 'St—'st—'st—and What's-his-name, and also You-know-who—
The task of filling up the blanks I'd rather leave to *you.*
But it really doesn't matter whom you put upon the list,
For they'd none of 'em be missed—they'd none of 'em be missed!


# I've Got My Captain Working for Me Now
W & M: IRVING BERLIN (1919)

1. Johnny Jones was a first class private
In the army last year;
Now he's back to bus'ness in his father's place,
Sunday night I saw him with a smiling face.

   When I asked why he felt so happy,
Johnny chuckled with glee;
He winked his eye
And made this reply:
"Something wonderful has happened to me."

   *Chorus:*
I've got the guy
who used to be my Captain
Working for me;
He wanted work, so I made him a clerk
In my father's factory.

   And bye and bye
I'm gonna have him wrapped in
Work up to his brow;
I make him open the office ev'ry morning at eight,
I come around about four hours late,
Ev'rything comes to those who wait,
I've got my Captain working for me now.

2. He's not worth what I have to pay him,
But I'll never complain;
I've agreed to give him fifty dollars per,
It's worth twice as much to hear him call me "Sir."

   While I sit in my cozy office,
He's outside working hard;
Out in the hall
At my beck and call,
With a feather duster standing on guard.

*Chorus:*
I've got the guy
   who used to be my Captain
Working for me;
He wanted work, so I made him a clerk
In my father's factory.

And bye and bye
   I'm gonna have him wrapped in
Work up to his brow;
   When I come into the office he gets up on his feet,
   Stands at attention and gives me his seat;
   Who was it said, "Revenge is sweet,"
I've got my Captain working for me now.


# I've Got Rings on My Fingers
## (Mumbo Jumbo Jijjiboo J. O'Shea)
W: R. P. WESTON & F. J. BARNES / M: MAURICE SCOTT (1909)

1. Jim O'Shea was cast away
   Upon an Indian isle,
The natives there they liked his hair,
   They liked his Irish smile,
So made him chief Panjandrum,
   The nabob of them all.
They call'd him Jijjiboo Jhai,
   And rigg'd him out so gay,
So he wrote to Dublin Bay
   To his sweetheart just to say:

   *Chorus:*
   "Sure, I've got rings on my fingers, bells on my toes,
   Elephants to ride upon, my little Irish Rose,
   So come to your nabob, and next Patrick's Day,
   Be Mistress Mumbo Jumbo Jijjiboo J. O'Shea."

2. O'er the sea went Rose McGee
   To see her nabob grand,
He sat within his palanquin,
   And when she'd kissed his hand,
He led her to his harem
   Where he had wives galore.
She started shedding a tear;
   Said he, "Now have no fear!
I'm keeping these wives here
Just for ornament, my dear":

172

[*to Chorus*]

3. Em'rald green he robed his queen,
   To share with him his throne,
   'Mid eastern charms and waving palms
   They'd shamrocks, Irish grown,
   Sent all the way from Dublin,
   To Nabob J. O'Shea.
   But in his palace so fine,
   Should Rose for Ireland pine,
   With smiles her face will shine,
   When he murmurs, "Sweetheart mine":

[*to Chorus*]

# I've Got Sixpence
BRITISH MARCHING SONG

1. I've got sixpence, jolly, jolly sixpence,
   I've got sixpence to last me all my life!
   I've got tuppence to spend,
   And tuppence to lend,
   And tuppence to send home to my wife
   (Poor wife!).

   No cares have I to grieve me,
   No pretty little gal to deceive me,
   I'm happy as a lark, believe me,
   As we go rolling, rolling home.
   (Rolling home!)

   Rolling home,
   (Rolling home!)
   Rolling home,
   (Rolling home!)
   By the light of the silvery moo-oo-oo-oon,
   Happy is the day
   When we go home with our pay,
   As we go rolling, rolling home!

2. I've got *fourpence*, jolly, jolly fourpence,
   I've got fourpence to last me all my life!
   I've got tuppence to spend,
   And tuppence to lend,
   And *no* pence to send home to my wife
   (Poor wife!).

No cares have I to grieve me,
No pretty little gal to deceive me . . .
(*etc., etc.*)

3. I've got *tuppence*, jolly, jolly tuppence,
I've got tuppence to last me all my life!
I've got tuppence to spend,
    And *no* pence to lend,
        And *no* pence to send home to my wife
        (Poor wife!).

No cares have I to grieve me,
No pretty little gal to deceive me . . .
(*etc., etc.*)

4. I've got *no* pence, jolly, jolly no pence,
I've got no pence to last me all my life!
I've got *no* pence to spend,
    And *no* pence to lend,
        And *no* pence to send home to my wife
        (Poor wife!).

No cares have I to grieve me,
No pretty little gal to deceive me . . .
(*etc., etc.*)

# I Want a Girl
## (Just Like the Girl That Married Dear Old Dad)
W: WILLIAM DILLON / M: HARRY VON TILZER (1911)

1. When I was a boy, my mother often said to me,
"Get married, boy, and see how happy you will be."
I have looked all over, but no girl can I find
Who seems to be just like the little girl I have in mind.
    I will have to look around
    Until the right one I have found.

    *Chorus:*
    I want a girl just like the girl
    That married dear old Dad.
    She was a pearl and the only girl
    That Daddy ever had.

    A good old-fashioned girl with heart so true.
    One who loves nobody else but you.
    I want a girl just like the girl
    That married dear old Dad.

174

**2.** By the old mill stream there sits a couple old and gray,
Though years have rolled away, their hearts are young to day.
Mother dear looks up at Dad with lovelight in her eye;
He steals a kiss, a fond embrace, while ev'ning breezes sigh.
They're as happy as can be,
So that's the kind of love for me.

[*to Chorus*]


# I Wonder Who's Kissing Her Now
W: WILL M. HOUGH & FRANK R. ADAMS
M: JOSEPH E. HOWARD & HAROLD ORLOB (1909)

**1.** You have loved lots of girls in the sweet long ago,
And each one has meant heaven to you.
You have vowed your affection to each one in turn,
And have sworn to them all you'd be true.

You have kissed 'neath the moon while the world seemed in tune,
Then you've left her to hunt a new game.
Does it ever occur to you later, my boy,
That's she's probably doing the same?

> *Chorus:*
> I wonder who's kissing her now?
> Wonder who's kissing her now?
> Wonder who's looking into her eyes,
>     Breathing sighs,
>     Telling lies?
>
> I wonder who's buying the wine
> For lips that I used to call mine?
> Wonder if she ever tells him of me?
> I wonder who's kissing her now?

**2.** If you want to feel wretched and lonely and blue,
Just imagine the girl you love best
In the arms of some fellow who's stealing a kiss
From the lips that you once fondly pressed.

But the world moves a-pace and the loves of today
Flit away with a smile and a tear.
So you never can tell who is kissing her now,
Or just whom you'll be kissing next year.

[*to Chorus*]

# Jacob's Ladder

SPIRITUAL

1. We are climbing Jacob's ladder,
   We are climbing Jacob's ladder,
   We are climbing Jacob's ladder,
   Soldiers of the cross.

2. Ev'ry round goes higher, higher,
   Ev'ry round goes higher, higher,
   Ev'ry round goes higher, higher,
   Soldiers of the cross.

3. Brother, do you love my Jesus?
   (*etc.*)

4. If you love Him, you must serve Him,
   (*etc.*)

5. We are climbing higher, higher,
   (*etc.*)


# Ja Da
## (Ja Da, Ja Da, Jing Jing Jing!)
W & M: BOB CARLETON (1918)

1. You've heard all about your raggy melodies,
   Ev'rything from opera down to harmony;
   But I've a little song that I will sing to you,
   It's going to win you thru and thru.

   There ain't much to the words, but the music is grand,
   And you'll be singing it to beat the band.
   Now you've heard of your "Will o' the Wisp,"
   But give a little listen to this:
   It goes . . .

   *Chorus:*
   Ja Da, Ja Da,
   Ja Da, Ja Da, Jing Jing Jing,
   Ja Da, Ja Da,
   Ja Da, Ja Da, Jing Jing Jing.

   That's a funny little bit of melody,
   It's so soothing and appealing to me,
   It goes . . .
   Ja Da, Ja Da,
   Ja Da, Ja Da, Jing Jing Jing!

176

**2.** Now ev'ryone was singing a Hawaiian strain,
Ev'ryone seem'd to have it on their brain;
When Yaka Hicky Hoola Do was all the craze,
Why, that's the one that had 'em dazed.

The object now is for something new,
Something that will appeal to you;
And here's a little melody that you will find
Will linger, linger there in your mind:
    It goes . . .

    [*to Chorus*]

# J'ai du Bon Tabac

FRENCH CHILDREN'S PLAY SONG
*(Lyrics attributed to the Abbé Gabriel de l'Atteignant, 18th c.)*

J'ai du bon tabac dans ma tabatière,
J'ai du bon tabac, tu n'en auras pas.
    J'en ai du fin et du bien rapé,
    Mais ce n'est pas pour ton vilain nez.
J'ai du bon tabac dans ma tabatière,
J'ai du bon tabac, tu n'en auras pas.

# The Japanese Sandman

W: RAYMOND B. EGAN / M: RICHARD A. WHITING (1920)

**1.** Won't you stretch imagination
    for the moment and come with me,
Let us hasten to a nation
    lying over the western sea;
Hide behind the cherry blossoms,
    here's a sight that will please your eyes,
There's a baby with a lady of Japan
    singing lullabies,
    Night winds breathe her sighs.

*Chorus:*
Here's the Japanese Sandman,
Sneaking on with the dew,
Just an old second-hand man,
He'll buy your old day from you;

He will take ev'ry sorrow
Of the the day that is through,
And he'll give you tomorrow
Just to start life anew.

177

Then you'll be a bit older
In the dawn when you wake,
And you'll be a bit bolder
With the new day you make;

Here's the Japanese Sandman,
Trade him silver for gold,
Just an old second-hand man,
Trading new days for old.

2. Just as silent as we came,
    we'll leave the land of the painted fan,
Wander lightly or you'll wake
    the little people of old Japan;
May repose and pleasant dreaming
    be their share while the hours are small,
Like an echo of the song
    hear the Japanese Sandman call,
    New days near for all.

[*to Chorus*]


# Jeanie with the Light Brown Hair
W & M: STEPHEN C. FOSTER (1854)

1. I dream of Jeanie with the light brown hair,
Borne, like a vapor, on the summer air;
I see her tripping where the bright streams play,
Happy as the daisies that dance on her way.

Many were the wild notes her merry voice would pour,
Many were the blithe birds that warbled them o'er;
Oh! I dream of Jeanie with the light brown hair,
Floating, like a vapor, on the soft summer air.

2. I long for Jeanie with the day-dawn smile,
Radiant in gladness, warm with winning guile;
I hear her melodies, like joys gone by,
Sighing 'round my heart o'er the fond hopes that die:

Sighing like the night wind and sobbing like the rain,
Wailing for the lost one that comes not again;
Oh! I long for Jeanie, and my heart bows low,
Never more to find her where the bright waters flow.

**3.** I sigh for Jeanie, but her light form strayed
Far from the fond hearts 'round her native glade;
Her smiles have vanished and her sweet songs flown,
Flitting like the dreams that have cheered us and gone.

Now the nodding wild flowers may wither on the shore,
While her gentle fingers will cull them no more;
Oh! I sigh for Jeanie with the light brown hair,
Floating, like a vapor, on the soft summer air.

# Jesus Loves Me
TRADITIONAL

**1.** Jesus loves me! This I know,
For the Bible tells me so;
Little ones to Him belong,
They are weak but He is strong.

    Yes, Jesus loves me!
    Yes, Jesus loves me!
    Yes, Jesus loves me!
    The Bible tells me so.

**2.** Jesus from His throne on high
Came into this world to die
That I might from sin be free,
Bled and died upon the tree.

    Yes, Jesus loves me!
    Yes, Jesus loves me!
    Yes, Jesus loves me!
    The Bible tells me so.

# Jim Crack Corn
## (The Blue Tail Fly)
W & M: F. D. BENTEEN (1846)

**1.** When I was young, I used to wait
At master's side and hand his plate,
And pass the bottle when he got dry,
And brush away the blue-tail fly.

    *Chorus:*
    Jim crack corn and I don't care,
    Jim crack corn and I don't care,
    Jim crack corn and I don't care,
    Ol' master's gone away.

**2.** Then after dinner he would sleep,
A vigil I would have to keep,
And when he wanted to shut his eye,
He told me, "Watch the blue tail fly."

   [*to Chorus*]

**3.** One day he rode around the farm,
The flies so num'rous, they did swarm.
One chanced a-bitin' him on the thigh,
The devil take the blue tail fly!

   [*to Chorus*]

**4.** The pony run, he jump and pitch,
And tumble master in the ditch.
He died, the jury they wondered why:
The verdict was "the blue tail fly."

   [*to Chorus*]

**5.** They laid him 'neath a 'simmon tree,
His epitaph is there to see:
"Beneath this stone I'm forced to lie,
A victim of the blue tail fly."

   [*to Chorus*]

**6.** Ol' master's gone, now let him rest,
They say that things are for the best.
I can't forget 'till the day I die
Ol' master and the blue tail fly.

   [*to Chorus*]

# Jingle Bells
## (One Horse Open Sleigh)
W & M: JAMES PIERPONT (1857)

**1.** Dashing thro' the snow
In a one-horse open sleigh;
O'er the fields we go,
Laughing all the way.

Bells on bobtail ring,
Making spirits bright;
What fun it is to ride and sing
A sleighing song tonight!

*Chorus:*
Jingle bells, jingle bells,
Jingle all the way.
O! what fun it is to ride
In a one-horse open sleigh.
(*repeat*)

2. A day or two ago
   I thought I'd take a ride,
   And soon Miss Fanny Bright
   Was seated by my side.

   The horse was lean and lank,
   Misfortune seemed his lot,
   He got into a drifted bank
   And we, we got upset.

   [*to Chorus*]

3. Now the ground is white,
   Go it while you're young;
   Take the girls tonight,
   And sing this sleighing song.

   Just get a bobtailed bay,
   Two-forty for his speed,
   Then hitch him to an open sleigh,
   And crack! you'll take the lead.

   [*to Chorus*]

# John Brown

TRADITIONAL CIVIL WAR SONG
(*A long, complex history of this melody and its various texts begins in
1857, with authorships remaining in doubt. The same melody was used for
"Battle Hymn of the Republic," "Say, Brothers, Will You Meet Us?" and
"John Brown's Baby Has a Cold upon His Chest." The music of the
"Glory Hallelujah" chorus is present in all instances. Strong evidence sug-
gests that the John Brown in the song was a sergeant at Fort Warren, near
Boston, before 1861, not the antislavery crusader famous for his raid on
Harpers Ferry in 1859.*)

1. John Brown's body lies a-mould'ring in the grave,
   John Brown's body lies a-mould'ring in the grave,
   John Brown's body lies a-mould'ring in the grave,
   His soul goes marching on!

*Chorus:*
Glory, glory hallelujah!
Glory, glory hallelujah!
Glory, glory hallelujah!
His soul is marching on.

2. The stars of heaven are looking kindly down,
   The stars of heaven are looking kindly down,
   The stars of heaven are looking kindly down,
   On the grave of old John Brown!

   [*to Chorus*]

3. He's gone to be a soldier in the army of the Lord,
   He's gone to be a soldier in the army of the Lord,
   He's gone to be a soldier in the army of the Lord,
   His soul is marching on!

   [*to Chorus*]

4. John Brown's knapsack is strapped upon his back,
   John Brown's knapsack is strapped upon his back,
   John Brown's knapsack is strapped upon his back,
   His soul is marching on!

   [*to Chorus*]

# John Henry

AMERICAN WORK SONG

1. When John Henry was about three days old,
   Just a-sittin' on his pappy's knee,
   He gave one loud and lonesome cry:
   "The hammer'll be the death of me,
   The hammer'll be the death of me."

2. Well, the captain said to John Henry one day:
   "Gonna bring that steam drill out on the job,
   Gonna whop that steel on down,
   Gonna whop that steel on down."

3. John Henry said to the captain:
   "Well, a man ain't nothin' but a man,
   And before I let a steam drill beat me down,
   Gonna die with the hammer in my hand."

4. John Henry went to the tunnel,
   And they put him in the lead to drive;
   The rock so tall and John Henry so small,
   He laid down his hammer and he cried.

5. John Henry said to his shaker:
   "Shaker, why don't you sing?
   For I'm swingin' twelve pounds
       from the hips on down,
   Just listen to that cold steel ring."

6. John Henry told his captain:
   "Look a-yonder what I see—
   Your drill's done broke
       and your hole's done choke',
   And you can't drive steel like me."

7. Well, the man that invented the steam drill,
   He thought he was mighty fine,
   But John Henry drove his fifteen feet,
   And the steam drill only made nine.

8. John Henry looked up at the mountain,
   And his hammer was striking fire,
   Well, he hammered so hard
       that he broke his poor old heart,
   He laid down his hammer and he died.

9. They took John Henry to the graveyard,
   And they laid him in the sand;
   Three men from the east
       and a woman from the west
   Came to see that old steel-drivin' man.

10. They took John Henry to the graveyard,
    And they laid him in the sand,
    And every locomotive come a-roarin' by
    Says: "There lies a steel-drivin' man."

# John Jacob Jingleheimer Schmidt

CHILDREN'S PLAY SONG

John Jacob Jingleheimer Schmidt,
His name is my name, too;
Whenever we go out
And people always shout,
"John Jacob Jingleheimer Schmidt"
*Dah dah dah dah dah dah dah . . .*

John Jacob Jingleheimer Schmidt,
His name is my name, too;
(*etc., etc.*)


# Johnny Get Your Gun

W & M: "F. BELASCO" [M. H. Rosenfeld] (1886)

1. One evenin' in de month of May,
   *Johnny get your gun, get your gun*
   I met old Peter on de way;
   *Johnny get your gun, get your gun*
   Moses wept and Abr'am cried,
   *Johnny get your gun, get your gun*
   Satan's coming, don't you hide.
   *Johnny get your gun, get your gun*

   *Refrain:*
   Johnny get your gun, get your gun today,
   Pigeons a-flying all the way,
   If you want to get to Heaven in de good ole way,
   Johnny get your gun, get your gun!

   *Chorus:*
   Rolling on,
   Rolling on to glory, children,
   Rolling on,
   Johnny get your gun, get your gun!

2. Oh, now good children, do yo' best,
   *Johnny get your gun, get your gun*
   And button on your golden vest;
   *Johnny get your gun, get your gun*
   Tell your Uncles and your Aunts,
   *Johnny get your gun, get your gun*
   Fetch along their linen pants.
   *Johnny get your gun, get your gun*

   [*to Refrain & Chorus*]

184

**3.** The way am rough wid briar roots,
   *Johnny get your gun, get your gun*
We'll shoot old Satan 'fore he scoots;
   *Johnny get your gun, get your gun*
When you hear de rascal yell,
   *Johnny get your gun, get your gun*
Aim your musket, give him well.
   *Johnny get your gun, get your gun*

   [*to Refrain & Chorus*]

**4.** I looked old Satan in de eye,
   *Johnny get your gun, get your gun*
Said he, "I'll want you by an' by;
   *Johnny get your gun, get your gun*
Fetch me up an Alderman,
   *Johnny get your gun, get your gun*
Put him in my frying pan."
   *Johnny get your gun, get your gun*

   [*to Refrain & Chorus*]


# John Peel
W: JOHN WOODCOCK GRAVES
M: "BONNIE ANNIE" (19th c. English folk song)

**1.** D'ye ken John Peel with his coat so gay?
D'ye ken John Peel at the break of day?
D'ye ken John Peel when he's far far away
With his hounds and his horn in the morning?

   *Chorus:*
   'Twas the sound of his horn got me up from bed
   And the cry of hounds which he oft-times led,
   It was Peel's "View hallo" would wake the dead
   Or the fox from his lair in the morning.

**2.** Yes, I ken John Peel, good old Ruby too,
And old Ranter, Ringwood and Bellman true,
From a find to a check, from a check to a view,
From a view to a death in the morning.

   [*to Chorus*]

185

3. D'ye ken John Peel with his coat so gay,
   When he lived at Troutbeck in olden days?
   Now he's gone away, and so far far away,
   We shall ne'er hear his voice in the morning.

   [*to Chorus*]


# Joshua Fought the Battle of Jericho
SPIRITUAL

*Chorus:*
Joshua fought the battle of Jericho,
Jericho, Jericho,
Joshua fought the battle of Jericho,
And the walls came tumbling down.

1. You may talk about your kings of Gideon,
   You may talk about your men of Saul,
   But there's none like good old Joshua
   At the battle of Jericho.

   [*to Chorus*]

2. Now the Lord commanded Joshua:
   "I command you, and obey you must;
   You just march straight to those city walls
   And the walls will turn to dust."

   [*to Chorus*]

3. Straight up to the walls of Jericho
   He marched with spear in hand,
   "Go blow that ram's horn," Joshua cried,
   "For the battle is in my hand."

   [*to Chorus*]

4. The lamb-ram-sheep horns began to blow,
   And the trumpets began to sound,
   And Joshua commanded, "Now, children, shout!"
   And the walls came tumbling down.

   [*to Chorus*]

# Joy to the World

W: ISAAC WATTS (1719) / M: ANON.

1. Joy to the world! The Lord is come!
   Let earth receive her King;
   Let ev'ry heart prepare Him room,
      And heav'n and nature sing,
      And heav'n and nature sing,
      And heav'n, and heav'n and nature sing.

2. Joy to the world! The Saviour reigns!
   Let men their songs employ;
   While field and floods, rocks, hills and plain
      Repeat the sounding joy,
      Repeat the sounding joy,
      Repeat, repeat the sounding joy.

3. He rules the world with truth and grace,
   And makes the nations prove
   The glories of His righteousness,
      And wonders of His love,
      And wonders of His love,
      And wonders, wonders of His love.


# Judgment Day Is Rolling 'Round

SPIRITUAL

> *Chorus:*
> Judgment, Judgment,
> Judgment Day is rolling 'round!
> Judgment, Judgment,
> O how I long to go.

1. I've got a good old mother in the heaven, my Lord,
   How I long to go there, too;
   I've got a good old mother in the heaven, my Lord,
   O how I long to go.

   [*to Chorus*]

2. King Jesus sitting in the heaven, my Lord,
   How I long to go there, too;
   King Jesus sitting in the heaven, my Lord,
   O how I long to go.

   [*to Chorus*]

187

**3.** There's a big camp-meeting in the heaven, my Lord,
How I long to go there, too;
There's a big camp-meeting in the heaven, my Lord,
O how I long to go.

   [*to Chorus*]

# Kalinka
RUSSIAN FOLK SONG

   *Chorus:*
   Kalinka, kalinka,
   Kalinka moia!
   V sadu iagoda
   Malinka, malinka moia!
   Akh! . . .

**1.** Pod sosnoiu,
Pod zelёnoiu,
Spat' polozhite
Vy menia!

   [*to Chorus*]

**2.** Akh! Sosёnushka ty zelёnaia,
Ne shumi zhe nado mnoi!
Ai—liuli, liuli, ai—liuli,
Ne shumi zhe nado mnoi!

   [*to Chorus*]

**3.** Akh! Krasavitsa, dusha-devitsa,
Pliubi zhe ty menia!
Ai—liuli, liuli, ai—liuli,
Poliubi zhe ty menia!

   [*to Chorus*]

# The Kerry Dance
W & M: JAMES LYMAN MOLLOY (1879)

**1.** *O, the days of the Kerry dancing,*
*O the ring of the piper's tune!*
*O, for one of those hours of gladness,*
*Gone, alas! like our youth, too soon:*

When the boys began to gather
  in the glen of a summer night,
And the Kerry piper's tuning
  made us long with wild delight:
    O, to think of it,
    O, to dream of it,
    fills my heart with tears!

*O, the days of the Kerry dancing,*
*O the ring of the piper's tune!*
*O, for one of those hours of gladness,*
*Gone, alas! like our youth, too soon.*

2. Was there ever a sweeter colleen
   In the dance than Eily More!
   Or a prouder lad than Thady,
   As he boldly took the floor!

   "Lads and lasses, to your places,
     up the middle and down again,"
   Ah! the merry-hearted laughter
     ringing through the happy glen!
       O, to think of it,
       O, to dream of it,
       fills my heart with tears!

*O, the days of the Kerry dancing,*
*O the ring of the piper's tune!*
*O, for one of those hours of gladness,*
*Gone, alas! like our youth, too soon.*

   [*epilogue*]
   Time goes on and the happy years are dead,
   And one by one the merry hearts are fled;
   Silent now is the wild and lonely glen,
   Where the bright glad laugh will echo ne'er again,
     Only dreaming of days gone by,
       in my heart I hear . . .

3. Loving voices of old companions,
   Stealing out of the past once more,
   And the sound of the dear old music,
   Soft and sweet as in days of yore:

   When the boys began to gather
     in the glen of a summer night . . .

   *(etc., etc. to end of refrain)*

189

# Kingdom Coming

W & M: HENRY CLAY WORK (1862)

1. Say, darkeys, hab you seen de massa,
   Wid de muffstash on his face,
   Go long de road some time dis mornin',
   Like he gwine to leab de place?

   He seen a smoke, way up de ribber,
   Whar de Linkum gumboats lay;
   He took his hat, an' lef berry sudden,
   An' I spec he's run away!

   *Chorus:*
   De massa run? ha, ha!
   De darkey stay? ho, ho!
   It mus' be now de kingdom comin',
   An' de year ob Jubilo!

2. He six foot one way, two foot tudder,
   An' he weigh tree hundred pound,
   His coat so big, he couldn't pay de tailor,
   An' it won't go half way round.

   He drill so much dey call him Cap'an,
   An' he get so drefful tann'd,
   I spec he try an' fool dem Yankees
   For to tink he's contraband.

   [*to Chorus*]

3. De darkeys feel so lonesome libing
   In de loghouse on de lawn,
   Dey move dar tings to massa's parlor
   For to keep it while he's gone.

   Dar's wine an' cider in de kitchen,
   An' de darkeys dey'll hab some;
   I spose dey'll all be cornfiscated
   When de Linkum sojers come.

   [*to Chorus*]

4. De oberseer he make us trouble,
   An' he dribe us round a spell;
   We lock him up in de smokehouse cellar,
   Wid de key trown in de well.

   De whip is lost, de han'cuff broken,
   But de massa'll hab his pay;
   He's ole enough, big enough, ought to know better
   Dan to went an' run away.

   [*to Chorus*]

# K-K-K-Katy
W & M: GEOFFREY O'HARA (1918)

1. Jimmy was a soldier brave and bold,
Katy was a maid with hair of gold;
   Like an act of fate,
   Kate was standing at the gate
Watching all the boys on dress parade.

Jimmy with the girls was just a-gawk,
Stuttered ev'ry time he tried to talk;
   Still that night at eight,
   He was there at Katy's gate,
Stuttering to her this lovesick cry:

   *Chorus:*
   "K-K-K-Katy, beautiful Katy,
   You're the only g-g-g-girl that I adore;
   And when the m-m-m-moon shines over the cow-shed,
   I'll be waiting at the k-k-k-kitchen door."

2. No one ever looked so nice and neat,
No one could be just as cute and sweet;
   That's what Jimmy thought
   When the wedding ring he bought,
Now he's off to France the foe to meet.

Jimmy thought he'd like to take a chance,
See if he could make the Kaiser dance,
   Stepping to a tune
   All about the silv'ry moon,
This is what they hear in far-off France:

   [*to Chorus*]

# Kookaburra
THREE-PART ROUND FROM AUSTRALIA
W: M. SINCLAIR / M: ANON.

*First Part*
   1. Kookaburra sits on an old gum tree,
   2. Kookaburra sits on an old gum tree.

*Second Part*
   1. Merry, merry king of the bush is he,
   2. Eating all the gum drops he can see.

*Third Part*
1. Laugh, Kookaburra, laugh, Kookaburra,
   Gay your life must be.
2. Stop! Kookaburra, stop! Kookaburra,
   Leave some there for me!


# Kumbayah
AFRICAN FOLK SONG

> *Chorus:*
> Kumbayah, my Lord,
>   Kumbayah,
> Kumbayah, my Lord,
>   Kumbayah,
> Kumbayah, my Lord,
>   Kumbayah,
> Oh, Lord,
>   Kumbayah.

1. Someone's singing, Lord,
     Kumbayah,
   Someone's singing, Lord,
     Kumbayah,
   Someone's singing, Lord,
     Kumbayah,
   Oh, Lord,
     Kumbayah.

2. Someone's weeping, Lord,
     Kumbayah,
     *(etc.)*
     [*then to Chorus*]

3. Someone's dancing, Lord,
     Kumbayah,
     *(etc.)*
     [*then to Chorus*]

4. Someone's praying, Lord,
     Kumbayah,
     *(etc.)*
     [*then to Chorus*]

# Lavender's Blue

ENGLISH FOLK SONG

1. Lavender's blue,
   *diddle diddle*
   Lavender's green,
   When I am king,
   *diddle diddle*
   You shall be queen.

2. Call up your men,
   *diddle diddle*
   Set them to work,
   Some to the plough,
   *diddle diddle*
   Some to the cart,

3. Some to make hay,
   *diddle diddle*
   Some to cut corn,
   While you and I
   *diddle diddle*
   Keep ourselves warm.


# Let Me Call You Sweetheart
## (I'm in Love with You)

W: BETH SLATER WHITSON / M: LEO FRIEDMAN (1910)

1. I am dreaming, dear, of you
   Day by day,
   Dreaming when the skies are blue,
   When they're gray.

   When the silv'ry moonlight gleams,
   Still I wander on in dreams
   In a land of love, it seems,
   Just with you.

   *Chorus:*
   Let me call you "Sweetheart,"
   I'm in love with you;
   Let me hear you whisper
   That you love me, too.

   Keep the lovelight glowing
   In your eyes so true;
   Let me call you "Sweetheart,"
   I'm in love with you.

**2.** Longing for you all the while,
    More and more;
Longing for the sunny smile
    I adore.

Birds are singing far and near,
    Roses blooming ev'rywhere;
You, alone, my heart can cheer,
    You, just you.

    [*to Chorus*]


# Let the Rest of the World Go By

W: J. KEIRN BRENNAN / M: ERNEST R. BALL (1919)

**1.** Is the struggle and strife
We find in this life
    Really worthwhile after all?
I've been wishing today
I could just run away
    Out where the west winds call.

    *Chorus:*
    With someone like you,
    A pal good and true,
        I'd like to leave it all behind,
        And go and find
    Some place that's known
    To God alone,
        Just a spot to call our own.

We'll find a perfect peace,
Where joys never cease,
    Out there beneath a kindly sky;
We'll build a sweet little nest
Somewhere in the West,
        And let the rest of the world go by.

**2.** Is the future to hold
Just struggles for gold
    While the real world waits outside,
Away out on the breast
Of the wonderful West,
    Across the Great Divide?

    [*to Chorus*]

# Listen to the Mocking Bird

W: "ALICE HAWTHORNE" [Septimus Winner]
M: RICHARD MILBURN (1855)

1. I'm dreaming now of Hally,
      sweet Hally, sweet Hally;
   I'm dreaming now of Hally,
      for the thought of her is one that never dies.

   She's sleeping in the valley,
      the valley, the valley;
   She's sleeping in the valley,
      and the mocking bird is singing where she lies.

   *Chorus:*
   Listen to the mocking bird,
   Listen to the mocking bird,
   The mocking bird still singing o'er her grave.

   Listen to the mocking bird,
   Listen to the mocking bird,
   Still singing where the weeping willows wave.

2. Ah! well I yet remember,
      remember, remember,
   Ah! well I yet remember,
      when we gather'd in the cotton side by side.

   'Twas in the mild September,
      September, September,
   'Twas in the mild September,
      and the mocking bird was singing far and wide.

   [*to Chorus*]

3. When the charms of spring awaken,
      awaken, awaken,
   When charms of spring awaken,
      and the mocking bird is singing on the bough,

   I feel like one forsaken,
      forsaken, forsaken,
   I feel like one forsaken,
      since my Hally is no longer with me now.

   [*to Chorus*]

# Little Annie Rooney

W & M: MICHAEL NOLAN (1889)

1. A winning way, a pleasant smile,
   Dress'd so neat but quite in style;
   Merry chaff, your time to wile,
   Has Little Annie Rooney.

   Every evening, rain or shine,
   I make a call 'twixt eight and nine,
   On her who shortly will be mine,
   Little Annie Rooney.

   > *Chorus:*
   > She's my sweetheart! I'm her beau!
   > She's my Annie, I'm her Joe!
   > Soon we'll marry, never to part!
   > Little Annie Rooney is my sweetheart!

2. The parlor's small, but neat and clean,
   And set with taste so seldom seen;
   And you can bet the household queen
   Is Little Annie Rooney.

   The fire burns cheerfully and bright,
   As a family circle round each night
   We form, and every one's delight
   Is Little Annie Rooney.

   > [*to Chorus*]

3. We've been engaged close on a year,
   The happy time is drawing near;
   I'll wed the one I love so dear,
   Little Annie Rooney.

   My friends declare I 'm in a jest,
   Until the time comes will not rest;
   But one who knows its value best
   Is Little Annie Rooney.

   > [*to Chorus*]

# A Little Bit of Heaven
## (Shure They Call It Ireland)
W: J. KEIRN BRENNAN / M: ERNEST R. BALL (1914)

1. Have you ever heard the story
    of how Ireland got its name?
    I'll tell you so you'll understand
    from whence old Ireland came.

    No wonder that we're proud
    of that dear land across the sea,
    For here's the way me dear old mother
    told the tale to me:

    *Chorus:*
    Shure, a little bit of Heaven
        fell from out the sky one day,
    And nestled on the ocean
        in a spot so far away;

    And when the angels found it,
        shure, it looked so sweet and fair,
    They said, "Suppose we leave it
        for it looks so peaceful there";

    So they sprinkled it with star dust
        just to make the shamrocks grow;
    'Tis the only place you'll find them,
        no matter where you go;

    Then they dotted it with silver,
        to make its lakes so grand,
    And when they had it finished
        shure, they called it Ireland.

2. 'Tis a dear old land of fairies
    and of wond'rous wishing wells;
    And nowhere else on God's green earth
    have they such lakes and dells!

    No wonder that the angels
    loved its shamrock-bordered shore,
    'Tis a little bit of Heaven
    and I love it more and more.

    [*to Chorus*]

# The Little Brown Jug

W & M: "R. A. EASTBURN" [Joseph Winner] (1869)

1. My wife and I live all alone
   In a little hut we call our own;
   Now she loved gin and I loved rum,
   I tell you what, we'd lots of fun.

   *Chorus:*
   Ha ha ha, you and me,
   Little brown jug, don't I love thee;
   Ha ha ha, you and me,
   Little brown jug, don't I love thee.

2. 'Tis you who makes my friends and foes,
   And it's you who makes me wear old clothes;
   Now here you are so near my nose,
   So tip her up and down she goes.

   [*to Chorus*]

3. When I go toiling on my farm,
   I will take the brown jug in my arm;
   I place it 'neath a shady tree,
   My dear brown jug, 'tis you and me.

   [*to Chorus*]

4. If all the folks in Adam's race
   Were they here together in one place,
   Then I'd prepare to shed a tear
   Before I'd part from you, my dear.

   [*to Chorus*]

5. If I'd a cow that gave such milk,
   I would clothe her in the finest silk.
   I'd feed her on the choicest hay
   And milk her forty times a day.

   [*to Chorus*]

6. The rose is red, my nose is, too,
   But the vi'let's blue and so are you.
   And yet I guess before I stop,
   We'd better take another drop.

   [*to Chorus*]

# Little 'Liza Jane

AMERICAN FOLK SONG

You got a gal and I got none,
Little 'Liza Jane;
Come, my love, and be my one,
Little 'Liza Jane.

*Chorus:*
Oh, Eliza,
Little 'Liza Jane;
Oh, Eliza,
Little 'Liza Jane.


# Loch Lomond

SCOTTISH FOLK SONG

1. By yon bonnie banks and by yon bonnie braes,
   Where the sun shines bright on Loch Lomond,
   Where me and my true love were ever wont to gae,
   On the bonnie, bonnie banks of Loch Lomond.

   *Chorus:*
   Oh! ye'll take the high road, and I'll take the low road,
   And I'll be in Scotland a-fore ye,
   But me and my true love, we'll never meet again
   On the bonnie, bonnie banks of Loch Lomond.

2. 'Twas there that we parted in yon shady glen,
   On the steep, steep side of Ben Lomond,
   Where in purple hue the highlands hills we view,
   And the moon coming out in the gloaming.

   [*to Chorus*]

3. The wee birdies sing, and the wild flowers spring,
   And in sunshine the waters are sleeping,
   But the broken heart kens nae second spring again,
   Though the waeful may cease frae their greeting.

   [*to Chorus*]

# Lo, How a Rose E'er Blooming

W: ANON. GERMAN (16th c.)
ENGLISH VERSION BY DR. THEODORE BAKER
M: TRADITIONAL

Lo, how a Rose e'er blooming
From tender stem hath sprung!
Of Jesse's lineage coming
As men of old have sung.
  It came, a floweret bright,
  Amid the cold of winter,
  When half spent was the night.

Isaiah 'twas foretold it,
The Rose I have in mind,
With Mary we behold it,
The Virgin Mother kind.
  To show God's love aright,
  She bore to men a Saviour,
  When half spent was the night.

# London Bridge

ENGLISH CHILDREN'S PLAYING SONG

1.  London Bridge is falling down,
    Falling down, falling down,
    London Bridge is falling down,
    My fair lady!

2.  Build it up with iron bars,
    Iron bars, iron bars,
    Build it up with iron bars,
    My fair lady!

3.  Iron bars will bend and break,
    Bend and break (*etc.*)

4.  Build it up with gold and silver,
    Gold and silver *(etc.)*

5.  Gold and silver I've not got,
    I've not got (*etc.*)

6.  Here's a prisoner I have got,
    I have got (*etc.*)

7. What's the prisoner done to you?
   Done to you (*etc.*)

8. Stole my watch and broke my chain,
   Broke my chain (*etc.*)

9. What'll you take to set him free?
   Set him free (*etc.*)

10. One hundred pounds will set him free,
    Set him free (*etc.*)

11. One hundred pounds we have not got,
    Have not got (*etc.*)

12. Then off to prison he must go,
    He must go (*etc.*)


# Londonderry Air

TRADITIONAL IRISH

*The first known printing of this melody, 1855—most familiar as the tune
for "Danny Boy"—appeared without a title. It apparently acquired its
name as a result of a note indicating that the music was originally collected by a Miss J. Ross of the country of Londonderry, Ireland, from
the unpublished melodies of that country. The accompanying text is
anonymous.*

Would God I were the tender apple blossom
   That floats and falls from off the twisted bough,
To lie and faint within your silken bosom,
   Within your silken bosom, as that does now.

Or would I were a little burnished apple
   For you to pluck me, gliding by so cold,
While sun and shade your robe of lawn will dapple,
   Your robe of lawn and your hair's spun gold.

# Lonesome Valley

SPIRITUAL

1. Jesus walked this lonesome valley,
   He had to walk it by Himself;
   O nobody else could walk it for Him,
   He had to walk it by Himself.

2. We must walk this lonesome valley,
   We have to walk it by ourselves;
   O nobody else can walk it for us,
   We have to walk it by ourselves.

3. You must go and stand your trial,
   You have to stand it by yourself;
   O nobody else can stand it for you,
   You have to stand it by yourself.


# Long, Long Ago

W & M: THOMAS HAYNES BAYLY (1833)

1. Tell me the tales that to me were so dear,
   Long, long ago, long, long ago;
   Sing me the songs I delighted to hear
   Long, long ago, long ago.

   Now you are come, all my grief is removed,
   Let me forget that so long you have roved;
   Let me believe that you love as you loved,
   Long, long ago, long ago.

2. Do you remember the path where we met,
   Long, long ago, long, long ago?
   Ah, yes, you told me you ne'er would forget,
   Long, long ago, long ago.

   Then, to all others my smile you preferred,
   Love when you spoke gave a charm to each word;
   Still my heart treasures the praises I heard
   Long, long ago, long ago.

3. Though by your kindness my fond hopes were raised,
   Long, long ago, long, long ago;
   You, by more eloquent lips have been praised,
   Long, long ago, long ago.

But by long absence your truth has been tried,
Still to your accents I listen with pride;
Blest as I was when I sat by your side
Long, long ago, long ago.


# Looby Loo

CHILDREN'S PLAY-BATHING SONG

*(The verse texts—but not their tune—are strikingly similar to those of
"The Hokey Pokey," a traditional American "action song" and party
favorite.)*

> *Chorus:*
> Here we go looby loo,
> Here we go looby light,
> Here we go looby loo,
> All on a Saturday night.

1. Put your right hand in,
   Put your right hand out,
   Shake it a little, a little, a little,
   And turn yourself about.

   *[to Chorus]*

2. Put your left hand in,
   Put your left hand out,
   Shake it a little, a little, a little,
   And turn yourself about.

   *[to Chorus]*

3. Put your right foot in,
   *(etc.)*

4. Put your left foot in,
   *(etc.)*

5. Put your big head in,
   *(etc.)*

6. Put your whole self in,
   *(etc.)*

# Love Sends a Little Gift of Roses
W: LESLIE COOKE / M: JOHN OPENSHAW (1919)

1. Take thou my gift, my offering of roses,
   Cull'd from my garden, sweet with twilight dew;
   If just one flow'r upon your breast reposes,
   Life shall forever hold no rose but you.

   *Chorus:*
   Love sends a little gift of roses,
   Breathing a pray'r unto my posies,
   Torn from my heart as twilight closes,
       Asking this, only this:

   One heart to grow a little tender,
   Two eyes to glow with love's own splendor,
   Two lips to give in sweet surrender
       Just a kiss, just a kiss.

2. Take thou my gift, and be it joy or sorrow,
   Think e'er my roses fade and fall apart;
   With each sweet bloom that you may scorn tomorrow,
   I send to you for joy or pain my heart.

   [*to Chorus*]


# Love's Old Sweet Song
## (Just a Song at Twilight)
W: G. CLIFTON BINGHAM / M: JAMES L. MOLLOY (1884)

1. Once in the dear dead days beyond recall,
   When on the earth the mists began to fall,
   Out of dreams that rose in happy throng,
   Low to our hearts, love sang an old sweet song.

   And in the dusk where fell the firelight gleam,
   Softly it wove itself into our dream.

   *Chorus:*
   Just a song at twilight when the lights are low,
   And the flick'ring shadows softly come and go.
   Though the heart be weary, sad the day and long,
   Still to us at twilight comes love's old song,
       Comes love's old sweet song.

**2.** Even today we hear love's song of yore,
   Deep in our hearts it dwells forevermore.
   Footsteps may falter, weary grow the way,
   Still we can hear it at the close of day.

   So till the end, when life's dim shadows fall,
   Love will be found the sweetest song of all.

   [*to Chorus*]


# Ma
## (He's Making Eyes at Me)
W: SIDNEY CLARE / M: CON CONRAD (1921)

**1.** Little Lilly was oh! so silly and shy,
   And all the fellows knew
   She wouldn't bill and coo;
   Ev'ry single night some smart fellow would try
   To cuddle up to her,
   But she would cry:

   *Chorus:*
   "Ma, he's making eyes at me!
   Ma, he's awful nice to me!
   Ma, he's almost breaking my heart,
   I'm beside him, mercy! Let his conscience guide him!

   "Ma, he wants to marry me,
   Be my honey bee.
      Ev'ry minute he gets bolder,
      Now he's leaning on my shoulder,
   Ma, he's kissing me!"

**2.** Lilly was so good, ev'rybody could tell;
   You'd never see her roam,
   She'd always stay at home;
   All the neighbors knew little Lilly too well,
   For when the boys would call,
   They'd hear her yell:

   [*to Chorus*]

# Macnamara's Band

W: JOHN J. STAMFORD / M: SHAMUS O'CONNOR (1917)
*("American version by Red Latham, Wamp Carlson, Guy Bonham: 'The Three Jesters'")*

1. Oh! me name is Macnamara, I'm the leader of the band,
Although we're few in numbers, we're the finest in the land.
We play at wakes and weddings and at ev'ry fancy ball,
And when we play to funerals, we play the march from "Saul."

    *Chorus:*
    Oh! the drums go bang, and the cymbals clang,
        And the horns they blaze away;
    McCarthy pumps the old bazoon
        While I the pipes do play;
    And Hennessey Tennessee tootles the flute,
        And the music is somethin' grand—
    A credit to old Ireland is Macnamara's band.

2. Right now we are rehearsin' for a very swell affair,
The annual celebration, all the gentry will be there.
When General Grant to Ireland came, he took me by the hand,
Says he, "I never saw the likes of Macnamara's band."

    [*to Chorus*]

3. "Oh! my name is Uncle Yulius and from Sweden I have come,
To play with Macnamara's band and beat the big bass drum.
And when I march along the street, the ladies think I'm grand,
They shout, 'There's Uncle Yulius playing with an Irish band.'

4. "Oh! I wear a bunch of shamrocks and a uniform of green,
And I'm the funniest looking Swede that you have ever seen.
There's O'Briens and Ryans and Sheehans and Meehans,
    They come from Ireland,
But, by Yimminy, I'm the only Swede in Macnamara's band."

    [*now to Chorus*]


# Macushla

W: JOSEPHINE V. ROWE / M: DERMOT MACMURROUGH (1910)

Macushla! Macushla! your sweet voice is calling,
Calling me softly again and again.
Macushla! Macushla! I hear its dear pleading,
My blue-eyed Macushla, I hear it in vain.

Macushla! Macushla! your white arms are reaching,
I feel them enfolding, caressing me still.

Fling them out from the darkness, my lost love, Macushla,
Let them find me and bind me again if they will.

Macushla! Macushla! your red lips are saying
That death is a dream, and love is for aye.
Then awaken, Macushla, awake from your dreaming,
My blue-eyed Macushla, awaken to stay.


# Madelon
## (I'll Be True to the Whole Regiment)
W: ORIGINAL FRENCH BY LOUIS BOUSQUET
ENGLISH VERSION BY ALFRED BRYAN
M: CAMILLE ROBERT (1918)

1. There is a tavern 'way down in Brittany,
   Where weary soldiers take their liberty;
   The keeper's daughter whose name is Madelon
   Pours out the wine while they laugh and "carry on."

   And while the wine goes to their senses,
   Her sparkling glance goes to their hearts,
   Their admiration so intense as
   Each one his tale of love imparts.

   She coquettes with them all
   But favors none at all,
   And here's the way they banter
   Ev'ry time they call:

   *Chorus:*
   O Madelon, you are the only one,
   O Madelon, for you we'll carry on;
   It's so long since we have seen a miss,
   Won't you give us just a kiss?

   But Madelon, she takes it all in fun,
   She laughs and says, "You see it can't be done,
   I would like but how can I consent
   When I'm true to the whole regiment?"

   [Original French Chorus]
   *Quand Madelon vient nous servir à boire*
   *Sous la tonnelle on frôle son jupon,*
   *Et chacun lui raconte une histoire*
   *Une histoire à sa façon.*

*La Madelon pour nous n'est pas sévère*
*Quand on lui prend la taille ou le menton,*
*Elle rit, c'est tout l'mal qu'elle sait faire,*
*Madelon, Madelon, Madelon.*

2. He was a fair-hair'd boy from Brittany,
   She was a blue-eyed maid from Normandy;
   He said good-bye to this pretty Madelon,
   He went his way with the boys who carry on.

   And when his noble work was ended,
   He said farewell to his command,
   Back to his Madelon he wended
   To claim her little heart and hand.

   With lovelight in his glance,
   This gallant son of France
   He murmurs as she listens
   With her heart entranc'd:

   *Chorus:*
   O Madelon, you are the only one;
   Now that the foe is gone
   Let the wedding bells ring sweet and gay,
   Let this be our wedding day.

   O Madelon, sweet maid of Normandy,
   Like Joan of Arc you'll always be to me;
   All thru life for you I'll carry on,
   Madelon, Madelon, Madelon.


# Malbrouk s'en Va-t-en Guerre
FRENCH MARCHING SONG
*(same melody as "The Bear Went Over the Mountain"*
*as well as "For He's a Jolly Good Fellow")*

1. Malbrouk s'en va-t-en guerre,
   *Mironton, mironton, mirontaine:*
   Malbrouk s'en va-t-en guerre,
   Ne sait quand reviendra.
   Là bas—

   *Chorus:*
   Courez, courez, courez!
   Petite fille, jeune et gentille!
   Courez, courez, courez!
   Venez ce soir nous amuser!

**2.** Il viendra z'à Pâques,
*Mironton, mironton, mirontaine:*
Il viendra z'à Pâques,
Ou à la Trinité.
Là bas—

[*to Chorus*]

**3.** La Trinité se passe,
*Mironton, mironton, mirontaine:*
La Trinité se passe,
Malbrouk ne revient pas.
Là bas—

[*to Chorus*]

**4.** Madame à sa tour monte,
*Mironton, mironton, mirontaine:*
Madame à sa tour monte,
Si haut qu'elle peut monter.
Là bas—

[*to Chorus*]

**5.** Elle aperçoit son page . . .
*(etc., etc.)* . . .
Tout de noir habillé.
Là bas—

[*to Chorus*]

**6.** Beau page, ah! mon beau page . . .
*(etc., etc.)* . . .
Quell' nouvelle apportez?
Là bas—

[*to Chorus*]

**7.** Aux nouvelles que j'apporte . . .
*(etc., etc.)* . . .
Vos beaux yeux vont pleurer.
Là bas—

[*to Chorus*]

**8.** Monsieur Malbrouk est mort . . .
*(etc., etc.)* . . .
Est mort et enterré!
Là bas—

[*to Chorus*]

9. Je l'ai vu porter en terre . . .
   *(etc., etc.)* . . .
   Par quatre z'officiers.
   Là bas—

   [*to Chorus*]


# (The Man on) The Flying Trapeze
W: GEORGE LEYBOURNE / M: ALFRED LEE (1867)

1. Once I was happy, but now I'm forlorn,
   Like an old coat that is tatter'd and torn;
   Left on this wide world to fret and to mourn,
      betray'd by a maid in her teens.

   The girl that I lov'd, she was handsome,
   I tried all I knew, her to please;
   But I could not please her one quarter so well
      like that man upon the trapeze.

   *Chorus:*
   He'd fly thro' the air with the greatest of ease,
   A daring young man on the flying trapeze;
   His movements were graceful, all girls he could please,
   And my love he purloin'd away.

2. This young man by name was Signor Bona Slang;
   Tall, big and handsome, as well made as Chang;
   Where'er he appeared, the hall loudly rang
      with ovations from all people there.

   He'd smile from the bar on the people below,
   And one night he smiled on my love;
   She wink'd back at him, and she shouted "Bravo!"
      as he hung by his nose up above!

   [*to Chorus*]

3. Her father and mother were both on my side,
   And very hard tried to make her my own bride;
   Her father he sighed, and her mother she cried,
      to see her throw herself away.

   'Twas all no avail, she went there every night,
   And would throw him bouquets on the stage,
   Which caus'd him to meet her; how he ran me down,
      to tell you, would take a whole page.

   [*to Chorus*]

**4.** One night I as usual went to her dear home,
   Found there her father and mother alone;
   I ask'd for my love, and soon they made known,
      to my horror, that she'd run away!

She'd packed up her box, and eloped in the night
With him, with the greatest of ease;
From two stories high, he had lowered her down
   to the ground on his flying trapeze!

   [*to Chorus*]

**5.** Some months after this, I went to a hall;
   Was greatly surprised to see on the wall
   A bill in red letters, which did my heart gall,
      that she was appearing with him.

He taught her gymnastics, and dressed her in tights,
To help him to live at his ease,
And made her assume a masculine name,
   and now she goes on the trapeze!

   *Final Chorus:*
   She floats thro' the air with the greatest of ease,
   You'd think her a man on the flying trapeze;
   She does all the work, while he takes his ease,
   And that's what became of my love.


# The Man Who Broke the Bank at Monte Carlo
W & M: FRED GILBERT (1892)

**1.** I've just got here, through Paris, from the sunny southern shore;
   I to Monte Carlo went, just to raise my winter's rent.
   Dame Fortune smiled upon me as she'd never done before,
      And I've now such lots of money I'm a gent—
      Yes, I've now such lots of money I'm a gent.

   *Chorus:*
   As I walk along the *Bois Boolong,*
   With an independent air,
   You can hear the girls declare,
   "He must be a millionaire";

   You can hear them sigh
   And wish to die,
   You can see them wink the other eye
   At the man who broke the Bank at Monte Carlo.

211

**2.** I stay indoors till after lunch, and then my daily walk
   To the great Triumphal Arch is one grand triumphal march
   Observed by each observer with the keeness of a hawk;
     I'm a mass of money, linen, silk and starch—
     I'm a mass of money, linen, silk and starch.

   [*to Chorus*]

**3.** I patronized the tables at the Monte Carlo hell
   Till they hadn't got a sou for a Christian or a Jew.
   So I quickly went to Paris for the charms of mad'moiselle,
     Who's the loadstone of my heart—What can I do
     When with twenty tongues she swears that she'll be true?

   [*to Chorus*]


# Marching Through Georgia
W & M: HENRY CLAY WORK (1865)

**1.** Bring the good old bugle, boys! we'll sing another song—
   Sing it with a spirit that will start the world along—
   Sing it as we used to sing it, fifty thousand strong,
   While we were marching through Georgia.

   *Chorus:*
   "Hurrah! Hurrah! we bring the Jubilee!
   Hurrah! Hurrah! the flag that makes you free!"
   So we sang the chorus from Atlanta to the sea,
   While we were marching through Georgia.

**2.** How the darkeys shouted when they heard the joyful sound!
   How the turkeys gobbled, which our commissary found!
   How the sweet potatoes even started from the ground,
   While we were marching through Georgia.

   [*to Chorus*]

**3.** Yes, and there were Union men who wept with joyful tears
   When they saw the honor'd flag they had not seen for years;
   Hardly could they be restrained from breaking forth in cheers,
   While we were marching through Georgia.

   [*to Chorus*]

**4.** "Sherman's dashing Yankee boys will never reach the coast!"
So the saucy rebels said, and 'twas a handsome boast;
Had they not forgot, alas! to reckon with the host,
While we were marching through Georgia.

[*to Chorus*]

**5.** So we made a thoroughfare for Freedom and her train,
Sixty miles in latitude—three hundred to the main;
Treason fled before us, for resistance was in vain,
While we were marching through Georgia.

[*to Chorus*]

# Margie

W: BENNY DAVIS / M: CON CONRAD & J. RUSSEL ROBINSON (1920)

**1.** You can talk about your love affairs,
Here's one I must tell to you:
All night long they sit upon the stairs,
He holds her close and starts to coo:
     "My little . . .

> *Chorus:*
> ". . . Margie, I'm always thinking of you,
> Margie, I'll tell the world I love you;
> Don't forget your promise to me,
> I have a bought a home and ring and ev'rything,
>      For . . .
>
> ". . . Margie, you've been my inspiration,
> Days are never blue.
>      After all is said and done,
>      There is really only one,
> Oh! Margie, Margie, it's you."

**2.** You can picture me most ev'ry night,
I can't wait until they start,
Ev'rything he says just seems all right,
I want to learn that stuff by heart.
     "My little . . .

[*to Chorus*]

# The Marines' Hymn

W: L. Z. PHILLIPS (?) (1919)
*(uncertain authorship)*
M: JACQUES OFFENBACH
["Couplets des Deux Hommes d'Armes"
from the musical *Geneviève de Brabant*, 1868]

1. From the Halls of Montezuma
   To the shores of Tripoli,
   We fight our country's battles
   In the air, on land and sea.

   First to fight for right and freedom
   And to keep our honor clean,
   We are proud to claim the title
   Of United States Marine.

2. Our flag's unfurled to ev'ry breeze
   From dawn to setting sun,
   We have fought in ev'ry clime and place
   Where we could take a gun.

   In the snow of far off Northern lands
   And in sunny tropic scenes,
   You will find us always on the job,
   The United States Marines.

3. Here's health to you and to our Corps,
   Which we are proud to serve,
   In many a strife we've fought for life
   And never lost our nerve.

   If the Army and the Navy
   Ever look on heaven's scenes,
   They will find the streets are guarded
   By United States Marines.


# La Marseillaise

FRENCH NATIONAL ANTHEM
W & M: CLAUDE ROUGET DE LISLE (1792)

1. Allons, enfants de la patrie!
   Le jour de gloire est arrivé!
   Contre nous de la tyrannie
   L'étendard sanglant est levé!
   L'etendard sanglant est levé!

Entendez-nous, dans les campagnes,
Mugir ces feroces soldats?
Ils viennent jusque dans nos bras
Egorger nos fils, nos compagnes!

*Aux armes, citoyens!*
*Formez vos bataillons!*
*Marchons, marchons!*
*Qu'un sang impur*
*Abreuve nos sillons!*

2. Tremblez, tyrans! et vous, perfides,
L'opprobre de tous les partis,
Tremblez! vos projets parricides
Vont enfin recevoir leur prix!
Vont enfin recevoir leur prix!

Tout est soldat pour vous combattre.
S'ils tombent, nos jeunes héros,
La France en produit de nouveaux,
Contre vous tout prêts à se battre!

*Aux armes, citoyens!*
*Formez vos bataillons!*
*Marchons, marchons!*
*Qu'un sang impur*
*Abreuve nos sillons!*

3. Nous entrerons dans la carriere
Quand nos ainés n'y seront plus;
Nous y trouverons leur poussière
Et la trace de leurs vertus,
Et la trace de leurs vertus.

Bien moins jaloux de leur survivre
Que de partager leur cercueil,
Nous aurons le sublime orgueil
De les venger ou les suivre!

*Aux armes, citoyens!*
*Formez vos bataillons!*
*Marchons, marchons!*
*Qu'un sang impur*
*Abreuve nos sillons!*

# Mary Had a Baby

SPIRITUAL

1. Mary had a baby, my Lord,
   Mary had a baby, my Lord,
   Mary had a baby,
   Mary had a baby,
   Mary had a baby, my Lord.

2. Laid him in a manger, my Lord,
   *(etc.)*

3. She named him King Jesus, my Lord,
   *(etc.)*

4. Shepherds came to see him, my Lord,
   *(etc.)*


# Mary Had a Little Lamb

NURSERY SONG

1. Mary had a little lamb,
   Little lamb, little lamb,
   Mary had a little lamb,
   Its fleece was white as snow.

2. And ev'rywhere that Mary went,
   Mary went, Mary went,
   And ev'rywhere that Mary went,
   The lamb was sure to go.

3. He followed her to school one day,
   School one day, school one day,
   He followed her to school one day,
   That was against the rules.

4. It made the children laugh and play,
   Laugh and play, laugh and play,
   It made the children laugh and play,
   To see a lamb at school.

5. And so the teacher turned him out,
   *(etc.)*
   But still he lingered near.

**6.** He waited patiently about,
    *(etc.)*
    Till Mary did appear.

**7.** What makes the lamb love Mary so?
    *(etc.)*
    The eager children cry.

**8.** Mary loves the lamb, you know,
    *(etc.)*
    The teacher did reply.


# Maryland! My Maryland!

W: JAMES RYDER RANDALL (1861)
M: TRADITIONAL *(anonymous tune to the German poem
"O Tannenbaum, O Tannenbaum!")*

**1.** Thou wilt not cower in the dust,
    Maryland! My Maryland!
    Thy beaming sword shall never rust,
    Maryland! My Maryland!

    Remember Carroll's sacred trust,
    Remember Howard's war-like thrust,
    And all thy slumb'rers with the just,
    Maryland! My Maryland!

**2.** Thou wilt not yield the Vandal toll,
    Maryland! My Maryland!
    Thou wilt not crook to his control,
    Maryland! My Maryland!

    Better the fire upon thee roll,
    Better the shot, the blade, the bowl,
    Than crucifixion of the soul,
    Maryland! My Maryland!

**3.** I see no blush upon thy cheek,
    Maryland! My Maryland!
    Tho' thou wast ever bravely meek,
    Maryland! My Maryland!

    For life and death, for woe and weal,
    Thy peerless chivalry reveal,
    And gird thy beauteous limbs with steel,
    Maryland! My Maryland!

**4**. I hear the distant thunder hum,
Maryland! My Maryland!
The Old Line bugle, fife and drum,
Maryland! My Maryland!

Come! to thine heroic throng,
That stalks with Liberty along,
And ring thy dauntless slogan song,
Maryland! My Maryland!

# Mary's a Grand Old Name

W & M: GEORGE M. COHAN
[from *Forty-five Minutes from Broadway,* 1905]

**1**. My mother's name was Mary, she was so good and true,
Because her name was Mary she called me Mary, too.
She wasn't gay or airy but plain as she could be,
I hate to meet a fairy who calls herself Marie.

*Chorus:*
For it is Mary, Mary, plain as any name can be,
But with propriety society will say Marie.
But it was Mary, Mary, long before the fashions came.
And there is something there that sounds so square,
It's a grand old name.

**2**. Now when her name is Mary there is no falseness there,
When to Marie she'll vary, she'll surely bleach her hair.
Though Mary's ordinary, Marie is fair to see,
Don't ever fear sweet Mary, beware of sweet Marie.

[*to Chorus*]

# Massa's in de Cold, Cold Ground

W & M: STEPHEN C. FOSTER (1852)

**1**. 'Round de meadows am a-ringing
De darkey's mournful song,
While de mocking bird am singing,
Happy as de day am long.
Dare old massa am a-sleeping,
Sleeping in de cold, cold ground.

*Chorus:*
Down in de cornfield,
Hear dat mournful sound:
All the darkeys am a-weeping,
Massa's in de cold, cold ground.

2. When de autumn leaves are falling,
   When de days are cold,
   'Twas hard to hear old massa calling,
   'Cause he was so weak and old.

   Now de orange trees am blooming
   On de sandy shore,
   Now de summer days am coming,
   Massa nebber calls no more.

   [*to Chorus*]

3. Massa make de darkeys love him
   Cayse he was so kind,
   Now dey sadly weep above him,
   Mourning cayse he leave dem behind.

   I cannot work before to-morrow
   Cayse de tear-drop flow,
   I try to drive away my sorrow,
   Pickin' on de old banjo.

   [*to Chorus*]

# Meet Me in St. Louis, Louis

W: ANDREW B. STERLING / M: KERRY MILLS (1904)

1. Now Louis came home to the flat,
   He hung up his coat and his hat;
   He gazed all around but no wifey he found,
   So he said, "Where can Flossie be at?"

   A note on the table he spied;
   He read it just once, then he cried.
   It ran, "Louis dear, it's too slow for me here,
   So I think I will go for a ride."

   *Chorus:*
   "Meet me in St. Louis, Louis,
   Meet me at the fair.
   Don't tell me the lights are shining
   Any place but there.

"We will dance the Hoochee Koochee,
I will be your tootsie wootsie.
If you will meet me in St. Louis, Louis,
Meet me at the fair."

2. The dresses that hung in the hall
Were gone, she had taken them all;
She took all his rings and the rest of his things,
The picture he missed from the wall.

"What! moving?" the janitor said,
"Your rent is paid three months ahead."
"What good is the flat?" said poor Louis, "Read that,"
And the janitor smiled as he read:

[*to Chorus*]


# Meet Me To-night in Dreamland

W: BETH SLATER WHITSON / M: LEO FRIEDMAN (1909)

1. Dreaming of you, that's all I do,
Night and day for you I'm pining;
And in your eyes, blue as the skies,
I can see the lovelight softly shining.
Because you love me there, it seems,
Pray meet me in the land of dreams.

*Chorus:*
Meet me to-night in Dreamland,
Under the silv'ry moon;
Meet me to-night in Dreamland,
Where love's sweet roses bloom.

Come with the lovelight gleaming
In your dear eyes of blue;
Meet me in Dreamland,
Sweet, dreamy Dreamland,
There let my dreams come true.

2. Sighing all day when you're away,
Longing for you, dear, you only;
In blissful dreams, sweetheart, it seems
One is never sad and never lonely.
And if you'll come with me to stay,
We'll live in Dreamland night and day.

[*to Chorus*]

# Memories

W: GUSTAVE (GUS) KAHN / M: EGBERT VAN ALSTYNE (1915)

1. 'Round me at twilight come stealing
   Shadows of days that are gone;
   Dreams of the old days revealing
   Mem'ries of Love's golden yawn.

   *Chorus:*
   Memories, memories,
   Dreams of love, so true;
   O'er the Sea of Memory
   I'm drifting back to you.

   Childhood days, wildwood days,
   Among the birds and bees;
   You left me alone, but still you're my own!
   In my beautiful Memories.

2. Sunlight may teach me forgetting,
   Noonlight brings thoughts that are new;
   Twilight brings sighs and regretting,
   Moonlight means sweet dreams of you.

   [*to Chorus*]


# Michael Finnegan

CHILDREN'S NONSENSE SONG

1. There was an old man named Michael Finnegan,
   He had whiskers on his chinnegan;
   He cut 'em off but they grew in again!
   Poor old Michael Finnegan.

   *Spoken:*
   Begin again!

2. There was an old man named Michael Finnegan,
   He went fishing with a pin again;
   Caught a fish but it flopped in again!
   Poor old Michael Finnegan.

   *Spoken:*
   Begin again!

**3.** There was an old man named Michael Finnegan,
Ran a race and tried to win again;
He fell down and bumped his chin again!
  Poor old Michael,
  Poor old Michael,
Poor old Michael Finnegan.

  *Spoken:*
  Don't begin again!

# Michael, Row the Boat Ashore
SPIRITUAL

**1.** Michael, row the boat ashore, *Alleluia,*
Michael, row the boat ashore, *Alleluia.*

**2.** Michael's boat's a music boat, *Alleluia,*
Michael's boat's a music boat, *Alleluia.*

**3.** Sister, help to trim the sail, *Alleluia,*
Sister, help to trim the sail, *Alleluia.*

**4.** Jordan's River is deep and wide, *Alleluia,*
Kills the body but not the soul, *Alleluia.*

**5.** Jordan's River is deep and wide, *Alleluia,*
Meet my mother on the other side, *Alleluia.*

**6.** Gabriel, blow the trumpet horn, *Alleluia,*
Blow the trumpet loud and long, *Alleluia.*

# A Mighty Fortress Is Our God

*(This famous Protestant chorale is a setting of Martin Luther's "Ein' feste Burg ist unser Gott," 1529. Frederick H. Hedge wrote the English version. The melody is based on traditional plainchant.)*

**1.** A mighty fortress is our God,
A bulwark never failing;
Our Helper He, amid the flood
Of mortal ills prevailing.

For still our ancient foe
Doth seek to work us woe;
His craft and pow'r are great,

222

And armed with cruel hate,
   On earth is not his equal.

2. Did we in our own strength confide,
   Our striving would be losing,
   Were not the right man on our side,
   The man of God's own choosing.

   Dost ask who that may be?
   Christ Jesus, it is He;
   Lord Sabaoth is His name,
   From age to age the same,
      And He must win the battle.

3. And though this world, with devils filled,
   Should threaten to undo us,
   We will not fear, for God hath willed
   His truth to triumph through us.

   The prince of darkness grim,
   We tremble not for him;
   His rage we can endure,
   For lo! his doom is sure—
      One little word shall fell him.

4. That word above all earthly powers—
   No thanks to them—abideth;
   The Spirit and the gifts are ours
   Thro' Him who with us sideth.

   Let goods and kindred go,
   This mortal life also;
   The body they may kill;
   God's truth abideth still,
      His kingdom is forever.

# Mighty Lak' a Rose

W: FRANK L. STANTON / M: ETHELBERT NEVIN (1901)

Sweetest li'l feller,
Ev'rybody knows;
Dunno what to call him,
But he mighty lak' a rose!

Lookin' at his Mammy
Wid eyes so shiny blue,
Mek' you think that heav'n
Is comin' clost ter you!

W'en he's dar a-sleepin'
  In his li'l place,
Think I see de angels
  Lookin' thro' de lace.

W'en de dark is fallin',
  W'en de shadders creep,
Den dey comes on tiptoe
  Ter kiss 'im in his sleep.

Sweetest li'l feller . . .

  *(etc.: repeat stanzas 1 and 2)*


# The Minstrel Boy
W: THOMAS MOORE / M: ANON. (1813)

1. The Minstrel Boy to the war is gone,
     In the ranks of death you'll find him;
   His father's sword he has girded on,
     And his wild harp hung behind him.
   "Land of Song," said the Warrior Bard,
     "Tho' all the world betrays thee,
   One sword at least thy Right shall guard,
     One faithful Harp shall praise thee."

2. The Minstrel fell! but the foeman's chain
     Could not bring his proud soul under;
   The Harp he lov'd ne'er spoke again,
     For he tore its Chords asunder;
   And said, "No chains shall sully thee,
     Thou soul of Love and Bravery!
   Thy songs were made for the pure and free,
     They shall never sound in Slavery."


# M-I-S-S-I-S-S-I-P-P-I
W: BERT HANLON & BENNY RYAN
M: HARRY TIERNEY (1916)

1. When I was seven years of age I used to go to school,
   And when it came to spelling I was awful as a rule;

   I couldn't spell a single word when "S"s were concerned,
   I've tried to overcome my lisp and success came in return.

224

Now that word "Mississippi" was awful hard to spell,
But now I will convince you that I can spell it well:

*Chorus:*
M-I-S-S-I-S-S-I-P-P-I,
That used to be so hard to spell;
It used to make me cry,
But since I've studied spelling,
It's just like pumpkin pie:
M-I-S-S-I-S-S-I-P-P-I.

2. A lot of words would puzzle me—"bananas" was no cinch,
"Sas-a-pa-ril-la," that was hard, 'though I'd spell it in a pinch;

But words like "Cincinnati," "psychological" and such,
Gee, when it came to spelling those, I surely was in Dutch.

I can't spell "Cinderella," and "sausages," that's tough,
But I can spell "Mississippi," and believe me, that's enough.

[*to Chorus*]

## Missouri Waltz
W: "J. R. SHANNON" [James Royce]
M: FREDERICK KNIGHT LOGAN (1916)
*(Although Logan is credited as composer of the 1916 song, the music—*
*which was first published in 1914 as a piano instrumental—is thought to*
*have originated as an anonymous guitar tune.)*

Hushabye, ma baby, slumbertime is comin' soon;
Rest yo' head upon ma breast while Mammy hums a tune;
The sandman is callin'
Where shadows are fallin',
While the soft breezes sigh
As in days long gone by.

'Way down in Missouri where I heard this melody,
When I was a happy youngster on ma Mammy's knee;
The young folks were hummin',
Their banjos were strummin'
So sweet and low.

*Strum, strum, strum strum, strum*
Seems I hear those banjos playin' once again
*Hum, hum, hum hum, hum*
That same old plaintive strain.

Hear that mournful melody,
It just haunts you the whole day long;
    And you wander in dreams
    Back to Dixie, it seems,
When you hear that old-time song.

    *[Repeat first and second stanzas]*


# Molly Malone
## (Cockles 'n' Mussels)
POPULAR IRISH SONG (ca. 1850?)
*(Almost nothing is known of its origins. The refrain copies actual*
*vendors' street cries heard in Dublin.)*

1. In Dublin's fair city, where the girls are so pretty,
   I first set my eyes on sweet Molly Malone,
   As she wheeled her wheelbarrow thro' streets broad and narrow
   Cryin' 'Cockles and Mussels! alive, alive, O!'
       *Alive, alive, O! Alive, alive, O!*
       *Cryin' 'Cockles and Mussels! alive, alive, O!'*

2. She was a fishmonger, but sure 'twas no wonder,
   For so were her father and mother before,
   And they each wheeled their barrow thro' streets broad and narrow
   Cryin' 'Cockles and Mussels! alive, alive, O!'
       *Alive, alive, O! Alive, alive, O!*
       *Cryin' 'Cockles and Mussels! alive, alive, O!'*

3. She died of a fever, and no one could save her,
   And that was the end of sweet Molly Malone.
   But her ghost wheels her barrow thro' streets broad and narrow
   Cryin' 'Cockles and Mussels! alive, alive, O!'
       *Alive, alive, O! Alive, alive, O!*
       *Cryin' 'Cockles and Mussels! alive, alive, O!'*


# Molly, Put the Kettle On!
ENGLISH FOLK SONG

1. Molly, put the kettle on!
       Molly, put the kettle on!
         Molly, put the kettle on,
           And let's drink tea.

Sukey, take it off again!
Sukey, take it off again!
Sukey, take it off again;
They're all gone away!

2. Now put down the ginger cake,
Now put down the ginger cake,
Stir the fire and let it bake,
And we'll all take tea.

Put the muffins down to roast,
Put the muffins down to roast,
Blow the fire and make a toast,
And we'll all take tea.

3. Dolly, set the table out,
Dolly set the table out,
Move the dishes all about,
And we'll all take tea.

Pass around the pumpkin pie,
Pass around the pumpkin pie,
And the fritters made of rye,
And we'll all take tea.

# Moonlight Bay
W: EDWARD MADDEN / M: PERCY WENRICH (1912)

1. Voices hum, crooning over Moonlight Bay;
Banjos strum, tuning while the moonbeams play.
All alone, unknown they find me,
Memories like these remind me
Of the girl I left behind me,
Down on Moonlight Bay.

*Chorus:*
We were sailing along
On Moonlight Bay,
We could hear the voices ringing,
They seemed to say,
"You have stolen her heart,
Now don't go 'way!"
As we sang Love's Old Sweet Song
On Moonlight Bay.

**2.** Candle lights gleaming on the silent shore;
Lonely nights, dreaming till we meet once more.
   Far apart, her heart is yearning,
   With a sigh for my returning,
   With the light of love still burning,
As in days of yore.

   [*to Chorus*]


# M-O-T-H-E-R
## (A Word That Means the World to Me)
W: HOWARD JOHNSON / M: THEODORE F. MORSE (1915)

**1.** I've been around the world, you bet,
But never went to school;
Hard knocks are all I seem to get,
Perhaps I've been a fool.

But still, some educated folks,
Supposed to be so swell,
Would fail if they were called upon
A simple word to spell.

   Now, if you'd like to put me to the test,
   There's one dear name that I can spell the best:

   *Chorus:*
   "M" is for the million things she gave me,
   "O" means only that she's growing old,
   "T" is for the tears were shed to save me,
   "H" is for her heart of purest gold;
   "E" is for her eyes, with lovelight shining,
   "R" means right, and right she'll always be;

      Put them all together, they spell "MOTHER,"
      A word that means the world to me.

**2.** When I was but a baby,
Long before I learned to walk,
While lying in my cradle,
I would try my best to talk.

It wasn't long before I spoke,
And all the neighbors heard;
My folks were very proud of me
For "Mother" was the word.

Although I'll never lay a claim to fame,
I'm satisfied that I can spell this name:

*Chorus:*
"M" is for the mercy she possesses,
"O" means that I owe her all I own,
"T" is for her tender, sweet caresses,
"H" is for her hands that made a home;
"E" means ev'rything she's done to help me,
"R" means real and regular, you see;

Put them all together, they spell "MOTHER,"
A word that means the world to me.


# Mother Machree
W: RIDA JOHNSON YOUNG
M: CHAUNCEY OLCOTT & ERNEST R. BALL (1910)

1. There's a spot in me heart which no colleen may own,
There's a depth in me soul never sounded or known;
There's a place in my mem'ry, my life, that you fill,
No other can take it, no one ever will.

*Chorus:*
Sure, I love the dear silver that shines in your hair,
And the brow that's all furrowed and wrinkled with care.
I kiss the dear fingers, so toil-worn for me,
Oh, God bless you and keep you, Mother Machree!

2. Ev'ry sorrow or care in the dear days gone by,
Was made bright by the light of the smile in your eye;
Like a candle that's set in a window at night,
Your fond love has cheered me, and guided me right.

[*to Chorus*]


# Mother, Pin a Rose on Me
W & M: DAVE LEWIS, PAUL SCHINDLER & BOB ADAMS (1905)

1. I love the country air, I love the summertime,
I love to linger in the shade or bask in the old sunshine.

I never borrow trouble, as long as I eat, you see,
For ev'ry day is Sunday, they all look alike to me.

229

*Chorus:*
Mother, mother, mother, pin a rose on me,
Mother, mother, mother, pin a rose on me;
It doesn't matter if it rains or snows,
My one ambition is to get the dough.

Mother, mother, mother, pin a rose on me,
Mother, mother, mother, pin a rose on me;
What would Rockefeller give to have
An appetite like mine.

2. I traveled all around to New York for a lark,
   I went to sleep upon a bench out in Central Park.

   But soon I was awakened—was funny, don't you see—
   It looked like a country orchard, a pear beneath each tree.

   *Chorus:*
   Mother, mother, mother, pin a rose on me,
   Mother, mother, mother, pin a rose on me;
   I say, old boy, you can plainly see
   The best thing for you is to "twenty-three."

   Mother, mother, mother, pin a rose on me,
   Mother, mother, mother, pin a rose on me;
   I was quite afraid some spooney girl
   Would pin a rose on me.

# The Mulberry Bush
CHILDREN'S PLAYING SONG

1. Here we go 'round the mulberry bush,
   The mulberry bush, the mulberry bush,
   Here we go 'round the mulberry bush
   On a cold and frosty morning.

2. This is the way we wash our hands,
   Wash our hands, wash our hands,
   This is the way we wash our hands
   On a cold and frosty morning.

3. This is the way we dry our hands,
   *(etc.)*

4. This is the way we clap our hands,
   *(etc.)*

5. This is the way we brush our teeth,
   *(etc.)*

6. This is the way we comb our hair,
   *(etc.)*

7. This is the way the ladies walk,
   *(etc.)*

8. This is the way the gentlemen walk,
   *(etc.)*

# My Bonnie Lies Over the Ocean
SCOTTISH SONG

*(Although both poet and composer are unknown, a substantially edited version of the song, published in 1882, credited authorship to "H. J. Fulmer," a pseudonym for Charles E. Pratt.)*

1. My Bonnie lies over the ocean,
   My Bonnie lies over the sea,
   My Bonnie lies over the ocean,
   Oh, bring back my Bonnie to me.

   > *Chorus:*
   > Bring back, bring back,
   > Bring back my Bonnie to me, to me.
   > Bring back, bring back,
   > Oh, bring back my Bonnie to me.

2. Last night as I lay on my pillow,
   Last night as I lay on my bed,
   Last night as I lay on my pillow,
   I dreamt that my Bonnie was dead.

   *[to Chorus]*

3. Oh, blow ye winds over the ocean,
   Oh, blow ye winds over the sea,
   Oh, blow ye winds over the ocean,
   Oh, bring back my Bonnie to me.

   *[to Chorus]*

4. The winds have blown over the ocean,
   The winds have blown over the sea,
   The winds have blown over the ocean
   And brought back my Bonnie to me.

   *[to Chorus]*

# My Buddy
W: GUS KAHN /M: WALTER DONALDSON (1922)

1. Life is a book that we study,
   Some of its leaves bring a sigh,
   There it was written, my Buddy.
   That we must part, you and I.

   > *Chorus:*
   > Nights are long since you went away,
   > I think about you all thru the day,
   > My Buddy, my Buddy,
   > No Buddy quite so true.
   >
   > Miss your voice, the touch of your hand,
   > Just long to know that you understand,
   > My Buddy, my Buddy,
   > Your Buddy misses you.

2. Buddies thru all of the gay days,
   Buddies when something went wrong;
   I wait alone thru the gray days,
   Missing your smile and your song.

   > [*to Chorus*]


# My Gal Sal
## (They Called Her Frivolous Sal)
W & M: PAUL DRESSER (1905)

1. Ev'rything is over and I'm feeling bad,
   I have lost the best pal that I ever had;
   'Tis but just a fortnight since she was here,
   Seems like she's gone though for twenty year.

   Oh, how I miss her, my old pal,
   Oh, how I'd kiss her, my gal Sal;
   Face not so handsome but eyes, don't you know,
   That shone just as bright as they did years ago.

   > *Chorus:*
   > They called her frivolous Sal,
   > A peculiar sort of a gal
   >     With a heart that was mellow,
   >     an all 'round good fellow
   > Was my old pal.

232

Your troubles, sorrows and care
She was always willing to share.
   A wild sort of devil,
    but dead on the level
Was my gal Sal.

2. Brought her little dainties just a-fore she died,
Promised she would meet me on the other side;
Told her how I loved her, she said, "I know, Jim,
Just do your best, leave the rest to Him."

Gently I pressed her to my breast,
Soon she would take her last long rest;
She looked at me and she murmured, "My pal,"
And softly I whispered, "Goodbye, dearest Sal."

   [*to Chorus*]


# My Heart's in the Highlands

W: ROBERT BURNS (ca. 1787)
M: TRADITIONAL SCOTTISH

   *Chorus:*
   My heart's in the Highlands, my heart is not here,
   My heart's in the Highlands, a-chasing the deer,
   A-chasing the wild deer and following the roe—
   My heart's in the Highlands, wherever I go!

1. Farewell to the Highlands, farewell to the North,
The birthplace of valour, the country of worth!
Wherever I wander, wherever I rove,
The hills and the Highlands for ever I'll love.

   [*to Chorus*]

2. Farewell to the mountains high cover'd with snow,
Farewell to the straths and green valleys below,
Farewell to the forests and wild-hanging woods,
Farewell to the waters and loud-pouring floods!

   [*to Chorus*]

233

# My Hero

ORIG. GER. WORDS: RUDOLPH BERNAUER & LEOPOLD JACOBSON
ENG. VERSION: STANISLAUS STRANGE / M: OSCAR STRAUS
[From *The Chocolate Soldier*, 1909 (American version of *Der tapfere Soldat*, 1908)]

1. I have a true and noble lover,
   He is my sweetheart, all my own;
   His like on earth who shall discover?
   His heart is mine and mine alone.

   We pledged our troth each to the other,
   And for happiness I pray;
   Our lives belong to one another—
     Oh happy, happy wedding day,
     Oh happy, happy wedding day.

   *Chorus:*
   Come! Come! I love you only,
   My heart is true;
   Come! Come! my life is lonely,
   I long for you.

   Come! Come! Naught can efface you,
   My arms are aching now to embrace you;
   Thou art divine!
   Come! Come! I love you only,
   Come, hero mine.

2. It is my duty to bow before thee,
   It is my duty to love, adore thee!
   It is my duty to love thee ever,
   To love thee ever, love thee ever.

   We pledged our troth each to the other,
   And for happiness I pray,
   Our lives belong to one another—
     Oh happy, happy wedding day,
     Oh happy, happy wedding day.

   [*to Chorus*]

# (My Luve Is Like) A Red, Red Rose

W: ROBERT BURNS (ca. 1787)
M: TRADITIONAL SCOTTISH

1. O, my luve is like a red, red rose,
    That 's newly sprung in June.
    O, my luve is like the melodie,
    That 's sweetly play'd in tune.

2. As fair art thou, my bonie lass,
    So deep in luve am I,
    And I will luve thee still, my dear,
    Till a' the seas gang dry.

3. Till a' the seas gang dry, my dear,
    And the rocks melt wi' the sun!
    And I will luve thee still, my dear,
    While the sands o' life shall run.

4. And fare thee weel, my only luve,
    And fare thee weel a while!
    And I will come again, my luve,
    Tho' it were ten thousand mile!


# My Melancholy Baby

W: GEORGE A. NORTON / M: ERNIE BURNETT (1912)

1. Come, sweetheart mine,
        Don't sit and pine,
    Tell me of the cares that make you feel so blue.
        What have I done?
        Answer me, Hon',
    Have I ever said an unkind word to you?

    My love is true,
        And just for you,
    I'd do almost anything at any time.
        Dear, when you sigh,
        Or when you cry,
    Something seems to grip this very heart of mine.

    *Chorus:*
    Come to me, my melancholy baby,
    Cuddle up and don't be blue;
    All your fears are foolish fancy, maybe,
    You know, dear, that I'm in love with you.

Ev'ry cloud must have a silver lining,
Wait until the sun shines through;
Smile, my honey dear,
While I kiss away each tear,
Or else I shall be melancholy, too.

(Now won't you . . .)

[*repeat Chorus*]

2. Birds in the trees,
Whispering breeze,
Should not fail to lull you into peaceful dreams.
So tell me why
Sadly you sigh,
Sitting at the window where the pale moon beams.

You shouldn't grieve,
Try to believe,
Life is always sunshine when the heart beats true.
Be of good cheer,
Smile thro' your tears,
When you're sad it make me feel the same as you.

[*to Chorus, repeated*]


# My Old Kentucky Home
W & M: STEPHEN C. FOSTER (1853)

1. The sun shines bright on the old Kentucky home,
'Tis summer, the darkies are gay.
The corn top's ripe and the meadow's in the bloom,
While the birds make music all the day.

The young folks roll on the little cabin floor,
All merry, all happy and bright.
By 'n' by hard times comes a-knocking at the door,
Then my old Kentucky home, good night.

*Chorus:*
Weep no more, my lady,
Oh, weep no more today.
We will sing one song for the old Kentucky home,
For the old Kentucky home far away.

2. They hunt no more for the 'possum and the 'coon,
On meadow, the hill and the shore.
They sing no more by the glimmer of the moon,
On the bench by that old cabin door.

The day goes by like a shadow o'er the heart,
With sorrow where all was delight.
The time has come when the darkies have to part,
Then my old Kentucky home, good night.

[*to Chorus*]

3. The head must bow and the back will have to bend
   Wherever the darky may go.
   A few more days and the trouble all will end
   In the field where sugar-canes may grow.

   A few more days for to tote the weary load,
   No matter, 'twill never be light.
   A few more days till we totter on the road,
   Then my old Kentucky home, good night.

   [*to Chorus*]


# My Wild Irish Rose

W & M: CHAUNCEY OLCOTT
[from *A Romance of Athlone*, 1899]

1. If you listen, I'll sing you a sweet little song
   Of a flower that's now drooped and dead;
   Yet it's dearer to me, yes, than all of its mates,
   Although each holds aloft its proud head.

   'Twas given to me by a girl that I know,
   Since we met, faith, I've known no repose.
   She is dearer by far than the world's brightest star,
   And I call her my wild Irish rose.

   *Chorus:*
   My wild Irish rose,
   The sweetest flow'r that grows;
   You may search ev'rywhere, but none can compare
   With my wild Irish rose.

   My wild Irish rose,
   The dearest flow'r that grows;
   And some day for my sake, she may let me take
   The bloom from my wild Irish rose.

2. They may sing of their roses which by other names
   They could smell just as sweetly, they say;
   But I know that my dear rose would never consent
   To have that sweet name taken away.

Her glances are shy just whene'er I pass by
At the bower where my true love grows;
And my one wish has been that some day I may win
The dear heart of my wild Irish rose.

[*to Chorus*]


# Nearer, My God, to Thee
W: SARAH F. ADAMS / M: LOWELL MASON (1859)

1. Nearer, My God, to Thee,
   Nearer to Thee!
   E'en tho' it be a cross
   That raiseth me,

   Still all my song shall be
   *Nearer, my God, to Thee,*
   *Nearer, my God, to Thee,*
   *Nearer to Thee!*

2. Tho' like the wanderer,
   The sun gone down,
   Darkness be over me,
   My rest a stone,

   Yet in my dreams I'd be
   *Nearer, my God, to Thee,*
   *Nearer, my God, to Thee,*
   *Nearer to Thee!*

3. Then with my waking tho'ts
   Bright with Thy praise,
   Out of my stormy griefs
   Bethel I'll raise,

   So by my woes to be
   *Nearer, my God, to Thee,*
   *Nearer, my God, to Thee,*
   *Nearer to Thee!*

4. Or if on joyful wing,
   Cleaving the sky,
   Sun, moon, and stars forgot,
   Upward I fly,

   Still all my song shall be
   *Nearer, my God, to Thee,*
   *Nearer, my God, to Thee,*
   *Nearer to Thee!*

# Nobody Knows
## (And Nobody Seems to Care)
W & M: IRVING BERLIN (1919)

**1**. I'm sad and lonely,
There's a good reason why:
Nobody cares about me,
That's why I'm sad as can be.

I long for someone,
Somebody, yes, indeed:
Lovin' kisses from one
Is exactly what I need.

> *Chorus:*
> Many's the time I feel so lonesome,
> > But nobody knows,
> > And nobody cares;
> I've grown so tired of being by my "own some,"
> > I want somebody to hug,
> > Cuddle and snug as comfy as a bug in a rug.
>
> Many's the time I feel like spooning,
> > But nobody knows,
> > And nobody cares;
> I guess I'll make out a little "ad"
> That I want some lovin' so bad,
> > 'Cause nobody knows,
> > And nobody seems to care.

**2**. I'd love a sweetie
Hanging around the place:
Someone to worry about
I'd never want to go out.

My home is gloomy,
Nobody's there, that's why:
I feel "bride and groomy,"
Can't you see it in my eye?

> [*to Chorus*]

# Nobody Knows the Trouble I've Seen
SPIRITUAL

Nobody knows the trouble I've seen,
Nobody knows but Jesus;
Nobody knows the trouble I've seen,
Glory Hallelujah!

Sometimes I'm up, sometimes I'm down,
O yes, Lord;
Sometimes I'm nearly to the ground,
O yes, Lord.

Nobody knows the trouble I've seen,
Nobody knows but Jesus;
Nobody knows the trouble I've seen,
Glory Hallelujah!


# "O" (Oh!)
W: BYRON GAY / M: BYRON GAY & ARNOLD JOHNSON (1919)

1. I'm in the air, in the air, meaning atmosphere;
   Gee! she's a bear, she's a bear, let me tell you here;
   I'll say she's there with a pair of most wonderful
   Lips that caress,
   Eyes that mean "yes."

   I want to cry, want to cry when she passes by;
   I want to die, want to die when I hear her sigh;
   Gee, gosh durn it,
   I'm looney I guess.
   Oh, lady . . .

   *Chorus:*
   "O,"
   How she can snuggle, she's as sweet as can be;
   And when I hold her "hannie,"
   "O,"
   The way she whispers pretty nothings to me
   Completely gets my "nannie."

   "O,"
   It isn't what she does, but
   "O,"
   The clever way she does it,
   Does that fascinating thing that rhymes with "dove."
   Sweet cookie . . .

240

"O,"
The way she vamps me with her go-get-'em eyes
And puts me in a flurry;
"O,"
The way I fall for all her beautiful lies,
Believe me, I should worry.

"O,"
The way she feeds me taffy,
"O,"
I think she'll drive me daffy,
O, O, O, O,
How my super-sentimental wonderful sweetie can love.

2. I'm glad I found, glad I found what I like the most;
I'll stick around, stick around, like an evening post;
I'll never stop till I cop and I marry my
Wonderful pet,
I'll get her yet.

There'll be a moon, be a moon, I mean honeymoon,
And we will spoon, we will spoon to a vampy tune;
We'll vamp,
Vamp till the wedding is set.

[*to Chorus*]

# O Canada!

CANADIAN NATIONAL ANTHEM
W & M: CALIXA LAVALLÉE, JUDGE ROUTHIER
& JUSTICE R. S. WEIR

1. O Canada! Our home and native land!
True patriot love in all thy sons command;
With glowing hearts we see thee rise,
The true North strong and free,
And stand on guard, O Canada,
We stand on guard for thee.

*Chorus:*
O Canada! Glorious and free,
O Canada! We stand on guard for thee,
O Canada! We stand on guard for thee.

**2.** O Canada! Where pines and maples grow,
Great prairies spread and lordly rivers flow;
How dear to us thy vast domain,
From east to western sea,
Thou land of hope for all who toil!
Thou true North strong and free.

[*to Chorus*]

French version:
*O Canada! Terre de nos aïeux,*
*Ton front est ceint de fleurons glorieux!*
*Car ton bras sait porter l'épée,*
*Il sait porter la croix!*
*Ton histoire est une épopée*
*Des plus brillants exploits.*

Chorus:
*Et ta valeur, de foi trempée,*
*Protégera nos foyers et nos droits,*
*Protégera nos foyers et nos droits.*

# O Christmas Tree

TRADITIONAL CAROL

*(This famous tune of unknown origin served as the melody for the tradi-
tional German text "O Tannenbaum, O Tannenbaum!" as well as the pro-
Confederacy poem "Maryland, My Maryland" by James Ryder Randall.
There are several English versions of the Christmas text; the present one
is by Charles F. Cofone and Stanley Appelbaum.)*

**1.** O Christmas Tree, O Christmas Tree,
How steadfast are your branches!
Your boughs are green in summer's clime
And through the snows of wintertime.
O Christmas Tree, O Christmas Tree,
How steadfast are your branches!

**2.** O Christmas Tree, O Christmas Tree,
What happiness befalls me
When oft at joyous Christmastime
Your form inspires my song and rhyme.
O Christmas Tree, O Christmas Tree,
What happiness befalls me.

**3.** O Christmas Tree, O Christmas Tree,
Your boughs can teach a lesson:
That constant faith and hope sublime
Lend strength and comfort through all time.
O Christmas Tree, O Christmas Tree,
Your boughs can teach a lesson.

# O Come All Ye Faithful

TRADITIONAL CHRISTMAS CAROL

*(The music and original Latin words—"Adeste fideles, laeti tri-
umphantes"—appear to have been written about 1750 by John Francis
Wade, a copier of plainchant working in France. There is some conflicting
evidence that the melody was actually composed by John Reading in
1780. The standard English translation—"O come all ye faithful"—was
made in 1852 by Frederick Oakeley, Canon of Westminster.)*

**1.** O come all ye faithful,
Joyful and triumphant,
O come ye, O come ye to Bethlehem.
Come and behold Him,
Born the King of Angels!
*O come, let us adore Him,
O come, let us adore Him,
O come, let us adore Him,
Christ the Lord.*

**2.** Sing alleluia,
All ye choirs of angels;
O sing, all ye blissful ones of heav'n above.
Glory to God
In the highest, glory!
*O come, let us adore Him,
O come, let us adore Him,
O come, let us adore Him,
Christ the Lord.*

**3.** Yea, Lord, we greet Thee,
Born this happy morning;
Jesus, to Thee be the glory giv'n.
Word of the Father,
Now in flesh appearing.
*O come, let us adore Him,
O come, let us adore Him,
O come, let us adore Him,
Christ the Lord.*

# O Come, O Come, Emmanuel

CHRISTMAS CAROL

*(The melody is based on a 9th-century plainchant. The English para-*
*phrase of a Latin text is by the Reverend John Mason Neale, ca. 1850,*
*author as well of the words to "Good King Wenceslas.")*

1. O come, o come, Emmanuel,
   And ransom captive Israel,
   That mourns in lonely exile here
   Until the Son of God appear.
       *Rejoice! Rejoice! Emmanuel*
       *Shall come to thee, O Israel.*

2. O come, thou Wisdom from on high,
   Who ord'rest all things mightily;
   To us the path of Knowledge show,
   And teach us in her ways to go.
       *Rejoice! Rejoice! Emmanuel*
       *Shall come to thee, O Israel.*

3. O come, thou Dayspring, come and cheer
   Our spirits by thine advent here;
   Disperse the gloomy clouds of night,
   And death's dark shadows put to flight.
       *Rejoice! Rejoice! Emmanuel*
       *Shall come to thee, O Israel.*

4. O come, Desire of Nations, bind
   In one the hearts of all mankind;
   Bid thou our sad divisions cease,
   And be thyself our King of Peace.
       *Rejoice! Rejoice! Emmanuel*
       *Shall come to thee, O Israel.*


# O God, Our Help in Ages Past

W: ISAAC WATTS / M: WILLIAM CROFT

1. O God, our help in ages past,
   Our hope for years to come,
   Our shelter from the stormy blast,
   And our eternal home!

2. Before the hills in order stood,
   Or earth received her frame,
   From everlasting Thou art God,
   To endless years the same.

3. A thousand ages in Thy sight
   Are like an evening gone,
   Short as the watch that ends the night
   Before the rising sun.

4. Time, like an ever-rolling stream,
   Bears all its sons away;
   They fly, forgotten, as a dream
   Dies at the op'ning day.

# Oh, Bury Me Not on the Lone Prairie
AMERICAN COWBOY SONG

1. "Oh, bury me not on the lone prairie,"
   These words came low and mournfully,
   From the pallid lips of a youth who lay
   On his dying bed at the close of day.

2. He had wailed in pain, till o'er his brow
   Death's shadows fast were gathering now,
   He thought of his home and his loved ones nigh,
   As the cowboys gathered to see him die.

3. "How oft I remember the well known words
   Of the free, wild winds, and the songs of birds,
   I think of my home, and the cottage in the bower,
   And the friends I loved in my childhood's hour.

4. "And there is another whose tears will be shed,
   For one who lies in a prairie bed,
   It pained me then, and it pains me now,
   She has curled these locks, she has kissed this brow.

5. "These locks she has curled, shall the rattlesnake kiss?
   This brow she has pressed, shall the cold grave press?
   For the sake of the loved ones who will weep over me,
   Oh, bury me not on the lone prairie.

6. "Oh, bury me not on the lone prairie,
   Where the wild coyotes will howl over me,
   Where the rattlesnakes hiss, and the crow flies free,
   Oh, bury me not on the lone prairie!"

7. They heeded not his dying prayer,
   They buried him there on the lone prairie,
   In a little box just six by three,
   His bones now rot on the lone prairie.

# Oh by Jingo! Oh by Gee!
## (You're the Only Girl for Me)

W: LEW BROWN / M: ALBERT VON TILZER
[from *Linger Longer Letty,* 1919]

1. In the land of San Domingo
   Lived a girl called Oh! by Jingo.
   *Ta da, da da da da da da,*
   *Umpa, umpa, umpa, umpa*

   From the fields and from the marshes
   Came the old and young by goshes.
   *Ta da, da da da da da da,*
   *Umpa, umpa, umpa, umpa*

   They all spoke with a diff'rent lingo,
   But they all loved Oh! by Jingo,
      And ev'ry night
      They sang in the pale moonlight:

      *Chorus:*
      Oh! by Gee! by Gosh, by Gum, by Juv,
      Oh! by Jingo, won't you hear our love;
         We will build for you a hut
         You will be our fav'rite nut,
      We'll have a lot of little Oh! by Gollies,
      Then we'll put them in the Follies.

   By Jingo said, by Gosh, by Gee,
   By Jiminy, please don't bother me;
      So they all went away singing,
      Oh! by Gee, by Gosh, By Juv, by Jingo,
   By Gee, you're the only girl for me.

2. Oh! by Jingo had a lover,
   He was always under cover.
   *Ta da, da da da da da da,*
   *Umpa, umpa, umpa, umpa*

   Ev'ry night she used to meet him,
   Oh, how nice she used to treat him.
   *Ta da, da da da da da da,*
   *Umpa, umpa, umpa, umpa*

   They eloped but both were collared,
   And the gang stood there and hollered,
      Don't raise a fuss,
      You've gotta take one of us.

      [*to Chorus*]

# Oh Dear, What Can the Matter Be?

ENGLISH FOLK SONG

1. Oh dear, what can the matter be?
Dear, dear, what can the matter be?
Oh dear, what can the matter be?
Johnny's so long at the fair.

He promised to give me a fairing to please me,
And then for a kiss, oh! he vowed he would tease me.
He promised to buy me a bunch of blue ribbons
To tie up my bonny brown hair. And now. . .

  *. . . Oh dear, what can the matter be?*
  *Dear, dear, what can the matter be?*
  *Oh dear, what can the matter be?*
  *Johnny's so long at the fair.*

2. Oh dear, what can the matter be?
Dear, dear, what can the matter be?
Oh dear, what can the matter be?
Johnny's so long at the fair.

He promised he'd buy me a basket of posies,
A garland of lilies, a garland of roses,
A little straw hat to set off the blue ribbons
That tie up my bonny brown hair. And now. . .

  *. . . Oh dear, what can the matter be?*
  *Dear, dear, what can the matter be?*
  *Oh dear, what can the matter be?*
  *Johnny's so long at the fair.*


# Oh, Dem Golden Slippers

W & M: JAMES BLAND (1879)

1. Oh, my golden slippers they are laid away,
I was savin' them until my wedding day.
An' my long-tail coat that I love so well,
I will wear up in the chariot in the morn.

And my long white robe that I had bought last June,
I am gonna change it 'cause it fits too soon.
An' the old grey horse that I used to drive,
I will hitch him to the chariot in the morn.

  *Chorus:*
  Oh, dem golden slippers,
  Oh, dem golden slippers,

Golden slippers I'm gonna wear
Because they look so neat.

Oh, dem golden slippers,
Oh, dem golden slippers,
Golden slippers I'm gonna wear
To walk the golden street.

2. Oh, my old banjo it hangs upon the wall
'Cause it ain't been tuned up ever since last fall.
But the folks say we'll have a real good time
When we ride up in the chariot in the morn.

There's my brother Ben and there's my sister Luce,
They will get the news to Uncle Bacco Juice.
What a great camp-meetin' we'll have that day
When we ride up in the chariot in the morn.

[*to Chorus*]

3. So it's goodbye children, I will have to go
Where the rain ain't fallin' or the wind don't blow,
An' your ulster coats, why you will not need
When you ride up in the chariot in the morn.

But your golden slippers must be nice and clean
An' your age must be a tender sweet sixteen,
An' your white kid gloves you will have to wear
When you ride up in the chariot in the morn.

[*to Chorus*]

# Oh! How I Hate to Get Up in the Morning

W & M: IRVING BERLIN
[from *Yip Yip Yaphank*, 1918]

1. The other day I chanced to meet a soldier friend of mine,
He'd been in camp for sev'ral weeks and he was looking fine;
His muscles had developed and his cheeks were rosy red,
I asked him how he liked the life, and this is what he said:

*Chorus:*
"Oh! how I hate to get up in the morning,
Oh! how I'd love to remain in bed;
For the hardest blow of all
is to hear the bugler call:
You've got to get up,
You've got to get up,
You've got to get up this morning!

Some day I'm going to murder the bugler,
Some day they're going to find him dead;
   I'll amputate his reveille,
   and step upon it heavily,
And spend the rest of my life in bed."

2. A bugler in the army is the luckiest of men,
   He wakes the boys at five and then goes back to bed again;
   He doesn't have to blow again until the afternoon,
   If ev'rything goes well with me, I'll be a bugler soon.

> *Chorus:*
> "Oh! how I hate to get up in the morning,
> Oh! how I'd love to remain in bed;
>    For the hardest blow of all
>    is to hear the bugler call:
>      You've got to get up,
>      You've got to get up,
>    You've got to get up this morning!

> Oh boy! the minute the battle is over,
> Oh boy! the minute the foe is dead,
>    I'll put my uniform away,
>    and move to Phil-a-del-phi-a,
> And spend the rest of my life in bed."

# Oh, How Lovely Is the Evening
THREE-PART ROUND FROM ENGLAND

*First Part*
> Oh, how lovely is the evening,
> Is the evening, is the evening,

*Second Part*
> When the bells are sweetly ringing,
> Sweetly ringing,

*Third Part*
> Ding dong,
> Ding dong,
> Ding.

# O Holy Night
## (Cantique de Noël)
W: ORIGINAL FRENCH BY CAPPEAU DE ROQUEMAURE
ENGLISH VERSION BY JOHN S. DWIGHT (19th c.)
M: ADOLPHE ADAM (ca. 1845?)

1. O holy night! The stars are brightly shining,
   It is the night of the dear Saviour's birth!
   Long lay the world in sin and error pining,
   Till he appear'd and the soul felt its worth.

   A thrill of hope the weary world rejoices,
   For yonder breaks a new and glorious morn!
   *Fall on your knees! O hear the angel voices!*
   *O night divine! O night when Christ was born!*
   *O night divine! O night, O night divine!*

2. Led by the light of Faith serenely beaming,
   With glowing hearts by his cradle we stand.
   So led by light of a star sweetly gleaming,
   Here came the wise men from Orient land.

   The King of Kings lay thus in lowly manger,
   In all our trials born to be our friend!
   *Fall on your knees! O hear the angel voices!*
   *O night divine! O night when Christ was born!*
   *O night divine! O night, O night divine!*

3. Truly he taught us to love one another;
   His law is love and his gospel is peace.
   Chains shall he break for the slave is our brother,
   And in his name all oppression shall cease.

   Sweet hymns of joy in grateful chorus raise we,
   Let all within us praise his holy name!
   *Fall on your knees! O hear the angel voices!*
   *O night divine! O night when Christ was born!*
   *O night divine! O night, O night divine!*


# Oh, Johnny Oh!
W: ED ROSE / M: ABE OLMAN (1916)

All the girls are crazy 'bout a certain little lad
Although he's very, very bad;
He could be, oh, so good when he wanted to.

Bad or good he understood 'bout love and other things,
For ev'ry girl in town
Followed him around,
Just to hold his hand and sing:

*Chorus:*
Oh, Johnny! Oh, Johnny!
How you can love!
Oh, Johnny! Oh, Johnny!
Heavens above!

You make my sad heart jump with joy,
And when you're near I just can't
Sit still a minute, I'm so,

Oh, Johnny! Oh, Johnny!
Please tell me dear,
What makes me love you so?

You're not handsome, it's true,
But when I look at you, I just
Oh, Johnny! Oh, Johnny, Oh!


# Oh, Promise Me!

W: CLEMENT SCOTT / M: REGINALD DE KOVEN
*(published as Opus 50, 1889)*

Oh, promise me that some day you and I
Will take our love together to some sky,
Where we can be alone and faith renew,
And find the hollows where those flowers grew,

Those first sweet violets of early spring,
Which come in whispers, thrill us both, and sing
Of love unspeakable that is to be;
Oh, promise me, oh, promise me!

Oh, promise me that you will take my hand,
The most unworthy in this lonely land,
And let me sit beside you, in your eyes
Seeing the vision of our paradise,

Hearing God's message while the organ rolls
Its mighty music to our very souls,
No love less perfect than a life with thee;
Oh, promise me, oh, promise me!

# Oh, Susanna

W & M: STEPHEN C. FOSTER (1848)

1. For I came from Alabama
   With a banjo on my knee,
   And I'm goin' to Lou'siana
   There my true love for to see.

   Now it rained all night the day I left,
   The weather it was dry,
   And the sun so hot I froze to death,
   Susanna, don't you cry.

   *Chorus:*
   Oh, Susanna,
   Oh, don't you cry for me,
   For I come from Alabama
   With a banjo on my knee.

2. When I jumped aboard the telegraph
   And travelled down the riv'r,
   The electric fluid magnified
   And killed five hundred chigg'r.

   When the bullgine bust, the horse run off,
   I really thought I'd die,
   So I shut my eyes to hold my breath,
   Susanna, don't you cry.

   [*to Chorus*]

3. Now I had a dream the other night
   When ev'rything was still,
   And I thought I saw Susanna,
   She was comin' down the hill.

   Now the buckwheat cake was in her mouth,
   The tear was in her eye,
   So I says "I'm comin' from the South,
   Susanna, don't you cry."

   [*to Chorus*]

4. Now I soon will be in New Orleans
   And then I'll look around;
   When at last I find Susanna,
   I will fall upon the ground.

   But if I can never find her,
   Then I think I'd surely die.
   When I'm dead and gone and buried deep,
   Susanna, don't you cry.

   [*to Chorus*]

# Oh, What a Pal Was Mary

W: EDGAR LESLIE & BERT KALMAR / M: PETE WENDLING (1919)

1. Mary o' mine,
   Mary o' mine,
   Grew like a rose in a bower;
   Bloomed for a day,
   Faded away,
   I lost a beautiful flower;
   Sweetheart and friend
   Right to the end,
   That's why I miss her so.

   *Chorus:*
   Oh! what a gal was Mary,
   Oh! what a pal was she;
   An angel was born
   On Easter morn,
   And God sent her down to me.

   Heart of my heart was Mary,
   Soul of my soul divine;
   Though she is gone,
   Love lingers on
   For Mary, old pal of mine.

2. Mary o' mine,
   Mary o' mine,
   My little playmate of childhood;
   Symbol of love
   Sent from above,
   Staunch as an oak in the wildwood;
   Mem'ries of old,
   Purer than gold,
   Fill me with love sublime.

   [*to Chorus*]

# Oh, Where, Oh, Where Has My Little Dog Gone?

W: ENGLISH VERSION BY SEPTIMUS WINNER (1864)

M: GERMAN FOLK SONG

*(The anonymous melody, originally known as "Zu Lauterbach Hab' Ich Mein Strumpf Verloren"—"At Lauterbach I Lost My Sock"—dates from the early 19th century. Similar tunes are found in Beethoven's "Pastorale" Symphony and in a 13th-century manuscript of English dances. Winner's American edition is subtitled "A Deitcher's Dog.")*

1. Oh, where, oh, where has my little dog gone?
   Oh, where, oh, where can he be?
   With his tail cut short and his ears cut long,
   Oh, where, oh, where can he be?

2. My little dog always waggles his tail
   Whenever he wants his grog;
   And if the tail were more strong than he,
   Why the tail would waggle the dog.


# Oh, Won't You Sit Down?

STATEMENT-AND-RESPONSE SPIRITUAL

> *Chorus:*
> Oh, won't you sit down?
> *Lord, I can't sit down.*
> Oh, won't you sit down?
> *Lord, I can't sit down.*
> Oh, won't you sit down?
> *Lord, I can't sit down*
> *'Cause I just got to heaven,*
> *Goin' to look around.*

1. Who's that yonder dressed in red?
   *Must be the children that Moses led.*
   Who's that yonder dressed in white?
   *Must be the children of the Israelite.*

   [*to Chorus*]

2. Who's that yonder dressed in blue?
   *Must be the children that are comin' through.*
   Who's that yonder dressed in black?
   *Must be the hypocrites a-turnin' back.*

   [*to Chorus*]

# Oh! You Beautiful Doll

W: A. SEYMOUR BROWN / M: NAT D. AYER (1911)

1. Honey dear, want you near,
   Just turn out the light and then come over here;
   Nestle close up to my side,
   My heart's a-fire with love's desire.

   In my arms, rest complete,
   I never thought that life could ever be so sweet
   Till I met you, sometime ago,
   But now you know I love you so.

   *Chorus:*
   Oh! You beautiful doll,
   You great, big beautiful doll!
   Let me put my arms about you,
   I could never live without you.

   Oh! You beautiful doll,
   You great, big beautiful doll!
   If you ever leave me how my heart will ache,
   I want to hug you but I fear you'd break.
     Oh, oh, oh, oh,
     Oh, you beautiful doll!

2. Precious prize, close your eyes,
   Now we're goin' to visit lovers' paradise;
   Press your lips again to mine,
   For love is king of ev'rything.

   Squeeze me, dear, I don't care!
   Hug me just as if you were a grizzly bear.
   This is how I'll go through life,
   No care or strife when you're my wife.

   [*to Chorus*]


# Old Black Joe

W & M: STEPHEN C. FOSTER (1860)

1. Gone are the days when my heart was young and gay;
   Gone are my friends from the cotton field away;
   Gone from the earth to a better land, I know,
   I hear their gentle voices calling "Old Black Joe!"

   *Chorus:*
   I'm coming, I'm coming,
   For my head is bending low;

255

I hear their gentle voices calling,
"Old Black Joe!"

2. Why do I weep when my heart should feel no pain?
   Why do I sigh that my friends come not again?
   Grieving for forms now departed long ago,
   I hear their gentle voices calling "Old Black Joe!"

   [*to Chorus*]

3. Where are the hearts once so happy and so free?
   The children so dear that I held upon my knee?
   Gone to the shore where my soul has longed to go,
   I hear their gentle voices calling "Old Black Joe!"

   [*to Chorus*]

# The Old Chisholm Trail
AMERICAN COWBOY SONG

1. Well, come along, boys, and listen to my tale,
   I'll tell you of my troubles on the Old Chisholm Trail,
   *Come a ti-yi yippee, yippee yeah, yippee yeah,*
   *Come a ti-yi yippee, yippee yeah.*

2. Now, a ten-dollar horse and a forty-dollar saddle,
   I'm a-going to punching Texas cattle.
   *Come a ti-yi yippee, yippee yeah, yippee yeah,*
   *Come a ti-yi yippee, yippee yeah.*

3. My horse throwed me off, just like I was a bird,
   He throwed me off near the 2-U herd.
   *Come a ti-yi yippee, yippee yeah, yippee yeah,*
   *Come a ti-yi yippee, yippee yeah.*

4. Last time I saw him, he was goin' on the level,
   A-kickin' up his heels and running like the devil!
   (*etc.*)

5. As soon as I recovered from the damned hard jolt,
   I got a job a-punchin' for old man Bolt.
   (*etc.*)

6. Old Ben Bolt was a fine old man,
   And you knowed there was whiskey wherever he'd land.
   (*etc.*)

7. Old Ben Bolt was a fine old boss,
But he'd go to see the gals on a sore-backed horse.
*(etc.)*

8. 'Twas early in the morning of October twenty-third,
When we started up the trail with the 2-U herd.
*(etc.)*

9. I woke up one morning on the Old Chisholm Trail,
A rope in my hand and a cow by the tail.
*(etc.)*

10. A-roping and a-tying and a-branding all day,
I'm working mighty hard for mighty little pay.
*(etc.)*

*One source for this cowboy classic presents thirty-three stanzas, ending with:*

With my feet in the stirrup and my seat in the sky,
I'll quit punchin' cows in the sweet bye-and-bye.


# Old Dan Tucker
AMERICAN SQUARE-DANCE SONG

1. Went to town the other night
To hear a noise and see a fight;
All the people were runnin' around
Sayin', "Old Dan Tucker's come to town."

> *Chorus:*
> Get out the way, Old Dan Tucker,
> You're too late to come for supper;
> Supper's over and dinner's cookin',
> And Old Dan Tucker just standin' there lookin'.

2. Old Dan Tucker's a fine old man,
Washed his face in a frying pan;
Combed his hair with a wagon wheel,
And died with a toothache in his heel.

> [*to Chorus*]

3. Old Dan Tucker come to town,
Ridin' a billy goat, leadin' a hound;
Hound barked and billy goat jumped,
Throwed Old Dan right straddle of a stump.

> [*to Chorus*]

**4.** Old Dan Tucker clumb a tree,
His Lord and Master for to see;
The limb broke and Dan got a fall,
Never got to see his Lord at all.

[*to Chorus*]

**5.** Old Dan Tucker he got drunk,
Fell in the fire and he kicked up a chunk;
Red-hot coal got in his shoe,
Lord Godamighty, how the ashes flew!

[*to Chorus*]

**6.** Old Dan Tucker he came to town,
Swingin' the ladies 'round and 'round,
First to the right and then to the left,
And then to the one that you love best.

[*to Chorus*]

# Old Folks at Home

W & M: STEPHEN C. FOSTER (1851)

**1.** 'Way down upon de Swanee ribber,
Far, far away,
Dere's wha my heart is turning ebber,
Dere's wha de old folks stay.

All up and down de whole creation,
Sadly I roam,
Still longing for de old plantation,
And for de old folks at home.

> *Chorus:*
> All de world am sad and dreary,
> Ebry where I roam,
> Oh! darkeys how my heart grows weary,
> Far from de old folks at home.

**2.** All 'round de little farm I wandered
When I was young,
Den many happy days I squandered,
Many de songs I sung.

When I was playing wid my brudder
Happy was I—
Oh! take me to my kind old mudder,
Dere let me live and die.

[*to Chorus*]

3. One little hut among de bushes,
   One dat I love,
   Still sadly to my mem'ry rushes,
   No matter where I rove.

   When will I see de bees a-humming
   All round de comb?
   When will I hear de banjo tumming
   Down in my good old home?

   [*to Chorus*]


# The Old Grey Mare
## (The Whiffle Tree)
TRADITIONAL AMERICAN
*(Background of this song and its many variants is discussed under*
*"Down in Alabam'".)*

1. Oh, the old grey mare, she ain't what she used t' be,
       Ain't what she used t' be,
       Ain't what she used t' be;
   The old grey mare, she ain't what she used t' be,
       Many long years ago . . .

   *Many long years ago,*
   *Many long years ago,*
   *The old grey mare, she ain't what she used t' be,*
   *Many long years ago.*

2. The old grey mare, she kicked on the whiffletree,
       Kicked on the whiffletree,
       Kicked on the whiffletree;
   The old grey mare, she kicked on the whiffletree,
       Many long years ago . . .

   *Many long years ago,*
   *Many long years ago,*
   *The old grey mare, she ain't what she used t' be,*
   *Many long years ago.*

# Old Hundred

W: PSALM 134 *(from the Genevan Psalter, edition of 1551)*
ENGLISH VERSION BY THOMAS STERNHOLDE (?) (1560)
M: LOUIS BOURGEOIS

(Doxology)
*Praise God, from whom all blessings flow,*
*Praise Him, all creatures here below;*
*Praise Him above, ye heav'nly host;*
*Praise Father, Son, and Holy Ghost.*

1. All people that on earth do dwell,
   Sing to the Lord with cheerful voice,
   Him serve with mirth, His praise forth tell,
   Come ye before Him and rejoice.

2. Know that the Lord is God indeed;
   Without our aid He did us make:
   We are His flock, He doth us feed,
   And for His sheep He doth us take.

3. Oh, enter then His gates with joy,
   Within His courts His praise proclaim;
   Let thankful songs your tongues employ,
   O bless and magnify His name.

4. Because the Lord our God is good,
   His mercy is forever sure;
   His truth at all times firmly stood,
   And shall from age to age endure.

   *Praise God, from whom all blessings flow,*
   *Praise Him, all creatures here below;*
   *Praise Him above, ye heav'nly host;*
   *Praise Father, Son, and Holy Ghost.*

# Old Joe Clarke

AMERICAN SQUARE-DANCE TUNE

*(This song is in the form of one refrain followed by one stanza. There are many variants of each.)*

*Refrain:*
'Round and 'round, old Joe Clarke,
'Round and 'round, I say,
'Round and 'round, old Joe Clarke,
I ain't got long to stay.

*Stanza:*
Old Joe Clarke he had a house,
Sixteen stories high;
Ev'ry story in that house
Was full of chicken pie.

*Some other refrains:*
Rock-a-rock, old Joe Clarke,
Rock-a-rock, I'm gone;
Rock-a-rock, old Joe Clarke,
And goodbye, Susan Brown.

Fly around, old Joe Clarke,
Fly around, I'm gone;
Fly around, old Joe Clarke,
With golden slippers on.

Row around, old Joe Clarke,
Sail away and gone;
Row around, old Joe Clarke,
With golden slippers on.

*Some other stanzas:*
Old Joe Clarke he had a dog
As blind as he could be;
Chased a redbug 'round a stump
And a coon up a hollow tree.

I went down to old Joe's house,
Never been there before;
He slept on the feather bed
And I slept on the floor.

If you see that girl of mine,
Tell her if you can,
Before she goes to make up bread
To wash those dirty hands.

# Old King Cole

ENGLISH CHILDREN'S SONG

Old King Cole was a merry old soul,
And a merry old soul was he.
And he called for his pipe, and he called for his bowl,
And he called for his fiddlers three.

Ev'ry fiddler had a fiddle fine,
A very fine fiddle had he,
Then twee-did-dle-dee went the fiddlers three,
And so merry we will be.

# Old MacDonald Had a Farm

NURSERY SONG

1. Old MacDonald had a farm,
    E-I-E-I-O!
   And on this farm he had some chicks.
    E-I-E-I-O!
   With a chick-chick here and a chick-chick there,
   Here a chick, there a chick, ev'rywhere a chick-chick.
    Old MacDonald had a farm,
    E-I-E-I-O!

2. And on this farm he had some turkeys.
    E-I-E-I-O!
   With a gobble-gobble here and a gobble-gobble there,
   Here a gobble, there a gobble, ev'rywhere a gobble-gobble.
    Old MacDonald had a farm,
    E-I-E-I-O!

3. And on this farm he had some pigs . . .
    (grunt, grunt)

4. And on this farm he had some sheep . . .
    (baa, baa)

5. And on this farm he had some cows . . .
    (moo, moo)

   *Commonly sung as an "accumulation song":*
   With a chick-chick here and a chick-chick there,
   Here a chick, there a chick, ev'rywhere a chick-chick.
   With a gobble-gobble here and a gobble-gobble there,
   Here a gobble, there a gobble, ev'rywhere a gobble-gobble.
   *(etc., etc.)*

# The Old Oaken Bucket

W: SAMUEL WOODWORTH (1817) / M: GEORGE KIALLMARK (1822)
*(The melody was originally known as "Araby's Daughter," a ballad from*
*Thomas Moore's celebrated poem "Lalla Rookh," 1817.)*

1. How dear to this heart are the scenes of my childhood,
   When fond recollection presents them to view:
   The orchard, the meadow, the deep tangled wildwood,
   And ev'ry lov'd spot which my infancy knew;

   The wide-spreading stream, the mill that stood near it,
   The bridge and the rock where the cataract fell;
   The cot of my father, the dairy house by it,
   And e'en the rude bucket that hung in the well.

   *Chorus:*
   . . . The old oaken bucket, the iron-bound bucket,
   The moss-cover'd bucket that hung in the well.

2. The moss-cover'd bucket I hail as a treasure,
   For often at noon when returned from the field,
   I found it the source of an exquisite pleasure,
   The purest and sweetest that nature can yield.

   How ardent I seized it with hands that were glowing,
   And quick to the white-pebbled bottom it fell;
   Then soon with the emblem of health overflowing,
   And dripping with coolness it rose from the well.

   [*to Chorus*]

3. How soon from the green mossy rim to receive it,
   As pois'd on the curb it reclin'd to my lips,
   Not a full flowing goblet could tempt me to leave it,
   Tho' fill'd with the nectar that Jupiter sips.

   And now far removed from the loved situation,
   The tear of regret will intrusively swell;
   As fancy reverts to my father's plantation,
   And sighs for the bucket that hung in the well.

   [*to Chorus*]

# The Old Rugged Cross

W & M: REV. GEORGE BENNARD (1913)

1. On a hill far away, stood an old rugged cross,
   The emblem of suff'ring and shame;
   And I loved that old cross where the dearest and best
   For a world of lost sinners was slain.

   *Chorus:*
   So I'll cherish the old rugged cross,
   Till my trophies at last I lay down;
   I will cling to the old rugged cross,
   And exchange it some day for a crown.

2. Oh, that old rugged cross, so despised by the world,
   Has a wond'rous attraction for me;
   For the dear Lamb of God left His glory above,
   To bear it to dark Calvary.

   [*to Chorus*]

3. In the old rugged cross, stained with blood so divine,
   A wond'rous beauty I see;
   For 'twas on that old cross Jesus suffered and died,
   To pardon and sanctify me.

   [*to Chorus*]

4. To the old rugged cross I will ever be true,
   Its shame and reproach gladly bear;
   Then He'll call me, some day, to my home far away,
   Where His glory forever I'll share.

   [*to Chorus*]


# O Little Town of Bethlehem

W: PHILLIPS BROOKS (1868) / M: LEWIS H. REDNER

1. O little town of Bethlehem,
   How still we see thee lie!
   Above thy deep and dreamless sleep
   The silent stars go by.

   Yet in thy dark streets shineth
   The everlasting Light;
   The hopes and fears of all the years
   Are met in thee tonight.

2. For Christ is born of Mary,
   And gathered all above,
   While mortals sleep, the angels keep
   Their watch of wond'ring love.

   O morning stars, together
   Proclaim the holy birth,
   And praises sing to God the King,
   And peace to men on earth!

3. How silently, how silently,
   The wondrous gift is giv'n!
   So God imparts to human hearts
   The blessings of his heav'n.

   No ear may hear his coming,
   But in this world of sin,
   Where meek souls will receive him still,
   The dear Christ enters in.

4. O Holy Child of Bethlehem,
   Descend to us, we pray;
   Cast out our sin and enter in;
   Be born in us today!

   We hear the Christmas angels
   The great glad tidings tell;
   O come to us, abide with us,
   Our Lord Emmanuel!

# On a Sunday Afternoon

W: ANDREW B. STERLING / M: HARRY VON TILZER (1902)

1. There's a day we feel gay,
       if the weather is fine;
   Ev'ry lad feels so glad,
       if the sun does shine.

   In his best he is dressed,
       and with smiling face,
   He goes with his Pearlie,
       his own little girlie,
       to some nice place.

*Chorus:*
On a Sunday afternoon,
   in the merry month of June,
Take a trip up the Hudson
   or down the bay,
Take a trolley to Coney
   or Rockaway.

On a Sunday afternoon,
   you can see the lovers spoon;
They work hard on Monday,
   but one day that's fun day
   is Sunday afternoon.

2. Coming home, starry dome,
   with a soft moon-shine,
Lovers kiss, oh, what bliss!
   Oh, what joy divine!

"Goodnight, Joe." "Goodnight, Flo,
   don't forget now, dear.
Next Sunday at two,
   I'll be waiting for you
   on the old Iron Pier."

[*to Chorus*]


# Once in Royal David's City
W: CECIL FRANCES ALEXANDER / M: ANON.

1. Once in royal David's city
   Stood a lowly cattle shed,
Where a mother laid her baby
In a manger for his bed;
   Mary was that mother mild
   Jesus Christ her little Child.

2. He came down to earth from heaven,
   Who is God and Lord of all,
And his shelter was a stable
And his cradle was a stall;
   With the poor, and mean, and lowly,
   Lived on earth our Saviour holy.

3. And through all his wondrous childhood,
   He would honour and obey,
   Love, and watch the lowly maiden
   In whose gentle arms he lay;
       Christian children all must be
       Mild, obedient, good as he.

4. For he is our childhood's pattern,
   Day by day like us he grew:
   He was little, weak, and helpless,
   Tears and smiles, like us he knew;
       And he feeleth for our sadness,
       And he shareth in our gladness.

5. And our eyes at last shall see him,
   Through his own redeeming love;
   For that Child, so dear and gentle,
   Is our Lord in heaven above;
       And he leads his children on
       To the place where he is gone.

6. Not in that poor lowly stable,
   With the oxen standing by,
   We shall see him, but in heaven,
   Set at God's right hand on high;
       When like stars his children rise
       Singing praises in the skies.


# One More River
SPIRITUAL

1. Old Noah built himself an ark,
      *There's one more river to cross*
   And built it all of hickory bark.
      *There's one more river to cross*

      *Chorus:*
      One more river,
      And that's the river of Jordan;
      One more river,
      There's one more river to cross.

2. The animals came two by two,
      *There's one more river to cross*
   The elephant and the kangaroo.
      *There's one more river to cross*

      [*to Chorus*]

267

**3.** The animals came three by three,
*There's one more river to cross*
The baboon and the chimpanzee.
*There's one more river to cross*

[*to Chorus*]

**4.** The animals came four by four,
*There's one more river to cross*
Old Noah got mad and hollered for more.
*There's one more river to cross*

[*to Chorus*]

**5.** The animals came five by five,
*There's one more river to cross*
The bees came swarming from the hive.
*There's one more river to cross*

[*to Chorus*]

**6.** The animals came six by six,
*There's one more river to cross*
The lion laughed at the monkey's tricks.
*There's one more river to cross*

[*to Chorus*]

**7.** When Noah found he had no sail,
*There's one more river to cross*
He just ran up his old coat tail.
*There's one more river to cross*

[*to Chorus*]

**8.** Before the voyage did begin,
*There's one more river to cross*
Old Noah pulled the gangplank in.
*There's one more river to cross*

[*to Chorus*]

**9.** They never knew where they were at,
*There's one more river to cross*
'Til the old ark bumped on Ararat.
*There's one more river to cross*

[*to Chorus*]

# O No, John!

OLD ENGLISH COURTING SONG

1. On yonder hill there stands a creature,
   Who she is I do not know;
   I go and court her for her beauty,
   She must answer Yes or No.
   *O No, John! No, John! No, John! No!*

2. "My father was a Spanish Captain,
   Went to sea a month ago;
   First he kiss'd me, then he left me,
   Bid me always answer No."
   *O No, John! No, John! No, John! No!*

3. O Madam, in your face is beauty,
   On your lips red roses grow;
   Will you take me for your lover?
   Madam, answer Yes or No.
   *O No, John! No, John! No, John! No!*

4. O Madam, I will give you jewels,
   I will make you rich and free;
   I will give you silken dresses.
   Madam, will you marry me?
   *O No, John! No, John! No, John! No!*

5. O Madam, since you are so cruel,
   And that you do scorn me so,
   If I may not be your lover,
   Madam, will you let me go?
   *O No, John! No, John! No, John! No!*

6. Then I will stay with you forever,
   If you will not be unkind.
   Madam, I have vowed to love you;
   Would you have me change my mind?
   *O No, John! No, John! No, John! No!*

# On the Banks of the Wabash, Far Away

W & M: PAUL DRESSER (1899)

1. 'Round my Indiana homestead wave the cornfields,
In the distance loom the woodlands clear and cool.
Oftentimes my thoughts revert to scenes of childhood
Where I first received my lessons, nature's school.

But one thing there is missing in the picture,
Without her face it seems so incomplete.
I long to see my mother in the doorway
As she stood there years ago, her boy to greet.

*Chorus:*
Oh, the moonlight's fair tonight along the Wabash,
From the fields there comes a breath of new mown hay,
Through the sycamores the candlelights are gleaming
On the banks of the Wabash far away.

2. Many years have passed since I strolled by the river,
Arm in arm with sweetheart Mary by my side.
It was there I tried to tell her that I loved her,
It was there I begged of her to be my bride.

Long years have passed since I strolled through the churchyard;
She's sleeping there, my angel, Mary dear.
I loved her but she thought I didn't mean it,
Still I'd give my future were she only here.

[*to Chorus*]


# On the Road to Mandalay

W: RUDYARD KIPLING / M: OLEY SPEAKS (1907)

1. By the old Moulmein Pagoda,
     lookin' eastward to the sea,
There's a Burma girl a-settin',
     and I know she thinks o' me;

For the wind is in the palm-trees,
     and the temple-bells they say:
'Come you back, you British soldier;
     Come you back to Mandalay,
     Come you back to Mandalay.'

*Chorus:*
Come you back to Mandalay,
Where the old Flotilla lay:

Can't you 'ear their paddles chunkin'
From Rangoon to Mandalay?

On the road to Mandalay,
Where the flyin'-fishes play,
And the dawn comes up like thunder
Outter China 'crost the Bay.

2. 'Er petticoat was yaller,
    an' 'er little cap was green,
An' 'er name was Supi-yaw-lat—
    jes' the same as Theebaw's Queen.

An' I seed her first a-smokin'
    of a whackin' white cheroot,
An' a-wastin' Christian kisses
    on an 'eathen idol's foot,
    on an 'eathen idol's foot.

*Chorus:*
Bloomin' idol made o' mud—
What they called the Great Gawd Budd—
Plucky lot she cared for idols
When I kissed 'er where she stud!

On the road to Mandalay,
Where the flyin'-fishes play,
And the dawn comes up like thunder
Outter China 'crost the Bay.

3. Ship me somewheres east of Suez
    where the best is like the worst,
Where there aren't no Ten Commandments,
    an' a man can raise a thirst;

For the temple-bells are callin',
    and it's there that I would be—
By the old Moulmein Pagoda,
    lookin' lazy at the sea,
    lookin' lazy at the sea.

*Chorus:*
Come you back to Mandalay
Where the old Flotilla lay,
Can't you 'ear the paddles chunkin'
From Rangoon to Mandalay?

On the road to Mandalay,
Where the flyin'-fishes play,
And the dawn comes up like thunder
Outter China 'crost the bay.

271

# On Top of Old Smoky

AMERICAN BALLAD

1. On top of Old Smoky,
   All covered with snow,
   I lost my true lover
   A-courtin' too slow.

2. A-courtin's a pleasure,
   A-partin' is grief,
   A false-hearted lover
   Is worse than a thief.

3. A thief he will rob you
   And take what you have,
   But a false-hearted lover
   Sends you to your grave.

4. They'll hug you and kiss you
   And tell you more lies
   Than the leaves on a willow
   Or the stars in the skies.

5. My sad heart is aching,
   I'm weary today;
   My lover has left me,
   I'm a-feelin' this way.

6. It's rainin', it's pourin',
   The moon gives no light;
   My horse he won't travel
   This dark lonesome night.

7. I'm goin' away, dear,
   I'll write you my mind;
   My mind is to marry
   And to leave you behind.

8. Come, all you young people,
   And listen to me:
   Don't place your affection
   On a green willow tree.

9. The leaves they will wither
   The roots they will die;
   You will be forsaken
   And never know why.

**10.** On top of Old Smoky,
   All covered with snow,
   I lost my true lover
   A-courtin' too slow.

# Onward, Christian Soldiers

W: REV. SABINE BARING-GOULD / M: ARTHUR S. SULLIVAN (1864)

**1.** Onward, Christian soldiers,
   Marching as to war,
   With the cross of Jesus
   Going on before.

   Christ, the royal Master,
   Leads against the foe;
   Forward into battle,
   See, His banners go.

   *Chorus:*
   Onward, Christian soldiers,
   Marching as to war,
   With the cross of Jesus
   Going on before.

**2.** Like a mighty army,
   Moves the Church of God;
   Brothers, we are treading
   Where the saints have trod.

   We are not divided,
   All one body we;
   One in hope and doctrine,
   One in charity.

   [*to Chorus*]

**3.** Crowns and throwns may perish,
   Kingdoms rise and wane,
   But the Church of Jesus
   Constant will remain.

   Gates of hell can never
   'Gainst that Church prevail;
   We have Christ's own promise,
   And that cannot fail.

   [*to Chorus*]

4. Onward, then, ye people,
   Join our happy throng;
   Blend with ours your voices
   In the triumph song.

   Glory, laud, and honor,
   Unto Christ the King;
   This, through countless ages,
   Men and angels sing.

   [*to Chorus*]


# Oranges and Lemons

ENGLISH NURSERY TUNE
*(naming all the bell towers in the City of London)*

1. Oranges and lemons,
       say the bells of St. Clement's.
   You owe me five farthings,
       say the bells of St. Martin's.

   When will you pay me?
       say the bells of Old Bailey.
   When I grow rich,
       say the bells of Shoreditch.

   When will that be?
       say the bells of Stepney.
   I do not know,
       says the great bell of Bow.

   *Chorus:*
   Here comes a candle
   to light you to bed,
   And here comes a chopper
   to cut off your head.

   *Chop chop chop*
   *Chop chop chop*
   *Chop chop chop*
   *CHOP!*

2. Pancakes and fritters,
   say the bells of St. Peter's.
Two sticks and an apple,
   say the bells of Whitechapel.
Old Father Baldpate,
   say the bells of Aldgate.
Poker and tongs,
   say the bells of St. John's.
Kettles and pans,
   say the bells of St. Ann's.
Brickbats and tiles,
   say the bells of St. Giles'.

   [*to Chorus*]


# 'O Sole Mio!

W: GIOVANNI CAPURRO / M: EDOARDO DI CAPUA (1899)

1. Che bella cosa è na jurnata 'e sole,
   'n'aria serena doppo 'na tempesta!
   Pe'll'aria fresca pare già 'na festa . . .
   che bella cosa 'na jurnata 'e sole.

   *Chorus:*
   Ma n'atu sole, cchiù bello, oi me
   'o sole mio, sta 'n fronte a te!
   'O sole, 'o sole mio
   sta 'n fronte a te,
   sta 'n fronte a te!

2. Lùceno e llastre d' 'a fenesta toia;
   'na lavannara canta e se ne vanta
   e pe' tramente torce, spanne e canta,
   lùceno e llastre d' 'a fenesta toia.

   [*to Chorus*]

3. Quanno fa notte e 'o sole se ne scenne,
   me vene quase 'na malincunia;
   sotto 'a fenesta toia restarria
   quanno fa notte e 'o sole se ne scenne.

   [*to Chorus*]

275

# Over There

W & M: GEORGE M. COHAN (1917)

1. Johnnie get your gun, get your gun, get your gun;
   Take it on the run, on the run, on the run;
   Hear them calling you and me,
   Ev'ry son of liberty.

   Hurry right away, no delay, go today;
   Make your daddy glad, to have had such a lad;
   Tell your sweetheart not to pine,
   And be proud her boy's in line.

   *Chorus:*
   Over there, over there,
   Send the word, send the word over there,
   That the Yanks/(boys) are coming, the Yanks/(boys) are coming,
   The drums rum-tumming ev'rywhere.

   So prepare, say a pray'r,
   Send the word, send the word to prepare,
   We'll be over, we're coming over,
   And we won't come back till it's over over there.

2. Johnnie get your gun, get your gun, get your gun;
   Johnnie show the Hun, you're a son-of-a-gun;
   Hoist the flag and let her fly,
   Like true heroes do or die.

   Pack your little kit, show some grit, do your bit;
   Soldiers to the ranks from the towns and the tanks;
   Make your mother proud of you,
   And to liberty be true.

   [*to Chorus*]


# Over the River and Through the Woods

W: LYDIA MARIA CHILD
*(originally published in 1844 as "Thanksgiving Day," a 12-stanza poem)*
M: FRENCH FOLK TUNE

1. Over the river and through the woods,
   To grandfather's house we go;
   The horse knows the way to carry the sleigh,
   Through the white and drifted snow.

Over the river and through the woods,
Oh, how the wind does blow!
It stings the toes, and bites the nose,
As over the ground we go.

2. Over the river and through the woods,
To have a first-rate play;
Oh, hear the bells ring, "Ting-a-ling-ling!"
Hurrah for Thanksgiving Day.

Over the river and through the woods,
Trot fast, my dapple gray!
Spring over the ground like a hunting hound,
For this is Thanksgiving Day!

3. Over the river and through the woods,
And straight through the barnyard gate;
We seem to go extremely slow,
It is so hard to wait!

Over the river and through the woods,
Now grandmother's cap I spy!
Hurrah for the fun! Is the pudding done?
Hurrah for the pumpkin pie!


# Pack Up Your Troubles in Your Old Kit-Bag and Smile, Smile, Smile

W: "GEORGE ASAF" [George Henry Powell] / M: FELIX POWELL (1915)

1. Private Perks is a funny little codger
With a smile, a funny smile.
Five feet none, he's an artful little dodger
With a smile, a funny smile.

Flush or broke, he'll have his little joke,
He can't be suppressed.
All the other fellows have to grin
When he gets this off his chest:
[*shout*] Hi!

*Chorus:*
"Pack up your troubles in your old kit-bag,
And smile, smile, smile.
While you've a lucifer to light your fag,
Smile, boys, that's the style.

"What's the use of worrying?
It never was worthwhile, so
Pack up your troubles in your old kit-bag,
And smile, smile, smile."

2. Private Perks went a-marching into Flanders
With his smile, his funny smile.
He was loved by the privates and commanders
For his smile, his funny smile.

When a throng of Bosches came along,
With a mighty swing
Perks yelled out, "This little bunch is mine!
Keep your heads down, boys, and sing:
    [*shout*] Hi!

[*to Chorus*]

3. Private Perks he came back from Bosche-hunting
With his smile, his funny smile.
'Round his home he then set about recruiting
With his smile, his funny smile.

He told all his pals, the short, the tall,
What a time he'd had;
And as each enlisted like a man,
Private Perks said, "Now, my lad:
    [*shout*] Hi!

[*to Chorus*]


# Paddle Your Own Canoe

W: HARRY CLIFTON / M: M. HOBSON (ca. 1912?)

1. I've travel'd about a bit in my time,
    And of troubles I've seen a few;
But found it better in ev'ry clime
    To paddle my own canoe.

My wants are small, I care not at all
    If my debts are paid when due;
I drive away strife in the ocean of life
    While I paddle my own canoe.

*Chorus:*
Then love your neighbor as yourself
As the world you go travelling through,
And never sit down with a tear or a frown,
But paddle your own canoe.

**2.** I have no wife to bother my life,
  No lover to prove untrue;
But the whole day long with a laugh and a song,
  I paddle my own canoe.

I rise with the lark and from daylight till dark
  I do what I have to do;
I'm careless of wealth if I've only the health
  To paddle my own canoe.

  [*to Chorus*]

**3.** It's all very well to depend on a friend,
  That is, if you've proved him true;
But you'll find it better by far in the end
  To paddle your own canoe.

To "borrow" is dearer by far than to "buy,"
  A maxim though old still true;
You never will sigh if you only will try
  To paddle your own canoe.

  [*to Chorus*]

**4.** If a hurricane rise in the midday
  And the sun is lost to view,
Move steadily by, with a steadfast eye to the skies,
  And paddle your own canoe.

The daisies that grow in the bright green fields
  Are blooming so sweet for you;
So never sit down with a tear or a frown,
  But paddle your own canoe.

  [*to Chorus*]


# Peg o' My Heart
W: ALFRED BRYAN / M: FRED FISCHER (1913)

**1.** Oh! my heart's in a whirl over one little girl,
  I love her, I love her, yes I do;
Altho' her heart is far away,
  I hope to make her mine some day.

Ev'ry beautiful rose, ev'ry violet knows,
  I love her, I love her fond and true,
And her heart fondly sighs, as I sing to her eyes,
  Her eyes of blue, sweet eyes of blue, my darling!

*Chorus:*
Peg o' my heart, I love you,
We'll never part, I love you,
Dear little girl, sweet little girl,
Sweeter than the rose of Erin,
Are your winning smiles endearin';

Peg o' my heart, your glances,
With Irish art entrance us,
Come, be my own,
Come, make your home in my heart!

2. When your heart's full of fears, and your eyes full of tears,
I'll kiss them, I'll kiss them all away;
For, like the gold that's in your hair,
Is all the love for you I bear,

O, believe in me, do, I'm as lonesome as you,
I miss you, I miss you all the day;
Let the light of love shine from your eyes into mine,
And shine for aye, sweetheart of aye, my darling!

[*to Chorus*]


# Polly-Wolly-Doodle
AMERICAN MINSTREL SONG

1. Oh, I went down South for to see my Sal,
   *Singin' Polly-Wolly-Doodle all the day*
For my Sally she was a spunky gal.
   *Sing Polly-Wolly-Doodle all the day*

   *Chorus:*
   Fare thee well, fare thee well,
   Fare thee well, my fairy fay,
   For I'm off to Lou'siana for to see my Susy Anna,
   Singin' Polly-Wolly-Doodle all the day.

2. Oh, my Sally was such a maiden fair,
   *Singin' Polly-Wolly-Doodle all the day*
With her curly eyes and her laughing hair.
   *Sing Polly-Wolly-Doodle all the day*

   [*to Chorus*]

**3.** Oh, a grasshopper sat on a railroad track,
   *Singin' Polly-Wolly-Doodle all the day*
Was a-pickin' his teeth with a carpet tack.
   *Sing Polly-Wolly-Doodle all the day*

   [*to Chorus*]

**4.** Oh, I went to bed but it weren't no use,
   *Singin' Polly-Wolly-Doodle all the day*
'Cause my feet stuck out for a chicken roost.
   *Sing Polly-Wolly-Doodle all the day*

   [*to Chorus*]

**5.** From behind the barn, down upon my knees,
   *Singin' Polly-Wolly-Doodle all the day*
I could swear I heard that old chicken sneeze.
   *Sing Polly-Wolly-Doodle all the day*

   [*to Chorus*]

**6.** An' he sneezed so hard with the whoopin' cough,
   *Singin' Polly-Wolly-Doodle all the day*
That he sneezed his head an' his tail right off.
   *Sing Polly-Wolly-Doodle all the day*

   [*to Chorus*]

# Pop Goes the Weasel
W: ANON. (1856?)
M: OLD ENGLISH DANCING TUNE (1853?)

**1.** All around the cobbler's bench
The monkey chased the weasel,
The monkey thought 'twas all in fun,
   *Pop goes the weasel!*

I've no time to wait and sigh,
No patience to wait till bye 'n' bye,
So kiss me quick, I'm off, good-bye,
   *Pop goes the weasel!*

**2.** A nickel for a spool of thread,
A penny for a needle,
That's the way the money goes,
   *Pop goes the weasel!*

You may try to sew and sew
And never make something regal,
So roll it up and let it go,
   *Pop goes the weasel!*

3. I went to a lawyer today
   For something very legal,
   He asked how much I'm willing to pay,
      *Pop goes the weasel!*

   I will bargain all my days
   But never again so feeble,
   I paid for ev'ry legal phrase,
      *Pop goes the weasel!*

4. A painter would his lover to paint,
   He stood before the easel,
   A monkey jumped all over the paint,
      *Pop goes the weasel!*

   When his lover she did laugh
   His temper got very lethal,
   He tore the painting up in half,
      *Pop goes the weasel!*

5. I went hunting up in the woods,
   It wasn't very legal,
   The dog and I were caught with the goods,
      *Pop goes the weasel!*

   I said I don't hunt or sport,
   The warden looked at my beagle,
   He said to tell it to the court,
      *Pop goes the weasel!*

6. My son and I went to the fair
   And there were lots of people,
   We spent a lot of money, I swear,
      *Pop goes the weasel!*

   I got sick from all the sun,
   My sunny boy got the measles,
   But still we had a lot of fun,
      *Pop goes the weasel!*

7. I went up and down on the coast
   To find a golden eagle,
   I climbed the rocks and thought I was close,
      *Pop goes the weasel!*

   But, alas, I lost my way,
   Saw nothing but just a seagull,

I tore my pants and killed the day,
*Pop goes the weasel!*

8. I went to a grocery store,
I thought a little cheese'll
Be good to catch a mouse in the floor,
*Pop goes the weasel!*

But the mouse was very bright,
He wasn't a mouse to wheedle,
He took the cheese and said "Good night."
*Pop goes the weasel!*

# Pretty Baby

W: GUS KAHN / M: TONY JACKSON & EGBERT VAN ALSTYNE
[from *The Passing Show of 1916*]

1. You ask me why I'm always teasing you,
You hate to have me call you Pretty Baby;
I really thought that I was pleasing you,
For you're just a baby to me.

Your cunning little dimples and your baby stare,
Your baby talk and baby walk and curly hair,
Your baby smile makes life worthwhile,
You're just as sweet as you can be.

> *Chorus:*
> Ev'rybody loves a baby, that's why I'm in love with you,
> Pretty Baby, Pretty Baby;
> And I'd like to be your sister, brother, dad and mother, too,
> Pretty Baby, Pretty Baby.
>
> Won't you come and let me rock you in my cradle of love,
> And we'll cuddle all the time.
> Oh! I want a Lovin' Baby and it might as well be you,
> Pretty Baby of mine.

2. Your mother says you were the cutest kid—
No wonder, dearie, that I'm wild about you;
And all the cunning things you said and did—
Why I love to fondly recall.

And just like Peter Pan, it seems you'll always be
The same sweet, cunning, Little Baby dear to me;
And that is why I'm sure
I will always love you best of all.

> *[to Chorus]*

# A Pretty Girl Is Like a Melody

W & M: IRVING BERLIN
[from *Ziegfeld Follies of 1919*]

I have an ear for music,
And I have an eye for a maid;
I link a pretty girlie
With each pretty tune that's played.

They go together, like sunny weather
Goes with the month of May;
I've studied girls and music,
So I'm qualified to say:

*Chorus:*
A pretty girl is like a melody
That haunts you night and day;
   Just like the strain
   Of a haunting refrain,
She'll start upon a marathon
And run around your brain.

You can't escape, she's in your memory,
By morning, night and noon;
   She will leave you and then
   Come back again,
A pretty girl is just like a pretty tune.

# Put On Your Old Grey Bonnet

W: STANLEY MURPHY / M: PERCY WENRICH (1909)

1. On the old farmhouse veranda
There sat Silas and Miranda,
   Thinking of the days gone by.
Said he, "Dearie, don't be weary,
You were always bright and cheery,
   But a tear, dear, dims your eye."

Said she, "They're tears of gladness,
Silas, they're not tears of sadness,
   It is fifty years today since we were wed."
Then the old man's dim eyes brighten'd,
And his stern old heart it lighten'd,
   As he turn'd to her and said . . .

"Put on your old grey bonnet
With the blue ribbon on it,
While I hitch old Dobbin to the shay;
And through the fields of clover
We'll drive up to Dover
On our Golden Wedding day."

2. It was in the same old bonnet
   With the same blue ribbon on it,
       In the old shay, by his side,
   That he drove her up to Dover,
   Thro' the same old fields of clover,
       To become his happy bride.

The birds were sweetly singing
And the same old bells were ringing
    As they pass'd the quaint old church
        where they were wed;
And that night when stars were gleaming,
The old couple lay a-dreaming,
    Dreaming of the words he said . . .

[*to Chorus*]


# Put Your Arms Around Me, Honey
## (I Never Knew Any Girl Like You)
W: JUNIE Mc CREE / M: ALBERT VON TILZER (1910)

Shades of night are falling, ev'rything is still,
And the pale moon is shining from above.
I hear Cupid calling ev'ry Jack and Jill,
It's just about the time for making love.

*Chorus:*
Put your arms around me, honey,
    hold me tight,
Huddle up and cuddle up
    with all your might.
Oh, babe! Won't you roll dem eyes,
    eyes that I just idolize.

When they look at me,
    my heart begins to float,
Then it starts a-rockin'
    like a motor boat.
Oh! Oh! I never knew
    any girl/(boy) like you.

# Rally 'Round the Flag

CIVIL WAR MARCHING SONG

W: JAMES C. FIELDS / M: WILLIAM S. BRADBURY

1. Rally 'round the flag, boys,
   Give it to the breeze,
   That's the banner we love,
   On the land and seas.

   Brave hearts are under ours,
   Hearts that heed no brag,
   Gallant lads, fire away,
   And fight for the flag!
     Gallant lads, fire away,
     And fight for the flag.

   Rally 'round the flag, boys,
   Give it to the breeze,
   That's the banner we love,
   On the land and seas.

   Let our colors fly, boys,
   Guard them day and night,
   For victory is liberty,
   And God will bless the right!

     *Chorus:*
     Then rally 'round the flag, boys,
     Rally 'round, rally 'round,
     Rally 'round the flag, boys,
     Rally 'round the flag!

     Rally 'round the flag, boys,
     Rally 'round, rally 'round,
     Rally 'round the flag, boys,
     Rally 'round the flag!

2. Floating high above us,
   Glowing in the sun,
   Speaking loud to all hearts
   Of a freedom won.

   Who dares to sully it,
   Bought with precious blood?
   Gallant lads, we'll fight for it,
   Tho' ours should swell the flood,
     Gallant lads, we'll fight for it,
     Tho' ours should swell the flood.

   Their flag is but a rag,
   Ours is the true one,

Up with the Stars and Stripes,
Down with the new one.

Floating high above us,
Glowing in the sun,
Speaking loud to all hearts,
Of a freedom won!
    [*to Chorus*]


# The Red River Valley
W & M: JAMES J. KERRIGAN (1896)

1. From this valley they say you are going,
    We will miss your bright eyes and sweet smile,
    For they say you are taking the sunshine
    That will brighten our pathway a while.

    *Chorus:*
    Come and sit by my side if you love me,
    Do not hasten to bid me adieu;
    But remember the Red River Valley
    And the girl that has loved you so true.

2. As you go to your home by the ocean,
    May you never forget those sweet hours
    That we spent in the Red River Valley
    And the love we exchanged 'mid the flow'rs.

    [*to Chorus*]

3. From this valley you say you are going,
    When you go, may your darling go, too?
    Would you leave her behind unprotected
    When you know she loves no one but you?

    [*to Chorus*]

4. I have promised you, darling, that never
    Will a word from my lips cause you pain,
    And my life, it will be yours forever
    If you only will love me again.

    [*to Chorus*]

5. Won't you think of the valley you're leaving?
    Oh, how lonely, how sad it will be.
    Won't you think of the fond heart you're breaking
    And the grief you are causing for me?

    [*to Chorus*]

287

# Red Wing
## (An Indian Intermezzo)
W: THURLAND CHATTAWAY / M: KERRY MILLS (1907)

1. There once lived an Indian maid,
   A shy little prairie maid
   Who sang a lay, a love song gay,
   As on the plain she'd while away the day.

   She loved a warrior bold,
   This shy little maid of old,
   But brave and gay,
   He rode one day to battle far away.

   *Chorus:*
   Now, the moon shines tonight on pretty Red Wing,
   　　the breeze is sighing,
   　　the night bird's crying;
   For afar 'neath his star her brave is sleeping
   　　while Red Wing's weeping
   　　her heart away.

2. She watched for him day and night,
   She kept all the campfires bright;
   And under the sky, each night she would lie
   And dream about his coming by and by.

   But when all the braves returned,
   the heart of Red Wing yearned,
   For far, far away, her warrior gay
   Fell bravely in the fray.

   [*to Chorus*]


# Reuben and Rachel
W: HARRY BIRCH / M: WILLIAM GOOCH (1871)

*(Girls)*
Reuben, I have long been thinking,
What a grand world this would be
If the men were all transported
Far beyond the Northern Sea.

*(Boys)*
O my goodness gracious, Rachel,
What a strange world this would be
If the men were all transported
Far beyond the Northern Sea.

*(Girls)*
Reuben, I have long been thinking,
What a fine life girls would lead
If they had no men about them,
None to tease them, none to heed.

*(Boys)*
Rachel, I have long been thinking,
Men would have a merry time
If at once they were transported
Far beyond the salty brine!

# Rise and Shine
SPIRITUAL

> *Chorus:*
> Rise and shine, and give God the glory, glory,
> Rise and shine, and give God the glory, glory,
> Rise and shine, and give God the glory, glory,
> Children of the Lord.

1. The Lord said to Noah, "There's gonna be a flood-y, flood-y";
   The Lord said to Noah, "There's gonna be a flood-y, flood-y;
   Get your children out of the mud-dy, mud-dy!"
   Children of the Lord.

   [*to Chorus*]

2. So Noah, he built him, he built him an ark-y, ark-y;
   So Noah, he built him, he built him an ark-y, ark-y;
   Built it out of hick'ry bark-y, bark-y,
   Children of the Lord.

   [*to Chorus*]

3. The animals, they came, they came by two-sies, two-sies;
   The animals, they came, they came by two-sies, two-sies;
   Elephants and kangaroo-sies, roo-sies,
   Children of the Lord.

   [*to Chorus*]

4. It rained and poured for forty day-sies, day-sies;
   It rained and poured for forty day-sies, day-sies;
   Drove those animals nearly crazy, crazy,
   Children of the Lord.

   [*to Chorus*]

5. The sun came out and dried up the land-y, land-y;
   The sun came out and dried up the land-y, land-y;
   Ev'ryone felt fine and dandy, dandy,
   Children of the Lord.

   [*to Chorus*]


# Roamin' in the Gloamin'
W & M: HARRY LAUDER (1911)

1. I've seen lots o' bonnie lassies trav'llin' far and wide,
   But my heart is centred noo on bonnie Kate McBride.
   And altho' I'm no' a chap that throws a word away,
   I'm surprised mysel' sometimes at a' I've got to say.

   *Chorus:*
   Roamin' in the gloamin'
      on the bonnie banks o' Clyde,
   Roamin' in the gloamin'
      wae my lassie by my side.

   When the sun has gone to rest,
   That's the time that we love best.
   O, it's lovely roamin' in the gloamin'!

2. One nicht in the gloamin' we were trippin' side by side;
   I kissed her twice, and asked her once if she would be my bride.
   She was shy, so was I, we were baith the same,
   But I got brave and braver on the journey comin' hame.

   [*to Chorus*]

3. Last nicht efter strollin' we got hame at half-past nine;
   Sittin' at the kitchen fire I asked her to be mine.
   When she promised, I got up and danced the Hielan' fling.
   I've just been at the jew'ler's and I've picked a nice wee ring.

   [*to Chorus*]

# Rock-a-Bye, Baby

W & M: "EFFIE I. CANNING" [Effie I. Crockett] (1884)
*(original words—"Hush-a-bye, Baby"—published about 1765)*

1. Baby is sleeping so cozy and fair,
   While mother sits near in her old oaken chair;
   Her foot on the rocker the cradle she swings,
   And though baby slumbers he hears what she sings:

   *Lullaby:*
   Rock-a-bye, baby, on the tree top,
   When the wind blows the cradle will rock,
   When the bough breaks the cradle will fall,
   And down will come baby, cradle and all.

2. Grandma sitting knitting close by the fireplace,
   With snowy white hair and a smile on her face;
   The years have passed by, yet it does not seem long,
   Since she rocked baby's papa to sleep with that song:

   [*to Lullaby*]

3. Dear little baby, their joy and their pride,
   Long may he be with them whatever betide;
   The kitchen, the cradle, that tender refrain,
   In mem'ry will linger that lullaby strain:

   [*to Lullaby*]


# Rock-a-Bye Your Baby
## (With a Dixie Melody)

W: JOE YOUNG & SAM M. LEWIS / M: JEAN SCHWARTZ
[from *Sinbad,* 1918]

1. Mammy mine,
   Your little rollin' stone that rolled away, strolled away;
   Mammy mine,
   Your rollin' stone is rollin' home today, there to stay.

   Just to see your smilin' face,
   Smile a welcome sign;
   When I'm in your fond embrace,
   Listen, Mammy mine:

   *Chorus:*
   Rock-a-bye your baby with a Dixie melody;
   When you croon, croon a tune from the heart of Dixie.

Just hang my cradle, Mammy mine,
Right on the Mason-Dixon Line,
And swing it from Virginia
To Tennessee with all the love that's in yer.

"Weep no more, my lady," sing that song again for me,
And "Old Black Joe," just as though you had me on your knee;
A million baby kisses I'll deliver,
The minute that you sing the "Swanee River";
Rock-a-bye your rock-a-bye baby with a Dixie melody.

2. Any time
   I hear a Mammy sing her babe to sleep, slumber deep,
   That's the time
   The shadows 'round my heart begin to creep, and I weep.

   Wonder why I went away,
   What a fool I've been;
   Take me back to yesterday,
   In your arms again.

   [*to Chorus*]


# Rock-a My Soul

SPIRITUAL

*Chorus:*
Rock-a my soul in the bosom of Abraham,
Rock-a my soul in the bosom of Abraham,
Rock-a my soul in the bosom of Abraham,
Oh, rock-a my soul.

1. My Lord is so high, you can't get over Him,
   So low, you can't get under Him,
   So wide, you can't get around Him,
   You must go in at the door.

   [*to Chorus*]

2. His love is so high, you can't get over it,
   So low, you can't get under it,
   So wide, you can't get around it,
   You must go in at the door.

   [*to Chorus*]

# Rock'd in the Cradle of the Deep
W: EMMA H. WILLARD / M: JOSEPH P. KNIGHT (1840)

1. Rock'd in the cradle of deep,
   I lay me down in peace to sleep;
   Secure I rest upon the wave,
   For thou, Oh! Lord, hast power to save.

   I know thou wilt not slight my call,
   For thou dost mark the sparrow's fall!
   And calm and peaceful is my sleep,
   Rock'd in the cradle of the deep—
       And calm and peaceful is my sleep,
       Rock'd in the cradle of the deep.

2. And such the trust that still were mine,
   Tho' stormy winds swept o'er the brine,
   Or tho' the tempest's fiery breath
   Roused me from sleep to wreck and death!

   In ocean cave still safe with Thee,
   The germ of immortality;
   And calm and peaceful is my sleep,
   Rock'd in the cradle of the deep—
       And calm and peaceful is my sleep,
       Rock'd in the cradle of the deep.

# Rock of Ages
W: AUGUSTUS M. TOPLADY (1776) / M: THOMAS HASTINGS (1832)

1. Rock of ages, cleft for me,
   Let me hide myself in Thee;
       Let the water and the blood
       From Thy wounded side which flowed
   Be of sin the double cure,
   Save from wrath and make me pure.

2. Could my tears forever flow,
   Could my zeal no languor know,
       These for sin could not atone;
       Thou must save, and Thou alone;
   In my hand no price I bring,
   Simply to Thy cross I cling.

3. While I draw this fleeting breath,
   When my eyes shall close in death,
       When I rise to worlds unknown,
       And behold Thee on Thy throne,
   Rock of ages, cleft for me,
   Let me hide myself in Thee.


# Roll, Jordan, Roll
SPIRITUAL

>   *Chorus:*
>   Roll, Jordan, roll,
>   Roll, Jordan, roll;
>   I want to go to heaven when I die,
>   To hear Jordan roll.

1. Oh, brothers, you ought t'have been there;
   Yes, my Lord!
   A-sitting in the Kingdom,
   To hear Jordan roll.

   > [*to Chorus*]

2. Oh, preachers, you ought t'have been there;
   Yes, my Lord!
   A-sitting in the Kingdom,
   To hear Jordan roll.

   > [*to Chorus*]

3. Oh, sinners, you ought t'have been there . . .
   > (*etc.*) [*then to Chorus*]

4. Oh, mourners, you ought t'have been there . . .
   > (etc.) [*then to Chorus*]

5. Oh, seekers, you ought t'have been there . . .
   > (*etc.*) [*then to Chorus*]

6. Oh, mothers, you ought t'have been there . . .
   > (*etc.*) [*then to Chorus*]

7. Oh, sisters, you ought t'have been there . . .
   > (*etc.*) [*then to Chorus*]

# Romany Life
## (Song à la Czardas)

W: HARRY B. SMITH / M: VICTOR HERBERT

[from *The Fortune Teller,* 1898]

We have a home 'neath the forest shades,
Never any other have we.
Our campfires glow in the nooks and glades,
Where our tents are white to see,
Where our tents are white to see.

Wand'ring ever here and there,
Our roof is the sky above,
*Juche!* but the Romany eyes are rare,
And the Romany life is love.

> *Chorus:*
> Thro' the forest, wild and free,
> Sounds our Magyar melody;
> Ever dancing, none can be
> Half so merry as are we.

Thro' the forest, wild and free,
Sounds our Magyar melody;
Ever dancing, as they say,
None so merry, and none so gay.

> Faster twirling!
> *Juche!* with leap and bound,
> Ho! dance, Ay, dance,
> Zigeuner, to music's sound;

> Singing ever,
> *Juche!* Our song is gay,
> Ho! sing, Ay, sing,
> Zigeuner, while yet ye may.

Thro' the forest, wild and free,
Sounds our Magyar melody;
Ever dancing, as they say,
None so merry, and none so gay.

> Singing Romany, Ah!
> Sighing Romany ne'er, ah!

Thro' the forest, wild and free,
Sounds our Magyar melody;
Ever dancing, none can be
Half so merry as lads of Romany.

None so gay as we,
The lads of Romany,
None so gay as we,
The lads of Romany.
*Eljen! Eljen!* Ha!

# The Rosary

W: ROBERT CAMERON ROGERS / M: ETHELBERT NEVIN (1898)

The hours I spent with thee, dear heart,
Are as a string of pearls to me;
I count them over ev'ry one apart,
My rosary, my rosary.

Each hour a pearl, each pearl a pray'r,
To still a heart in absence wrung:
I tell each bead unto the end
And there a Cross is hung!

Oh, memories that bless and burn
O, barren gain and bitter loss!
I kiss each bead and strive at last to learn
To kiss the Cross, sweetheart! to kiss the cross.


# The Rose of Tralee

W: F. MORDAUNT SPENCER / M: CHARLES W. GLOVER (ca. 1845)

1. The pale moon was rising above the green mountain,
   The sun was declining beneath the blue sea,
   When I strayed with my love to the pure crystal fountain
   That stands in the beautiful vale of Tralee:

   She was lovely and fair as the rose of summer,
   Yet 'twas not her beauty alone that won me,
   Oh, no! 'twas the truth in her eye ever dawning,
   That made me love Mary, the Rose of Tralee.

2. The cool shades of ev'ning their mantle were spreading,
   And Mary all smiling was list'ning to me,
   The moon thro' the valley her pale rays was shedding,
   When I won the heart of the Rose of Tralee:

   Though lovely and fair as the rose of the summer,
   Yet 'twas not her beauty alone that won me,
   Oh, no! 'twas the truth in her eye ever dawning,
   That made me love Mary, the Rose of Tralee.

# Rose of Washington Square

W: BALLARD MACDONALD / M: JAMES F. HANLEY
[from *Ziegfeld Midnight Frolic,* 1920]

1. A garden that never knew sunshine
   Once shelter'd a beautiful rose;
   In the shadows it grew without sunlight or dew,
   As a child of the city grows.

   A butterfly flew to the garden
   From out of the blue sky above;
   The heart of the rose set a-flutter
   With a wonderful tale of love.

   He told her of birds and of bees,
   Of the brooks and the meadows and trees.
       He whisper'd:

   *Chorus:*
   Rose of Washington Square,
   A flower so fair
       Should blossom where the sun shines;

   Rose, for nature did not mean
   That you should blush unseen,
       But be the queen of some fair garden.

   Rose, I'll never depart,
   But dwell in your heart,
       Your love to care;

   I'll bring the sunbeams from the Heavens to you,
   And give you kisses that sparkle with dew,
       My Rose of Washington Square.

2. But after the summer comes autumn,
   When flowers their petals must close;
   For the songbirds are still and the breezes are chill,
   To the cheek of the blushing rose.

   The gay butterfly's wings are folded,
   The heart of the rose has grown cold;
   A butterfly lives but a season,
   And a rose in a week grows old.

   The meadows, the brooks and the trees,
   Like the birds and the flowers and bees,
       Need sunshine:

   [*to Chorus*]

Rose of Washington Square,
I'm withering there,
   In basement air I'm fading;

Pose in plain or fancy clothes,
They say my Roman nose
   It seems to please artistic people.

Beaux, I've plenty of those,
With second-hand clothes
   And nice long hair;

I've got those Broadway vampires lashed to the mast,
I've got no future, but oh! what a past,
   I'm Rose of Washington Square.

# Rose Room
## (In Sunny Roseland)
W: HARRY H. WILLIAMS / M: ART HICKMAN (1917)

1. I want to take you to a little room,
A little room where all the roses bloom.
I want to lead you into Nature's Hall,
Where ev'ry year the roses give a ball.

   They have an orchestra up in the trees,
   For their musicians are the birds and bees.
   And they will sing us a song
   As we are stolling along:

   *Chorus:*
   In sunny Roseland, where summer breezes are playing,
   Where the honeybees are "a-Maying,"
   There all the roses are swaying,
   Dancing while the meadow brook flows.

   The moon when shining is more than ever designing,
   For 'tis ever then I am pining,
   Pining to be sweetly reclining
   Somewhere in Roseland beside a beautiful rose.

2. The ball is over and the tulips meet,
Their little kisses are so short and sweet.
The lilies nod to the forget-me-nots,
When they're departing in their flower pots.

But all the roses with the spirits high
Remain to love until they droop and die.
And, dear, why shouldn't it be
Just so with you and with me?

[*to Chorus*]


# 'Round Her Neck She Wore a Yellow Ribbon
AMERICAN FOLK SONG

1. 'Round her neck she wore a yellow ribbon,
   She wore it fall and winter and in the month of May.
   And if you asked her why the heck she wore it,
   She'd say it's for her lover who is far, far away . . .

   *Far away, far away,*
   *She'd say it's for her lover who is far, far away;*
   *Far away, far away,*
   *She wore it for her lover who is far, far away.*

2. 'Round her neck she wore a golden locket,
   She wore it in the night time and wore it ev'ry day.
   And if you asked her why the heck she wore it,
   She'd say it's for her lover who is far, far away . . .

   *Far away, far away,*
   *She'd say it's for her lover who is far, far away;*
   *Far away, far away,*
   *She wore it for her lover who is far, far away.*

3. In her home she kept a fire burning,
   She kept it fall and winter and in the month of May.
   And if you asked her why the heck she kept it,
   She'd say it's for her lover who is far, far away . . .

   *Far away, far away,*
   *She'd say it's for her lover who is far, far away;*
   *Far away, far away,*
   *She kept it for her lover who is far, far away.*

4. Saved her heart and saved her sweet kisses,
   Saved them fall and winter and in the month of May.
   And if you asked her why the heck she saved them,
   She'd say they're for her lover who is far, far away . . .

   *Far away, far away,*
   *She'd say they're for her lover who is far, far away;*
   *Far away, far away,*
   *She saved them for her lover who is far, far away.*

# Row, Row, Row

W: WILLIAM JEROME / M: JIMMIE V. MONACO (1912)

1. Young Johnnie Jones, he had a cute little boat,
And all the girlies he would take for a float;
    He had girlies on the shore,
    Sweet little peaches by the score.

   But Johnnie was a Weisenheimer, you know,
   His steady girl was Flo,
       And ev'ry Sunday afternoon,
       She'd jump in his boat and they would spoon.

   *Chorus:*
   And then he'd row, row, row,
   'Way up the river he would row, row, row;
   A hug he'd give her,
       Then he'd kiss her now and then,
       She would tell him when,
   He'd fool around and fool around
       And then they'd kiss again.

   And then he'd row, row, row,
   A little further he would row, oh, oh, oh, oh;
       *(first time)*
       Then he'd drop both his oars,
       Take a few more encores,
       And then he'd row, row, row.
       *(second time)*
       With her head on his breast,
       Then there's twenty bars rest,
       And then he'd row, row, row.

2. Right in his boat he had a cute little seat,
And ev'ry kiss he stole from Flo was so sweet;
    And he knew just how to row,
    He was a rowing Romeo.

   He knew an island where the trees were grand,
   He knew just where to land,
       Then tales of love he'd tell to Flo
       Until it was time to go.

   [*to Chorus*]

# Row, Row, Row Your Boat

FOUR-PART ROUND

*First Part*
Row, row, row your boat,

*Second Part*
Gently down the stream,

*Third Part*
Merrily, merrily,
Merrily, merrily,

*Fourth Part*
Life is but a dream.


# Rule, Britannia

W: DAVID MALLET or JAMES THOMSON
M: THOMAS AUGUSTINE ARNE (1740)
*(This "celebrated Ode, in Honour of Great-Britain," was written
in commemoration of the accession of the House of Hanover.)*

1. When Britain first at Heav'n's command
   Arose from out the azure main,
   Arose from out the azure main, the azure main,
   This was the charter, the charter of the land,
   And guardian angels sung this strain:

   *Chorus:*
   Rule, Britannia,
   Britannia rules the waves!
   Britons never shall be slaves.

   [*repeat Chorus*]

2. The nations not so blest as thee,
   Shall in their turn to tyrants bend,
   Shall in their turn to tyrants bend, to tyrants bend,
   Whilst thou shalt flourish, shalt flourish great and free,
   And to the weak protection lend.

   [*to Chorus, repeated*]

3. To thee belongs the rural reign,
   Thy cities shall with commerce shine,
   Thy cities shall with commerce shine, with commerce shine,
   And lands far over, far o'er the spreading main,
   Shall stretch a hand to grasp with thine.

   [*to Chorus, repeated*]

# The St. Louis Blues

W & M: W. C. HANDY (1914)

1. I hate to see the ev'nin' sun go down,
   Hate to see the ev'nin' sun go down,
   'Cause my baby, he done left this town.

   Feelin' tomorrow like I feel today,
   Feel tomorrow like I feel today,
   I'll pack my trunk, make my getaway.

   St. Louis woman, with her diamond rings,
   Pulls that man around by her apron strings;
   Weren't for powder and for store-bought hair,
   The man I love wouldn't go nowhere.

   *Chorus:*
   Got the St. Louis Blues just as blue as I can be,
   That man's got a heart like a rock cast in the sea,
   Or else he wouldn't have gone so far from me.
   *(spoken) Doggone it!*

2. Been to the Gypsy to get my fortune told,
   To the Gypsy to get my fortune told,
   'Cause I'm most wild 'bout my Jelly Roll.

   Gypsy done told me, "Don't you wear no black."
   Yes, she done told me, "Don't you wear no black.
   Go to St. Louis, you can win him back."

   Help me to Cairo, make St. Louis by myself,
   Git to Cairo, find my old friend Jeff;
   Goin' to pin myself close to his side,
   If I flag his train, I sure can ride.

   *Chorus:*
   I love that man like a schoolboy loves his pie,
   Like a Kentucky Col'nel loves his mint and rye,
   I'll love my baby till the day I die.

3. You ought to see that stovepipe brown of mine,
   Like he owns the Diamond Joseph line;
   He'd make a cross-eyed old man go stone blind.

   Blacker than midnight, teeth like flags of truce,
   Blackest man in the whole St. Louis,
   Blacker the berry, sweeter the juice.

   About a crap game he knows a pow'rful lot,
   But when worktime comes, he's on the dot;
   Goin' to ask him for a cold ten spot,
   What it takes to get it, he's certainly got.

*Chorus:*
A black-headed gal makes a freight train jump the track,
Said a black-headed gal makes a freight train jump the track,
But a long tall gal makes a preacher ball the Jack.

# Saint Patrick's Day
W: THOMAS MOORE (ca. 1810) / M: ENGLISH FOLK TUNE

Though dark are our sorrows, today we'll forget them,
  And smile through our tears like a sunbeam in show'rs.
There never were hearts, if our rulers would let them,
  More formed to be grateful and blest than ours.

But just when the chain has ceased to pain,
  And hope has enwreathed it round with flow'rs,
There comes a new link, our spirit to sink!

  *Chorus:*
  The joy that we taste, like the light of the poles
  Is a flash amid darkness too brilliant to stay;
  But tho't were the last spark in our souls
  We must light it up now on our prince's day.

# Sally in Our Alley
W & M: HENRY CAREY (1902)

1. Of all the girls that are so smart,
     There's none like pretty Sally;
   She is the darling of my heart,
     And lives in our alley.
   There is no lady in the land
     That's half so sweet as Sally;
   She is the darling of my heart,
     And lives in our alley.

2. Her father he makes cabbage-nets,
     And through the streets does cry 'em;
   Her mother she sells laces long
     To such as please to buy 'em.
   But sure such folks could ne'er beget
     So sweet a girl as Sally!
   She is the darling of my heart,
     And lives in our alley.

3. When she is by, I leave my work,
   I love her so sincerely;
   My master comes like any Turk
   And bangs me most severely.
   But let him bang his bellyful—
   I'll bear it all for Sally,
   For she is the darling of my heart,
   And lives in our alley.

4. Of all the days that's in the week
   I dearly love but one day,
   And that's the day that comes betwixt
   The Saturday and Monday.
   For then I'm dressed all in my best
   To walk abroad with Sally;
   She is the darling of my heart,
   And lives in our alley.

5. My master carries me to church,
   And often am I blamed
   Because I leave him in the lurch
   As soon as text is named.
   I leave the church in sermon-time
   And slink away to Sally;
   She is the darling of my heart,
   And lives in our alley.

6. When Christmas comes about again,
   Oh, then I shall have money!
   I'll hoard it up, and box and all
   I'll give it to my honey.
   Oh, would it were ten thousand pounds!
   I'd give it all to Sally;
   She is the darling of my heart,
   And lives in our alley.

# Santa Lucia

W & M: TEODORO COTTRAU (ca. 1850)
*(St. Lucia is a shoreline neighborhood in Naples.)*

1. Sul mare luccica
   L'astro d'argento,
   Placida è l'onda,
   Prospero il vento.

Venite all'agile
Barchetta mia:
Santa Lucia!
Santa Lucia!

2. Con questo zeffiro
Così soave,
Oh! com'à bello,
Star sulla nave!

Su passeggeri,
Venite via,
Santa Lucia!
Santa Lucia!

3. O dolce Napoli,
O suol beato,
Ove sorridere
Volle il creato.

Tu sei l'impero
Dell'armonia,
Santa Lucia!
Santa Lucia!

# Scarborough Fair
ENGLISH FOLK SONG

1. Where are you going? To Scarborough Fair?
   *Parsley, sage, rosemary and thyme,*
   Remember me to a bonny lass there,
   *For once she was a true lover of mine.*

2. Tell her to make me a cambric shirt,
   *Parsley, sage, rosemary and thyme,*
   Without any needle or thread work'd in it,
   *And she shall be a true lover of mine.*

3. Tell her to wash it in yonder well,
   *Parsley, sage, rosemary and thyme,*
   Where water ne'er sprung nor a drop of rain fell,
   *And she shall be a true lover of mine.*

4. Tell her to plough me an acre of land,
   *Parsley, sage, rosemary and thyme,*
   Between the sea and the salt sea strand,
   *And she shall be a true lover of mine.*

**5.** Tell her to plough it with one ram's horn,
*Parsley, sage, rosemary and thyme,*
And sow it all over with one peppercorn,
*And she shall be a true lover of mine.*

**6.** Tell her to reap it with a sickle of leather,
*Parsley, sage, rosemary and thyme,*
And tie it all up with a tom-tit's feather,
*And she shall be a true lover of mine.*

**7.** Tell her to gather it all in a sack,
*Parsley, sage, rosemary and thyme,*
And carry it home on a butterfly's back,
*And she shall be a true lover of mine.*

# Schnitzelbank
GERMAN CHILDREN'S TRADITIONAL
"ACCUMULATION" SONG

*Ei du schöne, ei du schöne,*
*Ei du schöne Schnitzelbank.*

**1.** Ist das nicht eine Schnitzelbank?
*Ja, das ist eine Schnitzelbank.*
Ist das nicht eine kurz und lang?
*Ja, das ist eine kurz und lang.*
Kurz und lang un'er Schnitzelbank!

*Ei du schöne, ei du schöne,*
*Ei du schöne Schnitzelbank.*

**2.** Ist das nicht ein Hin und Her?
*Ja, das ist ein Hin und Her.*
Ist das nicht eine Lichtputzschere?
*Ja, das ist eine Lichtputzschere.*
Lichtputzschere,
Hin und Her,
Kurz und lang un'er Schnitzelbank!

*Ei du schöne, ei du schöne,*
*Ei du schöne Schnitzelbank.*

**3.** Ist das nicht ein gold'ner Ring?
*Ja, das ist ein gold'ner Ring.*
Ist das nicht ein schönes Ding?
*Ja, das ist ein schönes Ding.*

Schönes Ding,
Gold'ner Ring,
Lichtputzschere,
Hin und Her,
Kurz und lang un'er Schnitzelbank!
*Ei du schöne, ei du schöne,*
*Ei du schöne Schnitzelbank.*

4. Ist das nicht ein Krumm und Grad?
*Ja, das ist ein Krumm und Grad.*
Ist das nicht ein Wagenrad?
*Ja, das ist ein Wagenrad.*
Wagenrad,
Krumm und Grad,
Schönes Ding,
Gold'ner Ring,
Lichtputzschere,
Hin und Her,
Kurz und lang un'er Schnitzelbank!

*Ei du schöne, ei du schöne,*
*Ei du schöne Schnitzelbank.*

5. Ist das nicht ein Geisenbock?
*Ja, das ist ein Geisenbock.*
Ist das nicht ein Reifenrock?
*Ja, das ist ein Reifenrock.*
Reifenrock,
Geisenbock,
Wagenrad,
Krumm und Grad,
Schönes Ding,
Gold'ner Ring,
Lichtputzschere,
Hin und Her,
Kurz und lang un'er Schnitzelbank!

*Ei du schöne, ei du schöne,*
*Ei du schöne Schnitzelbank.*

6. Ist das nicht eine gute Wurst?
Ja, das ist eine gute Wurst.
Ist das nicht ein grosser Durst?
Ja, das ist ein grosser Durst.
Grosser Durst,
Gute Wurst,
Reifenrock,
Geisenbock,

Wagenrad,
Krumm und Grad,
Schönes Ding,
Gold'ner Ring,
Lichtputzschere,
Hin und Her,
Kurz und lang un'er Schnitzelbank!

*Ei du schöne, ei du schöne,*
*Ei du schöne Schnitzelbank.*


# School Days
## (When We Were a Couple of Kids)
W: WILL D. COBB / M: GUS EDWARDS (1906)

1. Nothing to do, Nellie darling;
   Nothing to do, you say?
   Let's take a trip on memory's ship,
   Back to the bygone days.

   Sail to the old village school house,
   Anchor outside the school door.
   Look in and see, there's you and there's me,
   A couple of kids once more.

   *Chorus:*
   School days, school days,
   Dear old golden rule days;
   Readin' and 'ritin' and 'rithmetic,
   Taught to the tune of a hick'ry stick.

   You were my queen in calico,
   I was your bashful barefoot beau,
   And you wrote on my slate, "I love you so,"
   When we were a couple of kids.

2. 'Member the hill, Nellie darling,
   And the oak tree that grew on its brow?
   They've built forty stories upon that old hill,
   And the oak's an old chestnut now.

   'Member the meadows so green, dear,
   So fragrant with color and maize?
   Into new city lots and preferred bus'ness plots,
   They've cut them up since those days.

   [*to Chorus*]

# Shall We Gather at the River?

W & M: REV. ROBERT LOWRY

1. Shall we gather at the river,
   Where bright angel feet have trod;
   With its crystal tide forever
   Flowing from the throne of God?

   *Chorus:*
   Yes, we'll gather at the river,
   The beautiful, the beautiful river,
   Gather with the saints at the river
   That flows from the throne of God.

2. On the margin of the river,
   Washing up its silver spray,
   We shall walk and worship ever
   All the happy, golden day.

   [*to Chorus*]

3. On the bosom of the river,
   Where the Saviour-King we own,
   We shall meet and sorrow never
   'Neath the glory of the throne.

   [*to Chorus*]

4. Soon we'll reach the shining river,
   Soon our pilgrimage will cease;
   Soon our happy hearts will quiver
   With the melody of peace.

   [*to Chorus*]


# Shalom Chaverim

EIGHT-PART ROUND FROM ISRAEL

Shalom chaverim,
Shalom chaverim,
Shalom, shalom.

L'hitraot,
L'hitraot,
Shalom, shalom.

***Sung as a round***

*First Part*
  Shalom chaverim,

*Second Part*
  Shalom chaverim,

*Third Part*
  Shalom,

*Fourth Part*
  Shalom,

*Fifth Part*
  L'hitraot,

*Sixth Part*
  L'hitraot,

*Seventh Part*
  Shalom,

*Eighth Part*
  Shalom.

# The Sheik of Araby

W: HARRY B. SMITH & FRANCIS WHEELER
M: TED SNYDER (1921)

1. Over the desert wild and free
     Rides the bold Sheik of Araby.
   His Arab band at his command
     Follow his love's caravan.
   Under the shadow of the palms,
     He sings to call her to his arms:

     *Chorus:*
     "I'm the Sheik of Araby,
       Your love belongs to me.
     At night when you're asleep,
       Into your tent I'll creep.
     The stars that shine above
       Will light our way to love;
     You'll rule this land with me,
       The Sheik of Araby."

2. While stars are fading in the dawn,
   Over the desert they'll be gone;
   His captured bride close by his side,
   Swift as the wind they will ride.
   Proudly he scorns her smile or tear,
   Soon he will conquer love by fear.

   [*to Chorus*]

# She Is More to Be Pitied Than Censured

W & M: WILLIAM B. GRAY (1898)
(*"A Story of Life's 'Other Side' Taken From An Actual Occurence"*)

1. At the old concert hall on the Bow'ry,
   'Round a table were seated, one night,
   A crowd of young fellows carousing;
   With them, life seemed cheerful and bright.

   At the very next table was seated
   A girl who had fallen to shame;
   All the young fellows jeered at her weakness
   'Till they heard an old woman exclaim:

   > *Chorus:*
   > "She is more to be pitied than censured,
   > She is more to be helped than despised;
   > She is only a lassie who ventured
   > On life's stormy path, ill-advised.
   >
   > "Do not scorn her with words fierce and bitter,
   > Do not laugh at her shame and downfall,
   > For a moment just stop and consider
   > That a man was the cause of it all."

2. There's an old-fashioned church 'round the corner,
   Where the neighbors all gathered one day,
   While the parson was preaching a sermon
   O'er a soul that had just passed away.

   'Twas this same wayward girl from the Bow'ry,
   Who a life of adventure had led;
   Did the clergyman jeer at her downfall?
   No, he asked for God's mercy, and said:

   [*to Chorus*]

311

# She'll Be Comin' 'Round the Mountain

*(Originally "When the Chariot Comes," 1899, the song was adapted and spread by railroad work gangs in the American midwest at the turn of the century.)*

1. She'll be comin' 'round the mountain when she comes,
   She'll be comin' 'round the mountain when she comes,
   She'll be comin' 'round the mountain,
   She'll be comin' 'round the mountain,
   She'll be comin' 'round the mountain when she comes.

2. She'll be drivin' six white horses when she comes . . .
   *(etc.)*

3. She'll be shinin' just like silver when she comes . . .
   *(etc.)*

4. Oh, we'll all go out to meet her when she comes . . .
   *(etc.)*

5. She'll be breathin' smoke and fire when she comes . . .
   *(etc.)*

6. We'll be singin' "Hallelujah" when she comes . . .
   *(etc.)*

7. We will kill the old red rooster when she comes . . .
   *(etc.)*

8. We'll have chicken and some dumplin's when she comes . . .
   *(etc.)*


# Shenandoah

AMERICAN RIVER SONG

*(lst version)*

1. Oh, Shenandoah, I long to hear you,
   *Away, you rolling river,*
   Oh, Shenandoah, I long to hear you.
   *Away, I'm bound away*
   *'Cross the wide Missouri.*

2. Oh, Shenandoah, I love your daughter,
   *Away, you rolling river,*
   I'll take her 'cross that rolling water.
   *Away, I'm bound away*
   *'Cross the wide Missouri.*

3. This white man loves your Indian maiden,
   *Away, you rolling river,*
   In my canoe with notions laden.
   *Away, I'm bound away*
   *'Cross the wide Missouri.*

4. Farewell, goodbye, I shall not grieve you,
   *Away, you rolling river,*
   Oh, Shenandoah, I'll not deceive you.
   *Away, we're bound away*
   *'Cross the wide Missouri.*

*(2nd version)*

1. O Shenandoah, I love to hear you,
   Hi-oh, you rolling river,
   I'll take her 'cross the rolling water,
   *Ah-hah, I'm bound away*
   *'Cross the wide Missouri.*

2. For seven years I courted Sally.
   Hi-oh, you rolling river,
   For seven more I longed to have her,
   *Ah-hah, I'm bound away*
   *'Cross the wide Missouri.*

3. She said she would not be my lover,
   Hi-oh, you rolling river,
   Because I was a dirty sailor,
   *Ah-hah, I'm bound away*
   *'Cross the wide Missouri.*

4. A-drinkin' rum and a-chewin' t'baccer,
   Hi-oh, you rolling river,
   A-drinkin' rum and a-chewin' t'baccer,
   *Ah-hah, I'm bound away*
   *'Cross the wide Missouri.*

# Shew! Fly, Don't Bother Me

W: BILLY REEVES / M: FRANK CAMPBELL (1869)

[A favorite of Negro troops during the Civil War, the song was revived
in the play *Captain Jinks of the Horse Marines,* 1900.]

1. I think I hear the angels sing,
   I think I hear the angels sing,
   I think I hear the angels sing,
   The angels now are on the wing.

   I feel, I feel, I feel,
   That's what my mother said,
   The angels pouring 'lasses down,
   Upon this nigger's head.

   > *Chorus:*
   > Shew! fly, don't bother me,
   > Shew! fly, don't bother me,
   > Shew! fly, don't bother me,
   > I belong to Comp'ny G.

   I feel, I feel, I feel,
   I feel like a morning star,
     I feel, I feel, I feel,
     I feel like a morning star,
       I feel, I feel, I feel,
       I feel like a morning star,
         I feel, I feel, I feel,
         I feel like a morning star.

2. If I sleep in the sun, this nigger knows,
   If I sleep in the sun, this nigger knows,
   If I sleep in the sun, this nigger knows,
   A fly come sting him on the nose.

   I feel, I feel, I feel,
   That's what my mother said,
   Whenever this nigger goes to sleep,
   He must cover up his head.

   [*to Chorus*]

# Shine On, Harvest Moon

W & M: NORA BAYES-NORWORTH & JACK NORWORTH
[from *Ziegfeld Follies of 1908*]

1. The night was mighty dark so you could hardly see,
   For the moon refused to shine.
   Couple sitting underneath a willow tree,
   For love they pine.

   Little maid was kind-a 'fraid of darkness, so
   She said, "I guess I'll go."
   Boy began to sigh, looked up at the sky,
   Told the moon his little tale of woe.
   Oh—

   *Chorus:*
   Shine on, shine on harvest moon, up in the sky;
   I ain't had no lovin' since April, January, June or July.
   Snow time ain't no time to stay outdoors and spoon;
   So shine on, shine on harvest moon, for me and my gal.

2. Oh, can't see why a boy should sigh, when by his side
   Is the girl he loves so true.
   All he has to say is "Won't you be my bride,
   For I love you."

   Why should I be telling you this secret,
   When I know that you can guess?
   Harvest moon will smile, shine on all the while,
   If the little girl should answer, "Yes."

   [*to Chorus*]


# Silent Night

W: ORIGINAL GERMAN ("Stille Nacht, Heilige Nacht!")
   BY JOSEPH MOHR (1818)
M: FRANZ GRUBER (1832)

1. Silent night, holy night!
   All is calm, all is bright!
   'Round yon Virgin Mother and Child,
   Holy Infant, so tender and mild,
   Sleep in heavenly peace!
   Sleep in heavenly peace!

2. Silent night, holy night!
   Shepherds quake at the sight.
   Glories stream from heaven afar,
   Heav'nly hosts sing "Alleluia!"
   > Christ the Saviour is born!
   > Christ the Saviour is born!

3. Silent night, holy night!
   Wondrous star, lend thy light!
   With the angel let us sing
   Alleluia to our King!
   > Christ the Saviour is here,
   > Jesus the Saviour is here!

4. Silent night, holy night!
   Son of God, love's pure light,
   Radiant beams from thy holy face,
   With the dawn of redeeming grace,
   > Jesus, Lord, at thy birth,
   > Jesus, Lord, at thy birth!

# Silver Threads among the Gold

W: EBEN E. REXFORD / M: HART P. DANKS (1873)

1. Darling, I am growing old,
   Silver threads among the gold,
   Shine upon my brow today;
   Life is fading fast away.

   But, my darling, you will be, will be
   Always young and fair to me;
   Yes! my darling, you will be
   Always young and fair to me.

   > *Chorus:*
   > Darling, I am growing old,
   > Silver threads among the gold,
   > Shine upon my brow today;
   > Life is fading fast away.

2. When your hair is silver white,
   And your cheeks no longer bright,
   With the roses of the May;
   I will kiss your lips and say—

Oh! my darling, mine alone, alone,
You have never older grown,
Yes! my darling, mine alone,
You have never older grown!

[*to Chorus*]

3. Love can never more grow old,
   Locks may lose their brown and gold;
   Cheeks may fade and hollow grow,
   But the hearts that love will know

   Never, never winter's frost and chill:
   Summer warmth is in them still—
   Never, never winter's frost and chill:
   Summer warmth is in them still.

   [*to Chorus*]

4. Love is always young and fair—
   What to us is silver hair,
   Faded cheeks, or steps grown slow,
   To the heart that beats below?

   Since I kissed you, mine alone, alone,
   You have never older grown—
   Since I kissed you, mine alone, alone,
   You have never older grown.

   [*to Chorus*]


# Sing a Song of Sixpence
NURSERY SONG

1. Sing a song of sixpence,
   A pocket full of rye,
   Four and twenty blackbirds
   Baked in a pie.

   When the pie was opened,
   The birds began to sing;
   Wasn't that a dainty dish
   To set before a king?

2. The king was in his counting house,
   Counting all his money;
   The queen was in the parlor,
   Eating bread and honey;

317

The maid was in the garden,
Hanging out the clothes;
Down flew a blackbird
And pecked off her nose.


# Skip to My Lou
DANCE SONG OF THE AMERICAN WEST

1. Lost my partner, what'll I do,
   Lost my partner, what'll I do,
   Lost my partner, what'll I do,
   Skip to my Lou, my darling.

2. I'll get 'nother one, pretty one, too . . .
   *(etc.)*

3. Can't get a red bird, jay bird'll do . . .
   *(etc.)*

4. Lou, Lou, skip skip skip . . .
   *(etc.)*

5. Flies in the buttermilk, shoo shoo shoo . . .
   *(etc.)*

6. Gone again, what'll I do . . .
   *(etc.)*

7. I'll get a partner better than you . . .
   *(etc.)*

8. Can't get a blue bird, black bird'll do . . .
   *(etc.)*

9. I got another one, skip skip skip . . .
   *(etc.)*

10. Flies in the sugar bowl, shoo fly shoo . . .
    *(etc.)*

11. Cat's in the cream jar, ooh ooh ooh . . .
    *(etc.)*

12. Off to Texas, two by two . . .
    *(etc.)*

# Smiles
W: J. WILL CALLAHAN / M: LEE S. ROBERTS (1917)

1. Dearie, now I know
Just what makes me love you so,
Just what holds me and enfolds me
In its golden glow.

Dearie, now I see
'Tis each smile so bright and free,
For life's sadness turns to gladness
When you smile on me.

> *Chorus:*
> There are smiles that make us happy,
> There are smiles that make us blue,
> There are smiles that steal away the teardrops
> As the sunbeams steal away the dew;
>
> There are smiles that have a tender meaning
> That the eyes of love alone may see,
> And the smiles that fill my life with sunshine
> Are the smiles that you give to me.

2. Dearie, when you smile
Ev'rything in life's worthwhile,
Love grows fonder as we wander
Down each magic mile.

Cheery melodies
Seem to float upon the breeze,
Doves are cooing while they're wooing
In the leafy trees.

> [*to Chorus*]

# Smilin' Through
W & M: ARTHUR A. PENN (1919)
[introduced in the motion picture version (1922) of the play *Smilin' Through*]

There's a little brown road windin' over the hill
To a little white cot by the sea;
There's a little green gate
At whose trellis I wait,
While two eyes o' blue
Come smilin' through
At me!

There's a gray lock or two in the brown of the hair,
There's some silver in mine, too, I see;
   But in all the long years
   When the clouds brought their tears,
   Those two eyes o' blue
   Kept smilin' through
     At me!

  And if ever I'm left in this world all alone,
I shall wait for my call patiently;
   For if Heaven be kind,
   I shall wake there to find
   Those two eyes o' blue
   Still smilin' through
     At me!

# So Long, Mary

W & M: GEORGE M. COHAN
[from *Forty-five Minutes from Broadway,* 1905]

1. "It's awf'ly nice of all you girls to see me to the train."
   *"So long, Mary."*
  "I didn't think you'd care if you should ne'er see me again."
   *"You're wrong, Mary."*

"This reminds me of my family,
On the day I left Schenectady,
To the depot then they came with me,
I seem to hear them say:

   *Chorus:*
   'So long, Mary;
   Mary, we will miss you so.
   So long, Mary,
   How we hate to see you go;

   'And we'll all be longing for you, Mary,
   While you roam;
   So long, Mary,
   Don't forget to come back home.'"

2. "It's awf'ly nice of all you boys to see me off today."
   *"So long, Mary."*
  "I didn't think you'd care if I should either go or stay."
   *"You're wrong, Mary."*

"Yes, I'm going to other lands to dwell,
Awf'ly nice of you to wish me well;
Hardly thought a soul in New Rochelle
Would even come to say:

[*to Chorus*]


# Somebody Stole My Gal
W & M: LEO WOOD (1918)

1. Gee, but I'm lonesome, lonesome and blue,
   I've found out something I never knew;
   I know now what it means to be sad,
   For I've lost the best gal/(pal) I ever had;
   She/(He) only left yesterday,
   Somebody stole her/(him) away.

   > *Chorus:*
   > Somebody stole my gal/(pal),
   > Somebody stole/(left) my gal/(pal),
   > Somebody came and took her/(him) away,
   > She/(He) didn't even say she/(he) was leavin'.

   The kisses I loved so
   He's/(She's) getting now, I know,
   > And Gee!
   > I know that she/(he)
   > Would come to me
   > If she/(he) could see
   Her/(His) broken-hearted lonesome pal/(gal);
   Somebody stole my gal/(pal).

2. Angels, they say, are only above,
   I know that's wrong because my old love
   Sure is an angel, take it from me,
   And she's/(he's) all the angel I want to see;
   Maybe she'll/(he'll) come back some day,
   All I can do now is pray.

   [*to Chorus*]

321

# Some of These Days

W & M: SHELTON BROOKS (1910)

1. Two sweethearts courted happily for quite a while
   'Midst simple life of country folk;
   When the lad told girlie he must go away,
   Her little heart with grief 'most broke.

   She said, "You know it's true, I love you best of all,
   So, honey, don't you go away."
       Just as he went to go,
       It grieved the girlie so,
   These words he heard her say:

       *Chorus:*
       "Some of these days, you'll miss me, honey;
       Some of these days, you'll feel so lonely.
       You'll miss my hugging,
       You'll miss my kissing,
       You'll miss me, honey,
       When you go away.

       "I feel so lonely just for you only,
       For you know, honey, you've had your way;
       And when you leave me
       I know 'twill grieve me,
       You'll miss your little baby,
       Yes, some of these days."

2. The little girlie, feeling blue, said, "I'll go, too,
   And show him two can play this game."
   When her honey heard this melancholy news,
   He quickly came back home again.

   But when he reached the house, he found his girl was gone;
   So down he rushes to the train.
       While it was pulling out,
       He heard his girlie shout
   This loving sweet refrain:

       [*to Chorus*]

322

# Sometimes I Feel Like a Motherless Child
SPIRITUAL

1. Sometimes I feel like a motherless child,
   Sometimes I feel like a motherless child,
   Sometimes I feel like a motherless child,
   A long ways from home,
   A long ways from home.

2. Sometimes I feel I'm almost gone,
   Sometimes I feel I'm almost gone,
   Sometimes I feel I'm almost gone,
   A long ways from home,
   A long ways from home.

# Sourwood Mountain
AMERICAN FOLK SONG

1. Chicken crowin' on Sourwood Mountain,
   *Hey de-ing dang, diddle-ally day*
   So many pretty girls, I can't count 'em.
   *Hey de-ing dang, diddle-ally day*

   My true love, she lives in Letcher,
   *Hey de-ing dang, diddle-ally day*
   She won't come and I won't fetch 'er.
   *Hey de-ing dang, diddle-ally day*

2. My true love's a blue-eyed daisy,
   *Hey de-ing dang, diddle-ally day*
   If I don't get her, I'll go crazy.
   *Hey de-ing dang, diddle-ally day*

   Big dogs bark and little ones bite you,
   *Hey de-ing dang, diddle-ally day*
   Big girls court and little ones slight you.
   *Hey de-ing dang, diddle-ally day*

3. My true love lives by the river,
   *Hey de-ing dang, diddle-ally day*
   A few more jumps and I'll be with 'er.
   *Hey de-ing dang, diddle-ally day*

   My true love lives up the hollow,
   *Hey de-ing dang, diddle-ally day*
   She won't come and I won't follow.
   *Hey de-ing dang, diddle-ally day*

# Standin' in the Need of Prayer

SPIRITUAL

*Chorus:*
It's me, it's me, O Lord,
Standin' in the need of prayer;
It's me, it's me, O Lord,
Standin' in the need of prayer.

1. Not my brother, not my sister,
    but it's me, O Lord,
Standin' in the need of prayer.
Not my brother, not my sister,
    but it's me, O Lord,
Standin' in the need of prayer.

    [*to Chorus*]

2. Not my father, not my mother,
    but it's me, O Lord,
Standin' in the need of prayer.
Not my father, not my mother,
    but it's me, O Lord,
Standin' in the need of prayer.

    [*to Chorus*]

3. Not my preacher, not my teacher,
    but it's me, O Lord,
Standin' in the need of prayer.
Not my preacher, not my teacher,
    but it's me, O Lord,
Standin' in the need of prayer.

    [*to Chorus*]

# The Star Spangled Banner
AMERICAN NATIONAL ANTHEM

W: FRANCIS SCOTT KEY (1814) / M: JOHN STAFFORD SMITH (1777?)

*(Smith's popular melody—originally known as* The Anacreontic Song,
*referring to the style of the Greek poet Anacreon—was used as the setting*
*for over 80 different printed American poems, almost all of a patriotic*
*nature, from 1790 to 1820. The melody, together with Key's poem, first*
*appeared in 1814.)*

1. Oh! say, can you see by the dawn's early light,
    What so proudly we hail'd at the twilight's last gleaming,
    Whose stripes and bright stars, thro' the perilous fight,
    O'er the ramparts we watch'd were so gallantly streaming!
      And the rocket's red glare, the bombs bursting in air,
      Gave proof thro' the night that our flag was still there.
      *Oh! say, does that star spangled banner yet wave,*
      *O'er the land of the free, and the home of the brave?*

2. On the shore, dimly seen through the mists of the deep,
    Where the foe's haughty host in dread silence reposes,
    What is that which the breeze o'er the towering steep,
    As it fitfully blows, half conceals, half discloses?
      Now it catches the gleam of the morning's first beam,
      In full glory reflected, now shines on the stream.
      *'Tis the star spangled banner; O! long may it wave*
      *O'er the land of the free, and the home of the brave.*

3. And where is the band who so vauntingly swore
    That the havoc of war and the battle's confusion,
    A home and a country should leave us no more?
    Their blood has washed out their foul footstep's pollution.
      No refuge could save the hireling and slave
      From the terror of flight or the gloom of the grave—
      *And the star spangled banner in triumph doth wave*
      *O'er the land of the free, and the home of the brave.*

4. O! thus be it forever when freemen shall stand
    Between their loved home and the war's desolation;
    Blest with vict'ry and peace, may the heaven-rescued land
    Praise the pow'r that hath made and preserved us a nation.
      Then conquer we must, when our cause it is just,
      And this be our motto, "In God is our trust!"
      *And the star spangled banner in triumph shall wave*
      *O'er the land of the free, and the home of the brave.*

# The Streets of New York

W: HENRY BLOSSOM / M: VICTOR HERBERT

[from *The Red Mill*, 1906]

1. In dear old New York, it's remarkable very!
   The name on the lamppost is unnecessary!
   You merely have to see the girls
   To know what street you're on!

   Fifth Avenue beauties and dear old Broadway girls!
   The tailormade shoppers, the Avenue "A" girls,
   They're strictly all right but they're different quite,
   In the diff'rent parts of town.

   *Chorus:*
   In old New York! In old New York!
   The peach crop's always fine!
   They're sweet and fair and on the square!
   The maids of Manhattan for mine!

   You cannot see in gay Paree,
   In London or in Cork
   The queens you'll meet on any street
   In old New York.

2. If a spare afternoon you should happen to have and you
   Start on a leisurely stroll up Fifth Avenue,
   There is where with haughty air
   You'll see them as they walk!

   With velvets and laces and sables enfolding them,
   Really you'll nearly fall dead on beholding them,
   Lucky's the earl that can marry a girl
   From Fifth Avenue, New York.

   [*to Chorus*]

3. Whatever the weather is shining or showery,
   That doesn't "cut any ice" on the Bowery;
   Every night till broad daylight,
   They dance and sing and talk!

   The girls are all game and they're jolly good fellows,
   They're not very swell but they're none of them jealous;
   They go it alone in a style of their own
   On the Bowery in New York.

   [*to Chorus*]

# Sucking Cider Through a Straw
AMERICAN FOLK SONG

1. The prettiest girl
   That ever I saw,
   Was sucking cider
   Through a straw.

   [*optional: repeat each verse*]

2. I told that gal
   I didn't see how
   She sucked the cider
   Through a straw.

3. And cheek by cheek
   And jaw by jaw,
   We sucked that cider
   Through that straw.

4. And all at once
   That straw did slip;
   I sucked some cider
   From her lip.

5. And now I've got
   Me a mother-in-law
   From sucking cider
   Through a straw.


# Sunbonnet Sue
## (When I Was a Kid So High)
W: WILL D. COBB / M: GUS EDWARDS (1908)

1. So that is your new Sunday bonnet?
   Well, Sue, it's becoming to you;
   With those wonderful things you have on it,
   You'll make them "some jealous," dear Sue.

   But somehow it sets me to dreaming
   Of the day we first said, "Howdy-do,"
       And I see you once more
       In the bonnet you wore
   When I nicknamed you "Sunbonnet Sue."

*Chorus:*
Sunbonnet Sue, Sunbonnet Sue,
Sunshine and roses ran second to you;
   You looked so nice,
   I kissed you twice
Under your sunbonnet blue.

It was only a kind of a "kid kiss,"
But it tasted lots nicer than pie,
   And the next thing I knew
   I was dead stuck on you,
When I was a kid so high.

2. So that is your new Sunday bonnet?
Well, Sue, I must "hand it to you";
It's a dream, and the day that you don it
They'll take them "some notice," dear Sue.

But though it's a crown for a queen, dear,
In my heart there's a soft spot or two
   For the knot that I tied,
   That tied my heart inside,
When I tied your old Sunbonnet Sue.

[*to Chorus*]


# Sur le Pont d'Avignon
FRENCH CHILDREN'S SONG

*Chorus:*
Sur le pont d'Avignon
L'on y danse, l'on y danse;
Sur le pont d'Avignon
L'on y danse tout en rond.

[*Bows and curtsies*]
Les belles dames font comme ça,
Et puis encore comme ça.

   [*repeat Chorus*]

Les beaux messieurs font comme ça,
Et puis encore comme ça.

   [*repeat Chorus*]

Les cordonniers font comme ça,
Et puis encore comme ça.

[*repeat Chorus*]

Les blanchisseuses font comme ça,
Et puis encore comme ça.

[*repeat Chorus*]

## Sussex Carol
TRADITIONAL ENGLISH

1. On Christmas night all Christians sing
   To hear the news the angels bring,
   *On Christmas night all Christians sing*
   *To hear the news the angels bring;*
   News of great joy, news of great mirth,
   News of our merciful King's birth.

2. Then why should men on earth be sad,
   Since our Redeemer made us glad,
   *Then why should men on earth be sad,*
   *Since our Redeemer made us glad,*
   When from our sins he set us free,
   All for to gain our liberty?

3. When sin departs before his grace,
   Then life and health come in its place,
   *When sin departs before his grace,*
   *Then life and health come in its place;*
   Angels and men with joy may sing,
   All for to see the newborn King.

4. All out of darkness we have light,
   Which made the angels sing this night,
   *All out of darkness we have light,*
   *Which made the angels sing this night:*
   "Glory to God and peace to men,
   Now and forevermore. Amen."

# Swanee

W: IRVING CAESAR / M: GEORGE GERSHWIN (1919)

1. I've been away from you a long time,
   I never thought I'd miss you so,
      Somehow I feel
      Your love was real,
   Near you I long to be.

   The birds are singing, it is song-time,
   The banjos strummin' soft and low;
      I know that you
      Yearn for me, too,
   Swanee, you're calling me.

   *Chorus:*
   Swanee, how I love you! how I love you!
   My dear old Swanee.
   I'd give the world to be
   Among the folks in D-I-X-I-Even know

   My Mammy's
   Waiting for me,
   Praying for me
   Down by the Swanee.

   The folks up north will see me no more
   When I go to the Swanee shore.

2. Among the city ways I wander,
   I know the sunshine and the cloud,
      Still all the while,
      My Mammy's smile
   Lives in my memory.

   I want my homeland over yonder,
   I'm just a stranger 'mid the crowd,
      Swanee, I know
      I've got to go,
   Swanee, you're calling me.

   *Trio:*
   Swanee, Swanee,
   I am coming back to Swanee,
   Mammy, Mammy,
   I love the old folks at home.

   [*to Chorus*]

# Sweet Adeline
## (You're the Flower of My Heart)
W: RICHARD H. GERARD / M: HARRY W. ARMSTRONG (1903)

1. In the evening when I sit alone a-dreaming
   Of days gone by, love, to me so dear,
   There's a picture that in fancy oft appearing
   Brings back the time, love, when you were near.

   It is then I wonder where you are, my darling,
   And if your heart to me is still the same,
   For the sighing wind and nightingale a-singing
   Are breathing only your own sweet name:

   > *Chorus:*
   > Sweet Adeline,
   > My Adeline,
   > At night, dear heart,
   > For you I pine.
   >
   > In all my dreams
   > Your fair face beams,
   > You're the flower of my heart,
   > Sweet Adeline.

2. I can see your smiling face as when we wandered
   Down by the brookside, just you and I;
   And it seems so real at times, 'til I awaken
   To find all vanished, a dream gone by.

   If we meet sometime in after years, my darling,
   I trust that I will find your love still mine,
   Tho' my heart is sad and clouds above are hov'ring,
   The sun again, love, for me would shine.

   > [*to Chorus*]


# Sweet and Low
W: ALFRED LORD TENNYSON (1850) / M: J. BARNBY (1863)

1. Sweet and low, sweet and low,
   Wind of the western sea;
   Low, low, breathe and blow,
   Wind of the western sea;

   Over the rolling waters go,
   Come from the dying moon and blow,
   Blow him again to me
   While my little one, while my pretty one sleeps.

2. Sleep and rest, sleep and rest,
   Father will come to thee soon;
   Rest, rest on mother's breast,
   Father will come to thee soon;

   Father will come to his babe in the nest,
   Silver sails all out of the west,
   Under the silver moon
   Sleep, my little one, sleep, my pretty one, sleep.

# Sweet Betsy from Pike
AMERICAN WAGON SONG

1. Oh, don't you remember sweet Betsy from Pike,
   Who crossed the big mountains with her lover, Ike,
   With two yoke of oxen, a large yellow dog,
   And a Shanghai rooster an' one spotted hog.

   *Chorus:*
   "Goodbye, Pike County,
   Farewell for awhile.
   We will come back again
   When we pan out our pile."

2. The Shanghai ran off an' the oxen all died.
   That morning, the last piece of bacon was fried.
   Poor Ike got discouraged an' Betsy got mad,
   An' the dog wagged his tail an' looked wond'rously sad.

   [*to Chorus*]

3. The wagon broke down with a terrible crash,
   And out on the prairie rolled all sorts of trash.
   A few little baby clothes done up with care
   Looked a little suspicious but all on the square.

   [*to Chorus*]

4. The Injuns came down in a wild yellin' horde,
   And Betsy was skeered they would scalp her adored.
   Behind the front wagon wheel Betsy did crawl,
   It was there she fought Injuns with musket and ball.

   [*to Chorus*]

**5.** They soon reached the desert, where Betsy gave out,
    An' down in the sand she lay rollin' about,
    While Ike in great horror looked on with surprise
    Saying, "Betsy, get up, you'll get sand in your eyes."

    [*to Chorus*]

**6.** Sweet Betsy got up with a great deal of pain,
    An' said she'd go back to Pike County again.
    But Ike gave a sigh and they fondly embraced
    An' they travelled along with his arm 'round her waist.

    [*to Chorus*]

# The Sweetest Story Ever Told
## (Tell Me, Do You Love Me)
W & M: R. M. STULTS (1892)

**1.** Oh answer me a question, love, I pray,
    My heart for thee is pining day by day;
    Oh answer me, my dearest, answer true,
    Hold me close as you were wont to do.

    Whisper once again the story old,
    The dearest, sweetest story ever told;
    Whisper once again the story old,
    The dearest, sweetest story ever told.

**2.** Oh tell me that your heart to me is true,
    Repeat to me the story ever new;
    Oh take my hand in yours and tell me, dear,
    Is it joy to thee when I am near?

    Whisper o'er and o'er the story old,
    The dearest, sweetest story ever told;
    Whisper o'er and o'er the story old,
    The dearest, sweetest story ever told.

# Sweet Genevieve

W: GEORGE COOPER / M: HENRY TUCKER (1869)

1. O, Genevieve, I'd give the world
   To live again the lovely past!
   The rose of youth was dew-impearled,
   But now it withers in the blast.

   I see thy face in ev'ry dream,
   My waking thoughts are full of thee;
   Thy glance is in the starry beam
   That falls along the summer sea.

   *Chorus:*
   O, Genevieve, sweet Genevieve,
   The days may come, the days may go,
   But still the hands of mem'ry weave
   The blissful dreams of long ago.

   *Coda ( ad lib ):*
   O, Genevieve!

2. Fair Genevieve, my early love,
   The years but make thee dearer far!
   My heart shall never, never rove:
   Thou art my only guiding star.

   For me the past has no regret
   Whate'er the years may bring to me;
   I bless the hour when first we met—
   The hour that gave me love and thee!

# The Sweetheart of Sigma Chi

W: BYRON D. STOKES / M: F. DUDLEIGH VERNOR (1912)

1. When the world goes wrong, as it's bound to do,
   And you've broken Dan Cupid's bow,
   And you long for the girl you used to love,
   The maid of the long ago,

   Why, light your pipe, bid sorrow avaunt,
   Blow the smoke from your altar of dreams,
   And wreathe the face of your dream-girl there,
   The love that is just what it seems.

*Chorus:*
The girl of my dreams is the sweetest girl
Of all the girls I know;
Each sweet co-ed, like a rainbow trail,
Fades in the afterglow.

The blue of her eyes and the gold of her hair
Are a blend of the western sky;
And the moonlight beams on the girl of my dreams,
She's the Sweetheart of Sigma Chi.

2. Ev'ry magic breeze wafts a kiss to you,
From the lips of your "Sweet Sixteen,"
And one by one, the maids you knew,
Bow to your Meerschaum Queen.

As years drift by on the tides of time,
And they all have forgotten but you,
Then the girl of your dreams the sweeter seems,
She's the girl who is always true.

[*to Chorus*]


# Sweethearts

W: ROBERT B. SMITH / M: VICTOR HERBERT
[from *Sweethearts*, 1913]

1. If you ask where love is found,
The sort of love that's fond and true,
I will bid you look around;
It may be very near to you.

Sometimes love is very trying,
But you really must not mind it;
If it comes not to your sighing,
There is always one place you may find it—

Seek the dwelling of two happy sweethearts,
You will find it there!

*Chorus* [*Waltz*]:
Sweethearts make love their very own,
Sweethearts can live on love alone;
For them the eyes where lovelight lies
Open the gates to Paradise!

All other love is doomed to fade,
It is like sunshine veiled in shade;
Such joys of life as love imparts
Are all of them yours, sweethearts!

2. Love that's real will come to stay,
And ev'ry kiss will feed the flame;
Love that lingers for a day
Is most unworthy of the name.

When it softly comes a-stealing
To your heart, then you will know it;
You may fight against revealing,
But a word, a sigh, a glance, will show it.

Still if you love like other sweethearts,
You have naught to fear.

[*to Chorus*]


# Sweet Rosie O' Grady

W & M: MAUDE NUGENT (1896)

1. Just down around the corner of the street where I reside,
There lives the cutest little girl that I have ever spied;
Her name is Rosie O'Grady and, I don't mind telling you,
That she's the sweetest little rose the garden ever grew.

*Chorus:*
Sweet Rosie O'Grady,
My dear little Rose,
She's my steady lady,
Most ev'ryone knows;

And when we are married,
How happy we'll be;
I love sweet Rosie O'Grady,
And Rosie O'Grady loves me.

2. I never shall forget the day she promised to be mine,
As we sat telling love-tales, in the golden summertime.
'Twas on her finger that I placed a small engagement ring,
While in the trees, the little birds this song they seemed to sing!

[*to Chorus*]

# Swing Low, Sweet Chariot
SPIRITUAL

*Chorus:*
Swing low, sweet chariot,
Comin' for to carry me home;
Swing low, sweet chariot,
Comin' for to carry me home.

1. I looked over Jordan and what did I see,
   *Comin' for to carry me home*
   A band of angels comin' after me,
   *Comin' for to carry me home.*

   [*to Chorus*]

2. And if you get up there before I do,
   *Comin' for to carry me home*
   Tell all my friends that I'm a-comin' too,
   *Comin' for to carry me home.*

   [*to Chorus*]

3. The brightest of bright days that ever I saw,
   *Comin' for to carry me home*
   When Jesus washed my mortal sins away,
   *Comin' for to carry me home.*

   [*to Chorus*]

4. Now sometimes I'm up, and sometimes I'm 'way down,
   *Comin' for to carry me home*
   But still my soul feels heavenly bound,
   *Comin' for to carry me home.*

   [*to Chorus*]


# Take Me Out to the Ball Game
W: JACK NORWORTH / M: ALBERT VON TILZER (1908)

1. Katie Casey was baseball mad,
   Had the fever and had it bad;
   Just to root for the hometown crew,
   Ev'ry sou Katie blew.

   On a Saturday, her young beau
   Called to see if she'd like to go
   To see a show, but Miss Kate said, "No,
   I'll tell you what you can do:

*Chorus:*
"Take me out to the ball game,
Take me out with the crowd,
Buy me some peanuts and cracker jack,
I don't care if I ever get back.

"Let me root, root, root for the home team,
If they don't win, it's a shame,
For it's one, two, three strikes, you're out
At the old ball game."

2. Katie Casey saw all the games,
Knew the players by their first names;
Told the umpire he was wrong
All along, good and strong.

When the score was just two to two,
Katie Casey knew what to do;
Just to cheer up the boys she knew,
She made the gang sing this song:

[*to Chorus*]

# Taps

W: GEN. DANIEL BUTTERFIELD (1862)
M: OLIVER WILLCOX NORTON
*( An alternative to the then-traditional "Extinguish Lights," this bugle call was not called "Taps" until years later. No sensible explanation of the title has been given.)*

Day is done;
Gone the sun
From the lake,
From the hills,
From the sky.

Soldier sleep/(Safely rest),
All is well,
God is nigh.

# Ta-ra-ra Boom-de-ay!

W & M: HENRY J. SAYERS (?) (1891)
*( An early version gives the title as "Ta-ra-ra Boom-der-é." )*

1. A smart and stylish girl you see,
   Belle of good society;
   Not too strict, but rather free,
   Yet as right as right can be!

   Never forward, never bold—
   Not too hot and not too cold,
   But the very thing, I'm told,
   That in your arms you'd like to hold!

   > *Chorus:*
   > Ta-ra-ra Boom-de-ay!
   > Ta-ra-ra Boom-de-ay!
   > Ta-ra-ra Boom-de-ay!
   > Ta-ra-ra Boom-de-ay!
   > (*repeat*)

2. I'm not extravagantly shy,
   And when a nice young man is nigh,
   For his heart I have a try—
   And faint away with fearful cry!

   When the good young man, in haste,
   Will support me 'round the waist;
   I don't come to, while thus embraced,
   Till of my lips he steals a taste!

   [*to Chorus*]

3. I'm a timid flow'r of innocence,
   Pa says that I have no sense—
   I'm one eternal big expense;
   But men say that I'm just immense!

   Ere my verses I conclude,
   I'd like it known and understood,
   Tho' free as air, I'm never rude—
   I'm not too bad and not too good!

   [*to Chorus*]

4. You should see me out with Pa,
   Prim, and most particular;
   The young men say, "Ah, there you are!"
   And Pa says, "That's peculiar!"

339

"It's like their cheek!" I say, and so
Off again with Pa I go—
He's quite satisfied—although,
When his back's turned—well, you know—

[*to Chorus*]

5. When with swells I'm out to dine,
All my hunger I resign;
Taste the food, and sip the wine—
No such daintiness as mine!

But when I am all alone,
For shortcomings I atone!
No old frumps to stare like stone—
Chops and chicken on my own!

[*to Chorus*]

6. Sometimes Pa says, with a frown,
"Soon you'll have to settle down—
Have to wear your wedding gown—
Be the strictest wife in town!"

Well, it must come by-and-by—
When wed, to keep quiet I'll try;
But till then I shall not sigh,
I shall still go in for my—

[*to Chorus*]


# Ten Little Fingers and Ten Little Toes
W: HARRY PEASE & JOHNNY WHITE
M: IRA SCHUSTER & ED G. NELSON (1921)

1. I've got ten little fingers and ten little toes,
  Down in Tennessee,
  Waiting there for me;
I never had a baby call me "Dada,"
  How proud I know I'll be
  When I hear it calling me, O gee!

I'll kiss ev'ry finger, I'll kiss ev'ry toe,
At Home Sweet Home I'll linger
  For they'll need me there, I know;
Altho' it only weighs ten pounds and just one day old,
I wouldn't give it up for all the world and its gold;

  For I've got ten little fingers and ten little toes,
  Waiting down in Tennessee for me.

**2.** I've got ten little fingers and ten little toes,
    Down in Tennessee,
    Waiting there for me;
  Oh, how I'll hold it, in my arms enfold it,
    When night-time shadows creep,
    I will lull it fast asleep;

And then I'll count ev'ry finger, I'll count ev'ry toe,
Close to his side I'll linger
For he'll want me there I know;
If he looks like his mother, what a child he must be,
But if he looks like me, then he's got my sympathy;

    For I've ten little fingers and ten little toes
    Waiting down in Tennessee for me.

# Ten Little Indians
CHILDREN'S COUNTING SONG

    *One* little, *two* little, *three* little Indians,
    *Four* little, *five* little, *six* little Indians,
    *Seven* little, *eight* little, *nine* little Indians,
    *Ten* little Indian boys.

    *Ten* little, *nine* little, *eight* little Indians,
    *Seven* little, *six* little, *five* little Indians,
    *Four* little, *three* little, *two* little Indians,
    *One* little Indian boy.

# Tenting on the Old Camp-Ground
W & M: WALTER KITTREDGE (ca. 1863)

**1.** We're tenting tonight on the old camp-ground;
    Give us a song to cheer
    Our weary hearts, a song of home
    And friends we love so dear.

    *Chorus:*
    Many are the hearts that are weary tonight,
    Wishing for the war to cease;
    Many are the hearts looking for the right,
    To see the dawn of peace.
      *Tenting tonight, tenting tonight,*
      *Tenting on the old camp-ground.*

2. We've been tenting tonight on the old camp-ground,
   Thinking of days gone by,
   Of the loved ones at home that gave us the hand,
   And the tear that said, "Good-by!"

   *[to Chorus]*

3. We are tired of war on the old camp-ground;
   Many are the dead and gone
   Of the brave and true who've left their homes;
   Others been wounded long.

   *[to Chorus]*

4. We've been fighting tonight on the old camp-ground,
   Many are lying near;
   Some are dead, and some are dying—
   Many are in tears.

   *Final Chorus:*
   Many are the hearts that are weary tonight,
   Wishing for the war to cease;
   Many are the hearts looking for the light,
   To see the dawn of peace.
       *Dying tonight, dying tonight,*
       *Dying on the old camp-ground.*


# There Is a Tavern in the Town

W & M: WILLIAM H. HILLS (?) (1883)
*(possibly originated as a song sung by Cornish miners: "There is an
ale-house in our town")*

1. There is a tavern in the town, in the town,
   And there my dear love sits him down, sits him down
   And drinks his wine 'mid joyous laughter free
   And never never thinks of me.

   *Chorus:*
   Fare thee well for I must leave thee,
   Do not let the parting grieve thee,
   And remember that the best of friends must part.

   Adieu, adieu, kind friends, adieu, sweet adieu.
   I can no longer stay with you, stay with you.
   I'll hang my harp on a weeping willow tree
   And may the world go well with thee.

2. He left me for a damsel dark, damsel dark,
   Each Friday night they used to spark, used to spark.
   And now my love, who once was true to me,
   Takes that dark damsel on his knee.

   [*to Chorus*]

3. Oh dig my grave both wide and deep, wide and deep,
   Put tombstones at my head and feet, head and feet,
   And on my breast carve just a turtle dove
   To signify I died of love.

   [*to Chorus*]


# There's a Little Wheel a-Turning
SPIRITUAL

1. There's a little wheel a-turning in my heart,
   There's a little wheel a-turning in my heart,
      In my heart, in my heart,
   There's a little wheel a-turning in my heart.

2. Oh, I feel so very happy in my heart,
   Oh, I feel so very happy in my heart,
      In my heart, in my heart,
   Oh, I feel so very happy in my heart.


# There's a Long, Long Trail
W: STODDARD KING / M: ZO ELLIOTT (1914)

1. Nights are growing very lonely,
   Days are very long;
   I'm a-growing weary only
   List'ning for your song.

   Old remembrances are thronging
   Thro' my memory,
   Till it seems the world is full of dreams
   Just to call you back to me.

      *Chorus:*
      There's a long, long trail a-winding
      Into the land of my dreams,
      Where the nightingales are singing
      And a white moon beams.

There's a long, long night of waiting
Until my dreams all come true,
Till the day when I'll be going down
That long, long trail with you.

2. All night long I hear you calling,
Calling sweet and low;
Seem to hear your footsteps falling
Ev'rywhere I go.

Tho' the road between us stretches
Many a weary mile,
I forget that you're not with me yet,
When I think I see you smile.

[*to Chorus*]

# They Didn't Believe Me

W: HERBERT REYNOLDS / M: JEROME KERN
[from *The Girl from Utah*, 1914]

1. (He)
Got the cutest little way,
Like to watch you all the day,
And it certainly seems fine
Just to think that you'll be mine.

When I see your pretty smile,
Makes the living worth the while,
So I've got to run around
Telling people what I've found.

*Chorus:*
And when I told them how beautiful you are,
They didn't believe me, they didn't believe me!
Your lips, your eyes, your cheeks, your hair
    are in a class beyond compare,
You're the loveliest girl that one could see!

And when I tell them, and I cert'n'ly am goin' to tell them,
That I'm the man whose wife one day you'll be,
They'll never believe me, they'll never believe me
That from this great big world you've chosen me!

2. (She)
Don't know how it happened quite,
May have been the summer night,
May have been, well, who can say?
Things just happen any way.

All I know is I said "yes!"
Hesitating more or less,
And you kissed me where I stood,
Just like any fellow would.

*Chorus:*
And when I told them how wonderful you are,
They didn't believe me, they didn't believe me!
Your lips, your eyes, your curly hair
    are in a class beyond compare,
You're the loveliest thing that one could see!

And when I tell them, and I cert'n'ly am goin' to tell them,
That I'm the girl whose boy one day you'll be,
They'll never believe me, they'll never believe me
That from this great big world you've chosen me!


# This Old Hammer
AMERICAN RAILROAD SONG

1. This old hammer
   Shine like silver,
   Shine like gold, boys,
   Shine like gold.

   *[repeat each verse]*

2. Well, don't you hear that
   Hammer ringing?
   Drivin' in steel, boys,
   Drivin' in steel.

3. Can't find a hammer
   On this old mountain,
   Rings like mine, boys,
   Rings like mine.

4. I've been working
   On this old mountain
   Seven long years, boys,
   Seven long years.

5. I'm going back to
   Swannanoa Town-o,
   That's my home, boys,
   That's my home.

6. Take this hammer,
   Give it to the captain,
   Tell him I'm gone, boys,
   Tell him I'm gone.

# This Old Man

CHILDREN'S COUNTING SONG

1. This old man, he played *one,*
   He played knick knack on his thumb.
   *Knick knack paddy whack, give your dog a bone,*
   *This old man came rolling home.*

2. This old man, he played *two,*
   He played knick knack on his shoe.
   *Knick knack paddy whack, give your dog a bone,*
   *This old man came rolling home.*

3. This old man, he played *three,*
   He played knick knack on his knee.
   (*etc.*)

4. This old man, he played *four,*
   He played knick knack on the floor.
   (*etc.*)

5. This old man, he played *five,*
   He played knick knack on his hives.
   (*etc.*)

6. This old man, he played *six,*
   He played knick knack on his sticks.
   (*etc.*)

7. This old man, he played *seven,*
   He played knick knack up to heaven.
   (*etc.*)

8. This old man, he played *eight,*
   He played knick knack on his pate.
   (*etc.*)

9. This old man, he played *nine,*
   He played knick knack on his spine.
   (*etc.*)

10. This old man, he played *ten,*
     He played knick knack now and then.
        (*etc.*)

# This Train
SPIRITUAL

1. This train is bound for glory,
       This train—
   This train is bound for glory,
       This train—
   This train is bound for glory,
       Don't ride nothin' but the good and holy,
   This train is bound for glory,
       This train!

2. This train don't pull no extras,
       This train—
   This train don't pull no extras,
       This train—
   This train don't pull no extras,
       Don't pull nothin' but the midnight special,
   This train don't pull no extras,
       This train!

# Three Blind Mice
NURSERY SONG SUNG AS A FOUR-PART ROUND
*(Believed to be the earliest printed secular song that is still well known.*
*Words and music, both anonymous, were published in 1609.)*

*First Part:*
    Three blind mice,
    Three blind mice,

*Second Part:*
    See how they run!
    See how they run!

*Third part:*
    They all ran after the farmer's wife,
    She cut off their tails with a carving knife!

*Fourth part:*
    Did you ever see such a sight in your life
    As three blind mice?

# Throw Him Down, McCloskey

W & M: JOHN W. KELLY (1890)

1. 'Twas down at Dan McDevitt's at the corner of this street,
    There was to be a prize fight and both parties were to meet.
   To make all the arrangements and see ev'rything was right,
    McCloskey and a nagur were to have a finish fight.

   The rules were London Prize Ring and McCloskey said he'd try
    To bate the nagur wid one punch or in the ring he'd die.
   The odds were on McCloskey tho' the betting it was small,
    'Twas on McCloskey ten to one—on the nagur, none at all.

   *Chorus:*
   "Throw him down, McCloskey," was to be the battle cry,
   "Throw him down, McCloskey, you can lick him if you try";
   And future generations, with wonder and delight,
   Will read on hist'ry's pages of the great McCloskey fight.

2. The fighters were to start in at a quarter after eight,
    But the nagur did not show up and the hour was getting late.
   He sent around a messenger who then went on to say
    That the Irish crowd would jump him and he couldn't get fair play.

   Then up steps Pete McCracken, and said that he would fight
    Stand-up or rough-and-tumble if McCloskey didn't bite.
   McCloskey says, "I'll go you," then the seconds got in place,
    And the fighters started in to decorate each other's face.

   [*to Chorus*]

3. They fought like two hyenas 'till the forty-seventh round,
    They scattered blood enough around, by gosh, to paint the town.
   McCloskey got a mouthful of poor McCracken's jowl,
    McCracken hollered 'murthur' and his seconds hollered "foul"!

   The friends of both the fighters that instant did begin
    To fight, and ate each other—the whole party started in.
   You couldn't tell the dif'rence in fighters if you'd try,
    McCracken lost his upper lip, McCloskey lost an eye.

   [*to Chorus*]

# Tiger Rag
## (Hold That Tiger!)
W: HARRY DE COSTA
M: D. J. LA ROCCA ("The Original Dixieland Jazz Band") (1917)

Where's that Tiger!
Where's that Tiger!
Where's that Tiger!
Hold that Tiger!

Hold that Tiger!
Hold that Tiger!
Hold that Tiger!
Hold that Tiger!

Choke him, poke him,
 kick him and soak him!
Where's that Tiger?
Where's that Tiger?
Where, oh where can he be?

Low- or high-brow,
They all cry now:
"Please play that Tiger Rag for me."


# Till the Clouds Roll By
W: JEROME KERN, P. G. WODEHOUSE & GUY BOLTON
M: JEROME KERN
[from *Oh Boy!*, 1917]

1. *(Jacky)*
 I'm so sad
 to think that I have had to
Drive you from your home so cooly.
*(George)*
 I've be gaining
 nothing by remaining,
What would Missus Grundy say?
 Her conventions,
 kindly recollect them!
We must please respect them duly.
*(Jacky)*
 My intrusion needs explaining:
 I felt my courage waning.

349

*(George)*
Please, I beg don't mention it!
I should not mind a bit,
But it has started raining.

*Chorus:*
Oh, the rain comes a pitter, patter,
And I'd like to be safe in bed.
  Skies are weeping
  While the world is sleeping
  Trouble heaping
On our head.

It is vain to remain and chatter,
And to wait for a clearer sky;
  Helter-skelter
  I must fly for shelter
Till the clouds roll by.

**2.** *(Jacky)*
What bad luck,
  it's coming down in buckets;
Have you an umbrella handy?
*(George)*
I've got a warm coat,
  waterproof, a storm coat;
I shall be all right, I know.
  Later on, too,
  I will ward the grippe off,
With a little nip of brandy.
*(Jacky)*
Or a glass of toddy draining,
  You'd find that more sustaining.
*(George)*
Don't be worried, I entreat,
I've rubbers for my feet,
So I don't mind it raining.

[*to Chorus*]

# Till We Meet Again
W: RAYMOND B. EGAN / M: RICHARD A. WHITING (1918)

1. There's a song in the land of the lily
   Each sweetheart has heard with a sigh,
   Over high garden walls
   This sweet echo falls,
   As a soldier boy whispers goodbye.

   *Chorus:*
   Smile the while you kiss me sad adieu,
   When the clouds roll by I'll come to you;
   Then the skies will seem more blue
   Down in lovers' lane, my dearie.

   Wedding bells will ring so merrily,
   Ev'ry tear will be a memory;
   So wait and pray each night for me
   Till we meet again.

2. Tho' "goodbye" means the birth of a teardrop,
   "Hello" means the birth of a smile,
   And the smile will erase
   The tear-blighting trace
   When we meet in the after-a-while.

   [*to Chorus*]

# 'Tis the Last Rose of Summer
W: THOMAS MOORE (1813) / M: IRISH AIR (ca. 1793)

1. 'Tis the last rose of summer,
   Left blooming alone;
   All her lovely companions
   Are faded and gone;

   No flower of her kindred,
   No rosebud is nigh,
   To reflect back her blushes,
   Or give sigh for sigh.

2. I'll not leave thee, thou lone one,
   To pine on the stem,
   Since the lovely are sleeping,
   Go sleep thou with them;

   Thus kindly I scatter
   Thy leaves o'er the bed,
   Where thy mates of the garden
   Lie scentless and dead.

3. So soon may I follow,
   When friendships decay,
   And from love's shining circle
   The gems drop away;

   When true hearts lie withered,
   And fond ones are flown,
   Oh, who would inhabit
   This bleak world alone.

# Tit-Willow

W: W. S. GILBERT / M: SIR ARTHUR SULLIVAN
[from *The Mikado*, 1885]

1. On a tree by a river, a little tom-tit sang
   *"Willow, tit-willow, tit-willow."*
   And I said to him, Dickie bird, why do you sit, singing
   *"Willow, tit-willow, tit-willow"*?

   "Is it weakness of intellect, birdie?" I cried,
   "Or a rather tough worm in your little inside?"
   With a shake of his poor little head, he replied,
   *"Oh willow, tit-willow, tit-willow!"*

2. He slapped at his chest as he sat on the bough, singing
   *"Willow, tit-willow, tit-willow."*
   And a cold perspiration bespangled his brow, oh,
   *"Willow, tit-willow, tit-willow!"*

   He sobbed and he sighed, and a gurgle he gave,
   Then he plunged himself into the billowy wave,
   And an echo arose from the suicide's grave,
   *"Oh willow, tit-willow, tit-willow!"*

3. Now I feel just as sure as I'm sure that my name isn't
   *"Willow, tit-willow, tit-willow"*
   That 'twas blighted affection that made him exclaim, oh,
   *"Willow, tit-willow, tit-willow!"*

   And if you remain callous and obdurate,
   I shall perish as he did and you will know why,
   Though I probably shall not exclaim as I die,
   *"Oh willow, tit-willow, tit-willow!"*

# Tom Dooley
AMERICAN BALLAD

1. I met her on the mountain,
   That's where I took her life;
   Met her upon the mountain,
   I stabbed her dead with my knife.

   *Chorus:*
   Hang down your head, Tom Dooley,
   Hang down your head and cry,
   Hang down your head, Tom Dooley,
   Poor boy, you're goin' to die.

2. This time tomorrow morning,
   Reckon where I will be,
   If it was not for Grayson,
   I'd be in Tennessee.

   [*to Chorus*]

3. This time tomorrow morning,
   This soldier boy will be
   Down in a lonesome valley,
   Hangin' from some white oak tree.

   [*to Chorus*]

4. They're gonna try Ann Melton,
   Can't see no reason why,
   There's only one who's guilty,
   And now I'm goin' to die.

   [*to Chorus*]


# Too-ra-loo-ra-loo-ral
## (That's an Irish Lullaby)
W & M: JAMES ROYCE SHANNON (1913)

1. Over in Killarney,
   Many years ago,
   Me Mither sang a song to me
   In tones so sweet and low,

   Just a simple little ditty,
   In her good ould Irish way,
   And I'd give the world if she could sing
   That song to me this day:

353

*Chorus:*
"Too-ra-loo-ra-loo-ral,
Too-ra-loo-ra-li,
Too-ra-loo-ra-loo-ral,
Hush now, don't you cry!

"Too-ra-loo-ra-loo-ral,
Too-ra-loo-ra-li,
Too-ra-loo-ra-loo-ral,
That's an Irish lullaby."

2. Oft, in dreams, I wander
   To that cot again,
   I feel her arms a huggin' me
   As when she held me then.

   And I hear her voice a-hummin'
   To me as in days of yore,
   When she used to rock me fast asleep
   Outside the cabin door:

   [*to Chorus*]


# Tourelay, Tourelay
IRISH LULLABY

1. Oh, papa is out breaking rocks on the street,
   And baby is sleeping so cozy and sweet;
   Oh, baby, don't cry now, but be very goot,
   And when papa comes home he'll bring you cigaroot.

   *Chorus:*
   Tourelay, tourelay,
   With my fillagadee, skinamaroosha,
   Balderalda boom-ta-de-ay,
   Tourelay, tourelay,
   And the pride of the house is papa's baby.

2. When papa has gumdrops and baby has none,
   If papa is foolish and gives baby one,
   When four o'clock comes, and the child sleeps no more,
   Then papa stays up all night pacing the floor!

   [*to Chorus*]

# Toyland

W: GLEN MacDONOUGH / M: VICTOR HERBERT

[from *Babes in Toyland,* 1903]

1. When you've grown up, my dears,
   And are as old as I,
   You'll often ponder on the years
   That roll so swiftly by, my dears,
      that roll so swiftly by.

   And of the many lands
   You will have journeyed through,
   You'll oft recall the best of all,
   The land your childhood knew!
      your childhood knew.

   > *Chorus:*
   > Toyland! Toyland!
   > Little girl-and-boy-land,
   > While you dwell within it
   > You are ever happy then.
   >
   > Childhood's Joyland,
   > Mystic, merry Toyland!
   > Once you pass its borders
   > You can ne'er return again.

2. When you've grown up, my dears,
   There comes a dreary day
   When 'mid the locks of black appears
   The first pale gleam of gray, my dears,
      the first pale gleam of gray.

   Then of the past you'll dream
   As gray-haired grownups do,
   And seek once more its phantom shore,
   The land your childhood knew!
      your childhood knew.

   [*to Chorus*]

# The Trail of the Lonesome Pine

W: BALLARD MACDONALD / M: HARRY CARROLL (1913)

On a mountain in Virginia
Stands a lonesome pine;
Just below is the cabin home
Of a little girl of mine.

Her name is June, and very, very soon
She'll belong to me;
For I know she's waiting there for me
'Neath that lone pine tree:

*Chorus:*
In the Blue Ridge Mountains of Virginia,
On the Trail of the Lonesome Pine,
In the pale moonshine
Our hearts entwine
Where she carved her name and I carved mine.

Oh! June, like the mountains I'm blue;
Like the pine I am lonesome for you,
In the Blue Ridge Mountains of Virginia
On the Trail of the Lonesome Pine.


# Tramp! Tramp! Tramp!

W & M: GEORGE F. ROOT (1865)

1. In the prison cell I sit,
    Thinking, mother dear, of you,
    And our bright and happy home
        so far away;

    And the tears they fill my eyes
    Spite of all that I can do,
    Though I try to cheer my comrades
        and be gay.

    *Chorus:*
    Tramp! tramp! tramp!
    The boys are marching,
    Cheer up, comrades,
    They will come;

    And beneath the starry flag,
    We shall breathe the air again
    Of the freeland in our own beloved home.

2. In the battle front we stood
   When their fiercest charge they made,
   And they swept us off
      a hundred men or more;

   But before we reached their lines
   They were beaten back, dismayed,
   And we heard the cry of vict'ry
      o'er and o'er.

   [*to Chorus*]

3. So, within the prison cell,
   We are waiting for the day
   That shall come to open wide
      the iron door;

   And the hollow eye grows bright,
   And the poor heart almost gay,
   As we think of seeing home
      and friends once more.

   [*to Chorus*]

# Turkey in the Straw
## (Zip Coon)
AMERICAN TRADITIONAL FIDDLE TUNE
*(authorship, ca. 1834, unresolved)*

1. As I was a-gwine down the road,
   Tired team and a heavy load,
   Crack my whip and the leader sprung;
   I says day-day to the wagon tongue.

   *Chorus:*
   Turkey in the straw, turkey in the hay,
   Roll 'em up and twist 'em up a high tuckahaw,
   And hit 'em up a tune called Turkey in the Straw.

2. Went out to milk and I didn't know how,
   I milked the goat instead of the cow;
   A monkey sittin' on a pile of straw
   A-winkin' at his mother-in-law.

   [*to Chorus*]

3. Met Mr. Catfish comin' down stream,
   Says Mr. Catfish, "What does you mean?"
   Caught Mr. Catfish by the snout
   And turned Mr. Catfish wrong side out.

   [*to Chorus*]

4. Came to the river and I couldn't get across,
   Paid five dollars for an old blind hoss
   Wouldn't go ahead, nor he wouldn't stand still,
   So he went up and down like an old saw mill.

   [*to Chorus*]

5. As I came down the new cut road
   Met Mr. Bullfrog, met Miss Toad,
   And every time Miss Toad would sing
   Ole Bullfrog cut a pigeon wing.

   [*to Chorus*]

6. O, I jumped in the seat, and I gave a little yell,
   The horses run away, broke the wagon all to hell;
   Sugar in the gourd and honey in the horn,
   I never was so happy since the hour I was born.

   [*to Chorus*]

# The Twelve Days of Christmas
TRADITIONAL ENGLISH

1. On the first day of Christmas,
   my true love sent to me
   A partridge in a pear tree.

2. On the second day of Christmas,
   my true love sent to me
   *Two* turtle doves
   And a partridge in a pear tree.

3. On the third day of Christmas,
   my true love sent to me
   *Three* French hens,
   *Two* turtle doves
   And a partridge in a pear tree.

4. On the fourth day of Christmas,
   my true love sent to me
   *Four* calling birds,
   *Three* French hens,
   *Two* turtle doves
   And a partridge in a pear tree.

5. On the fifth day of Christmas,
   my true love sent to me
   *Five* golden rings . . .
   *Four* calling birds,
   *Three* French hens,
   *Two* turtle doves
   And a partridge in a pear tree.

   [*etc., etc., including:*]

   *Six* geese a-laying . . .

   *Seven* swans a-swimming . . .

   *Eight* maids a-milking . . .

   *Nine* ladies dancing . . .

   *Ten* lords a-leaping . . .

   *Eleven* pipers piping . . .

   *Twelve* drummers drumming . . .

# Twinkle, Twinkle, Little Star

W: JANE TAYLOR (1806)
M: TRADITIONAL FRENCH
*(same melody as "Ah! Vous Dirai-je, Maman" and "The Alphabet Song")*

1. Twinkle, twinkle, little star,
   How I wonder what you are
   Up above the world so high,
   Like a diamond in the sky.
       *Twinkle, twinkle, little star,*
       *How I wonder what you are.*

2. When the blazing sun is gone,
   When he nothing shines upon,
   Then you show your little light,
   Twinkle, twinkle, all the night.
       *Twinkle, twinkle, little star,*
       *How I wonder what you are.*

**3.** Then the trav'ller in the dark
Thanks you for your tiny spark;
He could not see where to go
If you did not twinkle so.
*Twinkle, twinkle, little star,*
*How I wonder what you are.*

**4.** In the dark blue sky you keep
While you through my window peep,
And you never shut your eye
Till the sun is in the sky.
*Twinkle, twinkle, little star,*
*How I wonder what you are.*

# Under the Bamboo Tree
W & M: BOB COLE & J. ROSAMOND JOHNSON (1902)
*(original title: "If You Lak-a-me")*
[from *Sally in Our Alley,* 1902]

**1.** Down in the jungles lived a maid
Of royal blood though dusky shade,
A marked impression once she made
Upon a Zulu from Matabooloo;

And ev'ry morning he would be
Down underneath a bamboo tree,
Awaiting there his love to see,
And then to her he'd sing:

*Chorus:*
"If you lak-a-me, lak I lak-a-you,
And we lak-a-both the same,
I lak-a-say, this very day,
I lak-a-change your name;

"'Cause I love-a-you and love-a-you true
And if you-a love-a-me,
One live as two, two live as one
Under the bamboo tree."

**2.** And in this simple jungle way,
He wooed the maiden ev'ry day,
By singing what he had to say;
One day he seized her and gently squeezed her;

And then beneath the bamboo green,
He begged her to become his queen;
The dusky maiden blushed unseen
And joined him in his song:

[*to Chorus*]

3. This little story strange but true
   Is often told in Mataboo,
   Of how this Zulu tried to woo
   His jungle lady in tropics shady.

   Although the scene was miles away,
   Right here at home I dare to say,
   You'll hear some Zulu ev'ry day,
   Gush out this soft refrain:

   [*to Chorus*]


# Up on the Housetop
CHRISTMAS TRADITIONAL

1. Up on the housetop, reindeer pause,
   Out jumps good old Santa Claus,
   Down through the chimney with lots of toys,
   All for the little ones, Christmas joys.

   *Chorus:*
   Ho, ho, ho!
   Who wouldn't go!
   Ho, ho, ho!
   Who wouldn't go
   Up on the housetop,
   Click, click, click,
   Down through the chimney
   With good Saint Nick.

2. First comes the stock of little Nell;
   Oh, dear Santa, fill it well;
   Give her a dollie that laughs and cries,
   One that will open and shut her eyes.

   [*to Chorus*]

# Vilia

ENGLISH WORDS: ADRIAN ROSS / M: FRANZ LEHÁR (1907)
[Originally from *Die lustige Witwe,* 1905: w. Victor Léon & Leo Smith]

1. There once was a Vilia, a witch of the wood,
   A hunter beheld her alone as she stood.
   The spell of her beauty upon him was laid;
   He look'd and he long'd for the magical maid!

   For a sudden tremor ran
   Right thro' the love-bewildered man,
   And he sigh'd as a hapless lover can:

   > *Chorus:*
   > "Vilia, O Vilia! the witch of the wood!
   > Would I not die for you, dear, if I could?
   > Vilia, O Vilia, my love and my bride!"
   > Softly and sadly he sigh'd.

   > [*Repeat*]

2. The wood-maiden smiled, and no answer she gave,
   But beckon'd him into the shade of the cave;
   He never had known such a rapturous bliss,
   No maiden of mortals so sweetly can kiss!

   As before her feet he lay,
   She vanished in the wood away,
   And he called vainly till his dying day!:

   > [*to Chorus, repeated; then:*]
   >    Sadly he sigh'd,
   >    "Vilia."


# Vive la Compagnie
## (Vive l'Amour)

TRADITIONAL DRINKING SONG

1. Let ev'ry good fellow now fill up his glass,
   *Vive la compagnie*
   And drink to the health of our glorious class.
   *Vive la compagnie*

   > *Chorus:*
   > Vive la, vive la, vive l'amour,
   > Vive la, vive la, vive l'amour,
   > Vive l'amour, vive l'amour,
   > Vive la compagnie.

2. Now let every married man drink to his wife,
   *Vive la compagnie*
   The joy of his bosom and plague of his life.
   *Vive la compagnie*

   [*to Chorus*]

3. Come fill up your glass, I'll give you a toast,
   *Vive la compagnie*
   A health to our dear friend, our kind worthy host.
   *Vive la compagnie*

   [*to Chorus*]

4. Since all with good humor I've toasted so free,
   *Vive la compagnie*
   I hope it will please you to drink now with me.
   *Vive la compagnie*

   [*to Chorus*]


# Wabash Cannon Ball
AMERICAN RAILROADING SONG

1. From the great Atlantic Ocean to the wide Pacific shore,
   From the queen of flowing mountains to the balmy southern shore,
   She's mighty tall and handsome and quite well known by all,
   For she's the combination of the Wabash Cannon Ball.

2. Won't'cha listen to the jingle, and the rumble and the roar
   As she glides along the woodland through the hills and by the shore.
   Just hear the mighty engine, and lonesome hoboes squall
   While trav'llin' through the jungles on the Wabash Cannon Ball.

3. Now the train it is a wonder and it travels mighty fast,
   It is made of shining silver and it takes off like a blast.
   You leave Mobile at seven, at eight you reach St. Paul,
   And there's a lonely whistle on the Wabash Cannon Ball.

4. When she come on down from Memphis on a cold December day,
   As she rolled into the station you could hear the people say,
   "Why, there's a girl from Memphis, she's long and she is tall,
   And she came down from Memphis on the Wabash Cannon Ball."

5. Here's to hobo Daddy Claxton, may his name forever stand,
   It'll always be remembered in the courts of Alabam';
   His earthly race is over, the curtains 'round him fall,
   We'll take him home to vict'ry on the Wabash Cannon Ball.

**6.** Now the Eastern folks are dandies, so the Western folks will say,
But they never saw the Wabash 'cause it never passed their way.
We'll never take a hobo from Boston, big or small,
No dandy can be taken on the Wabash Cannon Ball.


# Waiting for the Robert E. Lee

W: L. WOLFE GILBERT / M: LEWIS F. MUIR (1912)

**1.** 'Way down on the levee,
In old Alabamy,
There's Daddy and Mammy,
There's Ephra'm and Sammy.

On a moonlight night you can find them all;
While they are waitin',
The banjos are syncopatin'.

What's that they're sayin'?
Oh, what's that they're sayin'?
The while they keep playin',
I'm hummin' and swayin';

    It's the good ship Robert E. Lee
    That's come to carry the cotton away.

    *Chorus:*
    Watch them shufflin' along,
    See them shufflin' along;
    Go take your best gal, real pal,
    Go down to the levee,
    I said to the levee!

    And then join that shufflin' throng,
    Hear that music and song;
    It's simply great, mate,
    Waitin' on the levee,
    Waitin' for the Robert E. Lee!

**2.** The whistles are blowin',
The smokestacks are showin',
The ropes they are throwin',
Excuse me, I'm goin' . . .

To the place where all is harmonious,
Even the preacher,
They say, is the dancin' teacher.

Have you been down there?
Say, were you aroun' there?
If you ever go there,
You'll always be found there.

Why, "doggone," here comes my baby
On the good old ship Robert E. Lee.

[*to Chorus*]


# Wait 'Till the Sun Shines, Nellie
W: ANDREW B. STERLING / M: HARRY VON TILZER (1905)

1. On a Sunday Morn, sat a maid forlorn,
With her sweetheart by her side.
Thro' the window pane she looked at the rain,
"We must stay home, Joe," she cried.

   "There's a picnic, too, at the Old Point View.
It's a shame it's raining today."
Then the boy drew near, kissed away each tear,
And she heard him softly say:

   *Chorus:*
"Wait 'till the sun shines, Nellie,
When the clouds go drifting by.
We will be happy, Nellie,
Don't you sigh.

   "Down Lover's Lane we'll wander,
Sweethearts, you and I.
Wait 'till the sun shines, Nellie,
Bye and bye."

2. "How I long," she sighed, "for a trolly ride,
Just to show my brand new gown."
Then she gazed on high with a gladsome cry
For the sun came shining down.

   And she looked so sweet on the big front seat
As the car sped on its way,
And she whispered low, "Say, you're all right, Joe,
You just won my heart today."

   [*to Chorus*]

# Wal, I Swan
## (Ebenezer Frye)

W & M: BENJAMIN HAPGOOD BURT
[from *The Yankee Tourist*, 1907]

1. I run the old mill over here to Reuben's-ville,
   My name's Joshua Ebenezer Frye.
   I know a thing or two,
   you bet your neck I do,
   They don't ketch me for I'm too darn sly.

   I've seen Bunco men, allus got the best o' them,
   Once I met a couple on the Boston train.
   They says, "How be you!"
   I says, "That'll do!
   Travel right along with your darn skin game."

   *Chorus:*
   Wal, I swan!
   I mus' be gittin' on!
   Git-dap, Napoleon! it looks like rain.
   Wal, I'll be switched!
   The hay ain't pitched,
   Come in when you're over to the farm again.

2. I drove the old mare over to the County Fair,
   Took first prize on a load of summer squash.
   Stopped at the cider mill
   coming over by the hill,
   Come home "tighter" than a drum, by gosh!

   I was so durn full, I give away the old bull,
   Dropped both my reins clean out on the fill.
   Got hum so darn late
   couldn't find the barn gate,
   Ma says, "Joshua, 'taint pos-si-bil."

   [*to Chorus*]

3. We had a big show here 'bout a week ago,
   Hitched up a tent by the old mill dam.
   Ma says let's go
   into the side-show,
   Jus' take a look at the tattooed man.

   I see a cus' look sharp at my pocket book,
   Says, "Gimme two tens for a five."
   I says, "You durn fool!
   I be the constabule!
   Now you're a'rested sure as yer live."

366

> Wal, I swan!
> I mus' be gittin' on!
> Git-dap, Napoleon! it looks like rain.
> Wal, I'll be durned!
> The butter ain't churned,
> Come in when you're over to the farm again.

4. I drove the old bay into town yesterday,
   Hitched by the track to the railroad fence.
     Tied her good and strong,
     But a train came along,
   And I ain't seen the "hoss" or the wagin sence.

   Had to foot it home so I started off alone,
   When a man says, "Hurry! yer barn's on fire."
     But I had the key
     in my pocket, you see,
   So I knew the cus' was a fool or a liar.

   [*to Chorus*]

5. My son Joshua went to Philadelphia,
   He wouldn't do a day's work if he could.
     Smoked cigarettes, too,
     way the city folks do,
   What he's a-coming to ain't no good.

   He didn't give a darn 'bout stayin' on the farm,
   Keeps writin' hum he's a-doin' right well.
     It seems sort of funny
     that he's allus out o' money,
   And Ma says the boy's up to some kind o' hell.

   [*to Chorus*]

# Waltz Me Around Again, Willie
## ('Round, 'Round, 'Round)
W: WILL D. COBB  /  M: REN SHIELDS (1906)

1. Willie Fitzgibbons,
     who used to sell ribbons,
   And stood up all day on his feet,
     Grew very spooney
     on Madeline Mooney,
   Who'd rather be dancing than eat.

Each evening she'd tag him,
to some dance hall drag him,
And when the band started to play,
She'd up like a silly
and grab tired Willie,
Steer him on the floor and she'd say:

*Chorus:*
"Waltz me around again, Willie,
Around, around, around.
   The music is dreamy,
     it's peaches and creamy,
Oh! don't let my feet touch the ground.

"I feel like a ship on an ocean of joy,
I just want to holler out loud, "Ship ahoy!"
Oh! waltz me around again, Willie,
Around, around, around."

**2.**   Willie DeVere
was a dry goods cashier,
At his desk he would sit all the day,
Till his doctor advised him
to start exercising,
Or else he would soon fade away.

One night this poor looney
met Madeline Mooney,
Fitzgibbons then shouted with joy,
"She's a good health regainer,
You've got a great trainer,
Just wait till she hollers, my boy":

[*to Chorus*]


# A Wandering Minstrel I
W: W. S. GILBERT / M: SIR ARTHUR SULLIVAN
[from *The Mikado,* 1885]

A wandering minstrel I—
   A thing of shreds and patches,
   Of ballads, songs and snatches,
And dreamy lullaby!

My catalogue is long,
   Through every passion ranging,
   And to your humours changing
I tune my supple song!

Are you in sentimental mood?
   I'll sigh with you,
      Oh, sorrow, sorrow!
On maiden's coldness do you brood?
   I'll do so, too—
      Oh, sorrow, sorrow!
I'll charm your willing ears
With songs of lovers' fears,
While sympathetic tears
   My cheeks bedew—
      Oh, sorrow, sorrow!

But if patriotic sentiment is wanted,
   I've patriotic ballads cut and dried;
For where'er our country's banner may be planted,
   All other local banners are defied!

Our warriors, in serried ranks assembled,
   Never quail—or they conceal it if they do—
And I shouldn't be surprised if nations trembled
   Before the mighty troops of Titipu!

*And if you call for a song of the sea,*
   *We'll heave the capstan round*
*With a yeo heave ho, for the wind is free,*
*Her anchor's a-trip and her helm's a-lee,*
   *Hurrah for the homeward bound!*

To lay aloft in a howling breeze
   May tickle a landsman's taste,
But the happiest hour a sailor sees
   Is when he's down
   At an inland town,
With his Nancy on his knees, yeo ho!
   And his arm around her waist!

*Then man the capstan—off we go,*
   *As the fiddler swings us 'round,*
*With a yeo heave ho,*
*And a rum below,*
   *Hurrah for the homeward bound!*

# 'Way Down Yonder in New Orleans

W & M: HENRY CREAMER & J. TURNER LAYTON (1922)

1. Guess! where do you think I'm goin'
    when the winds start blowin' strong?
    Guess! where do you think I'm goin'
    when the nights start growin' long?

    I ain't goin' East, I ain't goin' West,
        I ain't goin' over the cuckoo's nest;
    I'm bound for the town that I love best,
        Where life is one sweet song:

    > *Chorus:*
    > 'Way down yonder in New Orleans,
    > In the land of dreamy scenes,
    > There's a garden of Eden,
    > That's what I mean,
    >
    > Creole babies with flashing eyes
    > Softly whisper with tender sighs,
    > "Stop! Oh! won't you give your lady fair
    > A little smile?"
    >
    > Stop! You bet your life you'll linger there
    >     a little while,
    > There is Heaven right here on earth,
    >     (*2nd time:* They've got angels right here on earth,)
    > With those beautiful queens,
    >     (*2nd time:* Wearing little blue jeans,)
    > 'Way down yonder in New Orleans.

2. Guess! what do you think I'm thinkin'
    when you think I'm thinkin' wrong?
    Guess! what do you think I'm thinkin'
    when I'm thinkin' all night long?

    I ain't thinkin' this, I ain't thinkin' that,
        I cannot be thinkin' about your hat;
    My heart does not start to pit-a-pat
        Unless I hear this song:

    > [*to Chorus*]

# The Wayfaring Stranger
APPALACHIAN FOLK SONG

1. I'm just a poor wayfaring stranger
   A-travelin' through this world of woe,
   But there's no sickness, toil nor danger
   In that bright world to which I go.

   I'm goin' there to see my mother,
   I'm goin' there, no more to roam,
   I'm just a-goin' over Jordan,
   I'm just a-goin' over home.

2. My father lived and died a farmer,
   A-reapin' less than he did sow,
   And now I follow in his footsteps,
   A-knowin' less than he did know.

   I'm goin' there to see my father,
   I'm goin' there, no more to roam,
   I'm just a-goin' over Jordan,
   I'm just a-goin' over home.

3. I know dark clouds will gather 'round me,
   My way is steep and rough, I know,
   But fertile fields lie just before me
   In that fair land to which I go.

   I'm goin' there to see my brother,
   I'm goin' there, no more to roam,
   I'm just a-goin' over Jordan,
   I'm just a-goin' over home.


# We Are Coming, Father Abra'am
W: WILLIAM CULLEN BRYANT [or JAMES SLOAN GIBBONS?]
M: LUTHER ORLANDO EMERSON (1862)

1. We are coming, Father Abra'am, three hundred thousand more,
   From Mississippi's winding stream and from New England's shore;
   We leave our plows and workshops, our wives and children dear,
   With hearts too full for utterance, with but a silent tear;
   We dare not look behind us, but steadfastly before—
   We are coming, Father Abra'am, three hundred thousand more!

   *Chorus:*
   We are coming, we are coming,
   Our Union to restore;

We are coming, Father Abra'am,
With three hundred thousand more,
We are coming, Father Abra'am,
With three hundred thousand more.

2. If you look across the hilltops that meet the northern sky,
Long moving lines of rising dust your vision may descry;
And now the wind, an instant, tears the cloudy veil aside,
And floats aloft our spangled flag in glory and in pride;
And bayonets in the sunlight gleam, and bands brave music pour—
We are coming, Father Abra'am, three hundred thousand more!

   [*to Chorus*]

3. If you look all up our valleys, where the growing harvests shine,
You may see our sturdy farmer boys fast forming into line;
And children from their mother's knees are pulling at the weeds,
And learning how to reap and sow, against their country's needs;
And a farewell group stands weeping at every cottage door—
We are coming, Father Abra'am, three hundred thousand more!

   [*to Chorus*]

4. You have called us, and we're coming, by Richmond's bloody tide,
To lay us down for freedom's sake, our brothers' bones beside;
Or from foul treason's savage group, to wrench the murderous blade,
And in the face of foreign foes its fragments to parade;
Six hundred thousand loyal men and true have gone before—
We are coming, Father Abra'am, three hundred thousand more!

   [*to Chorus*]


# The Wearing of the Green

W: DION BOUCICAULT / M: "an Irish Ballad of 1798"
[from *Arrah Na Pogue*, 1865]

1. Oh! Paddy, dear, and did you hear the news that's goin' round,
   The Shamrock is forbid by law, to grow on Irish ground;
      Saint Patrick's Day no more we'll keep, his color can't be seen,
      For there's a bloody law agin' the Wearin' o' the Green;
   I met with Napper Tandy and he tuk me by the hand,
   And he said "How's poor ould Ireland, and how does she stand?"
      *She's the most distressful country that ever you have seen,*
      *They're hanging men and women there for "Wearin' o' the Green."*

2. Then since the color we must wear is England's cruel red,
   Sure Ireland's sons will ne'er forget, the blood that they have shed;
      You may take the Shamrock from your hut, and cast it on the sod,
      But 'twill take root and flourish still, tho' under foot 'tis trod;

When the law can stop the blades of grass from growing as they grow,
And when the leaves in summertime, their verdure dare not show,
*Then I will change the color I wear in my corbeen,*
*But 'till that day, please God, I'll stick to "Wearin' o' the Green."*

3. But if at last our color should be torn from Ireland's heart,
Her sons with shame and sorrow from the dear old soil will part;
I've heard whisper of a country that lies far beyant the say,
Where rich and poor stand equal, in the light of freedom's day;
Oh, Erin, must we lave you, driven by the tyrant's hand,
Must we ask a mother's welcome from a strange but happier land?
*Where the cruel cross of England's thraldom never shall be seen,*
*And where, thank God, we'll live and die, still "Wearin' o' the Green."*

# We Gather Together
## (Prayer of Thanksgiving)
*(This anonymous song may be based on the 17th c. Dutch hymn*
*"Dankgebet." The English version dates from 1894.)*

1. We gather together to ask the Lord's blessing,
He chastens and hastens his will to make known.
The wicked oppressing now cease to be distressing,
Sing praises to His name for He forgets not his own.

2. Beside us to guide us, Our God with us joining,
Ordaining, maintaining His kingdom divine.
So from the beginning, the fighting we were winning,
Thou, Lord, wast at our side, and all glory be Thine.

3. We all do extol Thee, Thou leader triumphant,
And pray that Thou still our defender wilt be.
Let Thy congregation escape all tribulation,
Thy name be ever praised in glory, Lord make us free.

# Were You There?
SPIRITUAL

1. Were you there when they crucified my Lord?
Were you there when they crucified my Lord?
*Oh! Sometimes it causes me*
*to tremble, tremble, tremble—*
Were you there when they crucified my Lord?

2. Were you there when they nailed Him to the tree?
Were you there when they nailed Him to the tree?
*Oh! Sometimes it causes me*
  *to tremble, tremble, tremble—*
Were you there when they nailed Him to the tree?

3. Were you there when the sun refused to shine?
Were you there when the sun refused to shine?
*Oh! Sometimes it causes me*
  *to tremble, tremble, tremble—*
Were you there when the sun refused to shine?

4. Were you there when they laid Him in the tomb?
Were you there when they laid Him in the tomb?
*Oh! Sometimes it causes me*
  *to tremble, tremble, tremble—*
Were you there when they laid Him in the tomb?


# We Three Kings of Orient Are

W & M: JOHN HENRY HOPKINS, JR. (ca. 1857)

1. [ALL]
We three kings of Orient are,
Bearing gifts we traverse afar,
Field and fountain, moor and mountain,
Following yonder star.
    O . . .

  *Chorus:*
  Star of wonder, star of night,
  Star with royal beauty bright,
  Westward leading, still proceeding,
  Guide us to thy perfect light.

2. [MELCHIOR]
Born a king on Bethlehem plain,
Gold I bring to crown Him again—
King forever, ceasing never,
Over us all to reign.
    O . . .

  [*to Chorus*]

**3.** [CASPAR]
Frankincense to offer have I;
Incense owns a Deity nigh:
Prayer and praising, all men raising,
Worship Him, God most high.
     O . . .

*[to Chorus]*

**4.** [BALTHAZAR]
Myrrh is mine; its bitter perfume
Breathes a life of gathering gloom;
Sorrowing, sighing, bleeding, dying,
Sealed in the stone-cold tomb.
     O . . .

*[to Chorus]*

**5.** [ALL]
Glorious now, behold Him arise,
King, and God, and Sacrifice!
Heaven sings "Alleluia!"
"Alleluia!" the earth replies:
     O . . .

*[to Chorus]*


# We Wish You a Merry Christmas
TRADITIONAL ENGLISH

**1.** We wish you a merry Christmas,
We wish you a merry Christmas,
We wish you a merry Christmas
And a happy New Year!

> *Chorus:*
> Glad tidings we bring
> To you and your kin;
> Glad tidings for Christmas
> And a happy New Year!

**2.** Please bring us some figgy pudding,
Please bring us some figgy pudding,
Please bring us some figgy pudding,
Please bring it right here!

*[to Chorus]*

3. We won't go until we get some,
   We won't go until we get some,
   We won't go until we get some,
   Please bring it right here!

   [*to Chorus*]

4. We wish you a merry Christmas,
   We wish you a merry Christmas,
   We wish you a merry Christmas
   And a happy New Year!

   [*to Chorus*]

# What Can We Do with a Drunken Sailor

SEA CHANTEY (17th c.)

1. What can we do with a drunken sailor,
   What can we do with a drunken sailor,
   What can we do with a drunken sailor
   Early in the mornin'?

   Hoist him aloft with a running' bowlin',
   Hoist him aloft with a running' bowlin',
   Hoist him aloft with a running' bowlin',
   Early in the mornin.'

   *Chorus:*
   Way, hey, and up she rises,
   Way, hey, and up she rises,
   Way, hey, and up she rises
   Early in the mornin'.

2. What can we do with a drunken sailor (*3 times*)
   Early in the mornin'?

   Into the scuppers, ahoy there, sailors, (*3 times*)
   Early in the mornin'.

   [*to Chorus*]

3. What can we do with a drunken sailor (*3 times*)
   Early in the mornin'?

   Give him a lick o' the bosun's flipper (*3 times*)
   Early in the mornin'.

   [*to Chorus*]

**4.** What can we do with a drunken sailor (*3 times*)
Early in the mornin'?

Take him an' shake him an' try to wake him (*3 times*)
Early in the mornin'.

[*to Chorus*]

**5.** What can we do with a drunken sailor (*3 times*)
Early in the mornin'?

Into the brig till he gets up sober (*3 times*)
Early in the mornin'.

[*to Chorus*]

# What Child Is This?
W: WILLIAM C. DIX / M: "GREENSLEEVES"

**1.** What child is this, who, laid to rest,
On Mary's lap is sleeping?
Whom angels greet with anthems sweet,
While shepherds watch are keeping?

> *Chorus:*
> This, this is Christ the King,
> Whom shepherds guard and angels sing:
> Haste, haste to bring him laud,
> The Babe, the Son of Mary.

**2.** Why lies he in such mean estate
Where ox and ass are feeding?
Good Christian, fear: for sinners here
The silent Word is pleading.

[*to Chorus*]

**3.** So bring him incense, gold, and myrrh,
Come, peasant, King to own him;
The King of Kings salvation brings,
Let loving hearts enthrone him.

[*to Chorus*]

# When Irish Eyes Are Smiling

W: CHAUNCEY OLCOTT & GEORGE GRAFF JR.

M: ERNEST R. BALL (1912)

1. There's a tear in your eye, and I'm wondering why,
   For it never should be there at all.
   With such pow'r in your smile, sure a stone you'd beguile,
   So there's never a teardrop should fall.

   When your sweet lilting laughter's like some fairy song,
   And your eyes twinkle bright as can be,
   You should laugh all the while and all other times smile
   And now smile a smile for me.

   *Chorus:*
   When Irish eyes are smiling,
   Sure it's like a morn in spring;
   In the lilt of Irish laughter,
   You can hear the angels sing.

   When Irish hearts are happy,
   All the world seems bright and gay,
   And when Irish eyes are smiling,
   Sure they steal your heart away.

2. For your smile is a part of the love in your heart,
   And it makes even sunshine more bright.
   Like the linnet's sweet song, crooning all the day long,
   Comes your laughter so tender and light.

   For the springtime of life is the sweetest of all,
   There is ne'er a real care or regret;
   And while springtime is ours throughout all of youth's hours,
   Let us smile each chance we get.

   [*to Chorus*]

# When I Saw Sweet Nellie Home

W & M: JOHN FLETCHER (1859)

1. In the sky the bright stars glittered,
   On the grass the moonlight fell,
   Hush'd the sound of daylight bustle,
   Closed the pin-eyed pimpernel.

   As a-down the moss-grown wood path
   Where the cattle love to roam,
   From an August evening party
   I was seeing Nellie home.

*Chorus:*
In the sky the bright stars glittered,
On the grass the moonlight shone,
From an August evening party
I was seeing Nellie home.

2. When the autumn tinged the greenwood,
   Turning all its leaves to gold,
   In the lawn by elders shaded
   I my love to Nellie told.

   As we stood together gazing
   On the star-bespangled dome,
   How I blessed the August evening
   When I saw sweet Nellie home.

   [*to Chorus*]

3. White hairs mingle with my tresses,
   Furrows steal upon my brow,
   But a love smile cheers and blesses
   Life's declining moments now.

   Matron in the snowy kerchief,
   Closer to my bosom come;
   Tell me, do'st thou still remember
   When I saw sweet Nellie home?

   [*to Chorus*]


# When I Was a Lad
W: W. S. GILBERT / M: SIR ARTHUR SULLIVAN
[Sir Joseph and Chorus from *H.M.S. Pinafore,* 1878]

1. When I was a lad I served a term
   As office boy to an attorney's firm.
   I cleaned the windows and I swept the floor
   And I polished up the handle of the big front door.
   *He polished up the handle of the big front door.*

   I polished up that handle so carefullee,
   That now I am the ruler of the Queen's Navee!
   *He polished up that handle so carefullee,*
   *That now he is the ruler of the Queen's Navee!*

2. As office boy I made such a mark
   That they gave me the post of a junior clerk.
   I served the writs with a smile so bland
   And I copied all the letters in a big, round hand.
   *He copied all the letters in a big, round hand.*

379

And I copied all the letters in a hand so free,
That now I am the ruler of the Queen's Navee!
*He copied all the letters in a hand so free,*
*That now he is the ruler of the Queen's Navee!*

3. In serving writs I made such a name
That an articled clerk I soon became.
I wore clean collars and a bran' new suit
For the pass examination at the institute.
*For the pass examination at the institute.*

That pass examination did so well for me,
That now I am the ruler of the Queen's Navee!
*That pass examination did so well for he,*
*That now he is the ruler of the Queen's Navee!*

4. Of legal knowledge I acquired such a grip
That they took me into the partnership,
And that junior partnership I ween
Was the only ship that I ever had seen.
*Was the only ship he ever had seen.*

But that kind of ship so suited me,
That now I am the ruler of the Queen's Navee!
*But that kind of ship so suited he,*
*That now he is the ruler of the Queen's Navee!*

5. I grew so rich that I was sent
By a pocket borough into parliament.
I always voted at my party's call,
And I never tho't of thinking for myself at all.
*He never tho't of thinking for himself at all.*

I tho't so little they rewarded me,
By making me the ruler of the Queen's Navee!
*He tho't so little they rewarded he,*
*By making him the ruler of the Queen's Navee!*

6. Now landsmen all, who ever you may be,
If you want to rise to the top of the tree,
If your soul isn't fettered to an office stool,
Be careful to be guided by this golden rule.
*Be careful to be guided by this golden rule:*

Stick close to your desks and never go to sea,
And you all may be rulers of the Queen's Navee!
*Stick close to your desks and never go to sea,*
*And you all may be rulers of the Queen's Navee!*

# When Johnny Comes Marching Home Again

W: "LOUIS LAMBERT" [Patrick S. Gilmore] (1863)
M: "JOHNNY, I HARDLY KNEW YE" (?) (Irish street song, ca. 1898)

1. When Johnny comes marching home again,
   Hurrah, hurrah,
   We'll give him a hearty welcome then,
   Hurrah, hurrah,
   The men will cheer, the boys will shout, the ladies they will all turn out,
   And we'll all feel gay when Johnny comes marching home. (*twice*)

2. The old church bell will peel with joy,
   Hurrah, hurrah,
   To welcome home our darling boy,
   Hurrah, hurrah,
   The village lads and lassies say with roses they will strew the way,
   And we'll all feel gay when Johnny comes marching home. (*twice*)

3. Get ready for the jubilee,
   Hurrah, hurrah,
   We'll give the hero three times three,
   Hurrah, hurrah,
   The laurel wreath is ready now to place upon his loyal brow,
   And we'll all feel gay when Johnny comes marching home. (*twice*)

4. Let love and friendship on that day
   Hurrah, hurrah,
   Their choicest treasures then display
   Hurrah, hurrah,
   And let each one perform some part to fill with joy the warrior's heart,
   And we'll all feel gay when Johnny comes marching home. (*twice*)


# When My Baby Smiles at Me

W: TED LEWIS & ANDREW B. STERLING / M: BILL MUNRO
[from *The Greenwich Village Follies*, 1920]

1. My baby's eyes are blue,
   As blue as summer skies;
   My baby's hair is golden-hued,
   The kind I idolize.

   And when my baby's near,
   I'm happy all the while,
   For there is nothing in this world
   Just like my baby's smile.

*Chorus:*
For when my baby smiles at me,
My heart goes roaming to paradise;
And when my baby smiles at me,
There's such a wonderful light in her eyes.

The kind of light that means just love,
The kind of love that brings sweet harmony;
I sigh, I cry, it's just a glimpse of Heaven
When my baby smiles at me.

2. My baby's lips are sweet,
As sweet as sugar cane,
And when my baby kisses me,
Well, I just can't explain.

It seems the sun comes out,
Keep shining all the while,
And all the world is filled with love,
Just like my baby's smile.

[*to Chorus*]


# When the Saints Go Marching In
SPIRITUAL

1. Oh, when the saints go marchin' in,
Oh, when the saints go marchin' in,
Lord, I want to be in that number
When the saints go marchin' in.

2. Oh, when they come on Judgment Day,
Oh, when they come on Judgment Day,
Lord, I want to be in that number
When they come on Judgment day.

3. When Gabriel blows that golden horn,
When Gabriel blows that golden horn,
Lord, I want to be in that number
When he blows that golden horn.

4. When they go through them Pearly Gates,
When they go through them Pearly Gates,
Lord, I want to be in that number
When they go through Pearly Gates.

**5.** Oh, when they ring them silver bells,
Oh, when they ring them silver bells,
Lord, I want to be in that number
When they ring them silver bells.

**6.** And when the angels gather 'round,
And when the angels gather 'round,
Lord, I want to be in that number
When the angels gather 'round.

**7.** Oh, into Heaven when they go,
Oh, into Heaven when they go,
How I want to be in that number
Into Heaven when they go.

**8.** And when they're singing "Hallelu,"
And when they're singing "Hallelu,"
How I want to be in that number
When they're singing "Hallelu."

**9.** And when the Lord is shakin' hands,
And when the Lord is shakin' hands,
How I want to be in that number
When the Lord is shakin' hands.

# When You and I Were Young, Maggie

W: GEORGE W. JOHNSON / M: JAMES A. BUTTERFIELD (1866)

**1.** I wandered today to the hill, Maggie,
To watch the scene below:
The creek and the old rusty mill, Maggie,
Where we sat in the long, long ago.

The green grove is gone from the hill, Maggie,
Where first the daisies had sprung;
The old rusty mill is now still, Maggie,
Since you and I were young.

> *Chorus:*
> And now we are aged and gray, Maggie,
> The trials of life nearly done;
> Let's sing of the days that are gone, Maggie,
> When you and I were young.

**2.** A city so silent and lone, Maggie,
Where the young and the gay and the best,
In polished white mansions of stone, Maggie,
Where they each found a place for their rest,

383

Is built where the birds used to play, Maggie,
And join in songs that were sung;
We sang just as gay as did they, Maggie,
When you and I were young.

[*to Chorus*]

3. They say I am feeble with age, Maggie,
My steps less spritely than then;
My face is a well-written page, Maggie,
But time alone was the pen.

They say we are aged and gray, Maggie,
As spray by white breakers flung,
But to me you're as fair as you were, Maggie,
When you and I were young.

[*to Chorus*]

# When You Were Sweet Sixteen

W & M: JAMES THORNTON (1898)

1. When first I saw the lovelight in your eye,
And heard thy voice, like sweetest melody,
Speak words of love to my enraptur'd soul,
The world had naught but joy in store for me.

E'en though we're drifting down life's stream apart,
Your face I still can see in dream's domain;
I know that it would ease my breaking heart
To hold you in my arms just once again.

*Chorus:*
I love you as I never lov'd before,
Since first I met you on the village green.
Come to me, or my dream of love is o'er.
I love you as I lov'd you
When you were sweet,
When you were sweet sixteen.

2. Last night I dreamt I held your hand in mine,
And once again you were my happy bride.
I kissed you as I did in Auld Lang Syne,
As to the church we wander'd side by side.

The love I bear for you can never die;
Without you, I had rather not been born;
And even tho' we never meet again,
I love you as the sunshine loves the morn.

[*to Chorus*]

384

# When You Wore a Tulip
## (And I Wore a Big Red Rose)
W: JACK MAHONEY / M: PERCY WENRICH (1914)

I met you in a garden in an old Kentucky town,
The sun was shining down, you wore a gingham gown.

I kissed you as I placed a yellow tulip in your hair,
Upon my coat you pinned a rose so rare.

Time has not changed your loveliness, you're just as sweet to me.
I love you yet, I can't forget the days that used to be:

*Chorus:*
When you wore a tulip, a sweet yellow tulip,
And I wore a big red rose,
When you caressed me, 'twas then Heaven blessed me,
What a blessing, no one knows.

You made life cheery when you called me Dearie,
'Twas down where the blue grass grows,
Your lips were sweeter than julep when you wore a tulip,
And I wore a big red rose.


# Where Are You Going, My Pretty Maid?
ENGLISH FOLK SONG

1. "Where are you going, my pretty maid?
   Where are you going, my pretty maid?"

   "I'se going a-milking, sir," she said;
   "I'se going a-milking, sir," she said.

2. "Shall I go with you, my pretty maid?
   Shall I go with you, my pretty maid?"

   "O! yes, if you please, kind sir," she said;
   "O! yes, if you please, kind sir," she said.

3. "What is your father, my pretty maid ?". . .
   "Father's a farmer, sir," she said. . . .

4. "Shall I marry you, my pretty maid?". . .
   "O! yes, if you please, kind sir," she said. . . .

5. "And what is your fortune, my pretty maid?". . .
   "My face is my fortune, sir," she said. . . .

6. "Then I can't marry you, my pretty maid.". . .
   "Nobody asked you, sir," she said. . . .

385

# Where the River Shannon Flows

W & M: JAMES I. RUSSELL (1905)

1. There's a pretty spot in Ireland
   I always claim for my land,
   Where the fairies and the blarney
   Will never, never die.

   It's the land of the shillalah,
   My heart goes back there daily
   To the girl I left behind me
   When we kissed and said good-bye.

   *Chorus:*
   Where dear old Shannon's flowing,
   Where the three-leaved shamrock grows,
   Where my heart is, I am going
   To my little Irish rose.

   And the moment that I meet her
   With a hug and kiss I'll greet her,
   For there's not a colleen sweeter,
   Where the River Shannon flows.

2. Sure, no letter I'll be mailing,
   For soon will I be sailing,
   And I'll bless the ship that takes me
   To my dear old Erin's shore.

   There I'll settle down forever,
   I'll leave the old sod never,
   And I'll whisper to my sweetheart,
   "Come and take my name, Asthore."

   [*to Chorus*]


# While Shepherds Watched Their Flocks by Night

W: NAHUM TATE (late 17th c.) / M: TRADITIONAL

1. While shepherds watched their flocks by night,
       All seated on the ground,
   The angel of the Lord came down,
       And glory shone around.
   "Fear not," said he, for mighty dread
       Had seized their troubled mind;
   "Glad tidings of great joy I bring
       To you and all mankind.

2. "To you in David's town this day
    Is born of David's line
  A Saviour, who is Christ the Lord,
    And this shall be the sign:
  The heavenly Babe you there shall find
    To human view displayed,
  All meanly wrapped in swathing bands,
    And in a manger laid."

3. Thus spake the seraph and forthwith
    Appeared a shining throng
  Of angels, praising God, who thus
    Addressed their joyful song:
  "All glory be to God on high,
    And to the earth be peace;
  Goodwill henceforth from heav'n to men
    Begin, and never cease."

# While Strolling in the Park One Day
## (The Fountain in the Park)
W & M: ED HALEY (1884)

1. While strolling through the park one day,
  All in the merry month of May,
    A roguish pair of eyes,
    They took me by surprise,
  In a moment my poor heart they stole away!

Oh, a sunny smile was all she gave to me . . .
    [*soft-shoe break*]
And of course we were as happy as could be . . .
    [*soft-shoe break*]
    So neatly I raised my hat,
    And made a polite remark,
I never shall forget that lovely afternoon,
When I met her at the fountain in the park.

2. We linger'd there beneath the trees,
  Her voice was like the fragrant breeze;
    We talked of happy love
    Until the stars above,
  When her loving "yes" she gave my heart to please.

Oh, a sunny smile was all she gave to me . . .

    *(etc., etc.)*

# Whispering

W & M: JOHN SCHONBERGER, RICHARD COBURN
& VINCENT ROSE (1920)

1. Honey, I have something to tell you,
   And it's worthwhile listening to;
   Put your little head on my shoulder
   So that I can whisper to you.

   *Chorus:*
   Whispering while you cuddle near me,
   Whispering so no one can hear me,
   Each little whisper seems to cheer me
       I know it's true
       There's no one, dear, but you.

   You're whispering why you'll never leave me,
   Whispering why you'll never grieve me,
   Whisper and say that you believe me,
   Whispering that I love you.

2. When the twilight shadows are falling
   And the weary world is at rest,
   Then I'll whisper just why I know, dear,
   Loving time is always the best.

   [*to Chorus*]


# White Coral Bells

TWO-PART ROUND FROM ENGLAND

*First Part*
1. White coral bells
   Upon a slender stalk,

2. Oh, don't you wish
   That you could hear them ring?

*Second Part*
1. Lilies of the valley
   Deck my garden walk,

2. That will happen
   Only when the fairies sing.

# Whoopee, Ti Yi Yo
## (Git Along, Little Dogies)
AMERICAN COWBOY SONG

1. As I was a-walking one morning for pleasure,
   I saw a cow-puncher come riding along;
   His hat was throwed back and his spurs was a-jingling,
   And as he approached he was singing this song:

   *Chorus:*
   Whoopee, ti yi yo, git along, little dogies!
   It's your misfortune and none of my own.
   Whoopee, ti yi yo, git along, little dogies!
   For you know Wyoming will be your new home!

2. Early in the spring we round up the dogies,
   Mark and brand and bob off their tails,
   Round up our horses, load up the chuck wagon,
   Then throw the dogies up on the trail:

   [*to Chorus*]

3. It's whooping and yelling and driving the dogies;
   O how I wish they would go on!
   It's whooping and punching and go on, little dogies,
   For you know Wyoming will be your new home:

   [*to Chorus*]


# Who Threw the Overalls
# in Mistress Murphy's Chowder?
W & M: GEORGE L. GEIFER (1898)

1. Mistress Murphy gave a party just about a week ago,
   Ev'rything was plentiful, the Murphys they're not slow.
   They treated us like gentlemen, we tried to act the same,
   Only for what happened, well, it was an awful shame.

   When Mrs. Murphy dished the chowder out, she fainted on the spot,
   She found a pair of overalls at the bottom of the pot.
   Tim Nolan he got ripping mad, his eyes were bulging out,
   He jumped upon the piano and loudly he did shout:

*Chorus:*
"Who threw the overalls in Mistress Murphy's chowder?"
Nobody spoke, so he shouted all the louder.
"It's an Irish trick, that's true, I can lick the mick that threw
The overalls in Mistress Murphy's chowder."

2. They dragged the pants from out the soup and laid them on the floor.
Each man swore upon his life he'd ne'er seen them before.
They were plastered up with mortar and were worn out at the knee,
They had their many ups and downs, as we could plainly see.

And when Mrs. Murphy she came to, she 'gan to cry and pout,
She had them in the wash that day and forgot to take them out.
Tim Nolan he excused himself for what he said that night,
So we put music to the words and sung with all our might:

[*to Chorus*]

# Woodman, Spare That Tree

W: GEORGE P. MORRIS / M: HENRY RUSSELL (1837)

1. Woodman, spare that tree!
    Touch not a single bough;
In youth it sheltered me,
    And I'll protect it now.
'Twas my forefather's hand
    That placed it near his cot;
There, woodman, let it stand,
    Thy axe shall harm it not!

2. That old familiar tree,
    Whose glory and renown
Are spread o'er land and sea,
    And wouldst thou hack it down?
Woodman, forbear thy stroke!
    Cut not its earthbound ties;
Oh! spare that aged oak,
    Now towering to the skies!

3. When but an idle boy,
    I sought its grateful shade;
In all their gushing joy
    Here, too, my sisters played.
My mother kiss'd me here;
    My father press'd my hand—
Forgive this foolish tear,
    But let that old oak stand!

**4.** My heart-strings 'round thee cling,
   Close as thy bark, old friend!
Here shall the wild-bird sing,
   And still thy branches bend.
Old tree! the storm still brave!
   And, woodman, leave the spot;
While I've a hand to save,
   Thy axe shall harm it not.

# The World Is Waiting for the Sunrise
W: EUGENE LOCKHART / M: ERNEST SEITZ (1919)

Down in the lazy west rides the moon,
Warm as a night in June;
Stars shimm'ring soft in a bed of blue,
While I am calling and calling you.

Sweetly you are dreaming,
As the dawn comes slowly streaming;
Waken love in your bower,
Greet our trysting hour.

*Chorus:*
Dear one, the world is waiting for the sunrise;
Ev'ry rose is heavy with dew.
The thrush on high, his sleepy mate is calling
And my heart is calling you!

# The Yama-Yama Man
W: "O. A. HAUERBACH" [Otto Harbach]
M: KARL HOSCHNA
[from *The Three Twins*, 1908]

**1.** Ev'ry little tot at night
   Is afraid of the dark, you know;
Some big Yama man they see
When off to bed they go.

*Chorus:*
Yama-Yama, the Yama man,
Terrible eyes and a face of tan.
   If you don't watch out,
      He'll get you without a doubt,
If he can.

Maybe he's hiding behind the chair,
Ready to spring out at you unaware.
Run to your mama,
For here come the Yama-
Yama man.

2. Great big stary eyes you see,
So you cover up your head;
But that Yama man is there
Standing beside your bed.

[*to Chorus*]

# Yankee Doodle

MARCHING SONG OF COLONIAL AMERICA

*(The written history of this song—unquestionably the one piece of music most firmly associated with colonial America—begins in the 1760's, when it was already well known in the colonies. While most authorities now conclude that the song is American in origin, its true authorship remains unknown.)*

1. Father'n I went down to camp
Along with Captain Gooding,
And there we saw the men and boys
As thick as hasty pudding.

> *Chorus:*
> Yankee Doodle, keep it up,
> Yankee Doodle Dandy;
> Mind the music and the step,
> And with the girls be handy.

2. There was Captain Washington
Upon a slapping stallion,
A-giving orders to his men,
There must have been a million.

[*to Chorus*]

3. Then I saw a swamping gun
As large as logs of maple
Upon a very little cart,
A load for father's cattle.

[*to Chorus*]

4. Ev'ry time they shot it off,
It took a horn of powder,
And made a noise like father's gun,
Only a nation louder.

[*to Chorus*]

5. There I saw a wooden keg
   With heads made out of leather,
   They knocked upon it with some sticks
   To call the folks together.

   [*to Chorus*]

6. Then they'd fife away like fun
   And play on cornstalk fiddles,
   And some had ribbons red as blood
   All bound around their middles.

   [*to Chorus*]

7. Troopers too would gallop up
   And shoot right in our faces,
   It scared me almost half to death
   To see them run such races.

   [*to Chorus*]

8. I can't tell you all I saw,
   They kept up such a smother,
   I took my hat off, made a bow,
   And scampered home to mother.

   [*to Chorus*]


# Yankee Doodle Boy

W & M: GEORGE M. COHAN
[from *Little Johnny Jones,* 1904]

1. I'm the kid that's all the candy,
   I'm a Yankee Doodle Dandy,
   I'm glad I am,
   So's Uncle Sam.

   I'm a real live Yankee Doodle,
   Made my name and fame and boodle
   Just like Mister Doodle did,
   By riding on a pony.

   I love to listen to the Dixie strain,
   I long to see the girl I left behind me.
   That ain't a josh,
   She's a Yankee, by gosh.
       Oh, say, can you see
       Anything about a Yankee that's a phoney?

*Chorus:*
I'm a Yankee Doodle Dandy,
A Yankee Doodle, do or die,
A real live nephew of my Uncle Sam's,
Born on the fourth of July.

I've got a Yankee Doodle sweetheart,
She's my Yankee Doodle joy.
Yankee Doodle came to London just to ride the ponies,
I am a Yankee Doodle boy.

2. Father's name was Hezekiah,
Mother's name was Ann Maria,
Yankees through and through,
Red, white and blue.

Father was so Yankee-hearted
When the Spanish war was started,
He slipped on his uniform
And hopped upon a pony.

My mother's mother was a Yankee true,
My father's father was a Yankee, too,
And that's going some
For the Yankee, by gum.
    Oh, say, can you see
    Anything about my pedigree that's phoney?

[*to Chorus*]


# The Yellow Rose of Texas
AMERICAN FOLK SONG

1. There's a yellow rose in Texas
That I am gonna see;
Nobody got to know her,
Nobody, only me.

She cried so when I left her,
It like to broke my heart;
And if I ever find her,
We never more will part.

    *Chorus:*
    She's the sweetest little flower
    I ever, ever knew;
    Her eyes are bright as diamonds,
    They sparkle like the dew.

You may talk about your Daisy May
And sing of Rosalee,
But the yellow rose of Texas
Is the girl I'm gonna see.

2. Where the Rio Grande is flowing
   And starry nights are bright,
   She walks along the river
   Each quiet summer night.

   She thinks of when we parted
   So very long ago,
   I promised I would come back,
   No more to leave her so.

   [*to Chorus*]

3. Now I'm goin' back and find her,
   My heart is full of woe.
   We'll sing the songs that we used
   To sing so long ago.

   I'll play the banjo daily,
   We'll sing forevermore,
   The yellow rose of Texas,
   The girl that I adore.

   [*to Chorus*]


# Yip-I-Addy-I-Ay!
W: WILL D. COBB / M: JOHN H. FLYNN
[from *The Merry Widow and the Devil*, 1908]

1. Young Herman Von Bellow, a musical fellow,
   Played on a big cello each night
   Sweet melodies rare, in a dance garden where
   Dancers danced 'round and 'round with delight.

   One night he saw dancing a maid so entrancing
   His heart caught on fire inside,
   And music so mellow he sawed on his cello,
   She waltzed up to him and she cried:

   *Chorus:*
   "E-Yip-I-Addy-I-Ay, I-Ay!
   E-Yip-I-Addy-I-Ay!
   I don't care what becomes of me,
   When you play me that sweet melody:
   E-Yip-I-Addy-I-Ay, I-Ay!

My heart wants to holler 'Hurray' (Hurray)
Sing of joy, sing of bliss, home was never like this,
Yip-I-Addy-I-Ay!"

2. Now, some kind of music makes me sick and you sick,
And some kind is "puffickly" grand,
But the tune that Von Bellow tore off on his cello
Was that "I'd leave home for you" brand.

So look not, Spring Valley, to welcome home Sally,
Who went to New York for the ride,
For the night that Von Bellow cut loose on his cello
She tore up her ticket and cried:

[*to Chorus*]

3. Now, music, it's known, has a charm all its own,
And Von Bellow he gurgled with glee,
"Here's when I win a wife and a partner for life,"
As he coaxed out a chord up in G.

He played and she tarried, that night they got married,
But even before break of day,
Poor sleepy Von Bellow heard his new wife yell-oh,
"For goodness sake, wake up and play!"

[*to Chorus*]


# You'd Be Surprised
W & M: IRVING BERLIN (1919)

1. Johnny was bashful and shy;
Nobody understood why
Mary loved him;
All the other girls passed him by.

Ev'ryone wanted to know
How she could pick such a beau;
With a twinkle in her eye,
She made this reply:

*Chorus:*
"He's not so good in a crowd but when you get him alone,
You'd be surprised.
He isn't much at a dance but when he takes you home,
You'd be surprised.

He doesn't look like much of a lover,
But don't judge a book by its cover;
He's got the face of an angel
But there's a devil in his eye.

He's such a delicate thing but when he starts in to squeeze,
You'd be surprised.
He doesn't look very strong but when you sit on his knee,
You'd be surprised.

At a party or at a ball,
I've got to admit he's nothing at all,
But in a morris chair,
You'd be surprised."

2. Mary continued to praise
Johnny's remarkable ways
To the ladies—
And you know advertising pays.

Now Johnny's never alone,
He has the busiest phone;
Almost ev'ry other day
A new girl will say:

*Chorus:*
"He's not so good in the house but on a bench in the park,
You'd be surprised.
He isn't much in the light but when he gets in the dark,
You'd be surprised.

I know he looks as slow as the Erie,
But you don't know the half of it, dearie;
He looks as cold as an Eskimo
But there's a fire in his eyes.

He doesn't say very much but when he starts in to speak,
You'd be surprised.
He's not so good at the start but at the end of a week,
You'd be surprised.

On a streetcar or in a train
You'd think he was born without any brain,
But in a taxicab,
You'd be surprised.

# You Made Me Love You
## (I Didn't Want to Do It)
W: JOE MC CARTHY / M: JAMES V. MONACO (1913)

1. I've been worried all day long,
   Don't know if I'm right or wrong,
   I can't help just what I say,
   Your love makes me speak this way.

   Why, oh! why should I feel blue?
   Once I used to laugh at you,
   But now I'm cryin', no use denyin',
   There's no one else but you will do.

   > *Chorus:*
   > You made me love you,
   > I didn't want to do it,
   >   I didn't want to do it,
   > You made me want you,
   > And all the time you knew it,
   >   I guess you always knew it.

   You made me happy sometimes,
   You made me glad,
   But there were times, dear,
   You made me feel so bad.

   You made me sigh, for
   I didn't want to tell you,
     I didn't want to tell you,
   I want some love that's true,
     Yes, I do, 'deed I do, you know I do.

   Gimme, gimme what I cry for,
   You know you got the brand of kisses
     That I'd die for,
   You know you made me love you.

2. I had pictured in my mind,
   Some day I would surely find
   Someone handsome, someone true,
   But I never thought of you.

   Now my dream of love is o'er,
   I want you and nothing more,
   Come on, enfold me,
   Come on and hold me
   Just like you never did before.

   > [*to Chorus*]

# You're a Grand Old Flag

W&M: GEORGE M. COHAN
*(Originally, "You've a Grand Old Rag")*
[from *George Washington, Jr.*, 1906]

1. There's a feeling comes a-stealing and it sets my brain a-reeling
   When I'm list'ning to the music of a military band.
   Any tune like "Yankee Doodle" simply sets me off my noodle,
   It's that patriotic something that no one can understand.

   "Way down South in the land of Cotton,"
   Melody untiring, ain't that inspiring?
   Hurrah! Hurrah! We'll join the jubilee,
   And that's going some for the Yankees, by gum.
   Red, white, and blue, I am for you.
   Honest, you're a grand old flag.

   > *Chorus:*
   > You're a grand old flag, you're a high flying flag,
   > And forever in peace may you wave.
   > You're the emblem of the land I love,
   > The home of the free and the brave.
   >
   > Ev'ry heart beats true under red, white, and blue,
   > Where there's never a boast or brag;
   > But should auld acquaintance be forgot
   > Keep your eye on the grand old flag.

2. I'm a cranky hanky panky, I'm a dead-square honest Yankee,
   And I'm proud of that old flag that flies for Uncle Sam.
   Though I don't believe in raving, ev'ry time I see it waving
   There's a chill runs down my back that makes me glad I'm what I am.

   Here's a land with a million soldiers,
   That's if we should need 'em, we'll fight for freedom.
   Hurrah! Hurrah! for ev'ry Yankee Tar and old G.A.R.,
   Ev'ry stripe, ev'ry star.
   Red, white, and blue, hats off to you,
   Honest, you're a grand old flag.

   *[to Chorus]*

# You're in the Army Now

SONG OF THE UNITED STATES ARMY BUGLE CORPS
W: TELL TAYLOR & OLE OLSEN (1917)
M: TRADITIONAL

You're in the army now,
You're not behind the plow,
You'll never get rich, you son of a bitch,
You're in the army now.

You're in the army now,
You're in the army now;
You'll never get rich, own mansions and sich,
You're in the army now.


# Your Eyes Have Told Me So

W: GUS KAHN & EGBERT VAN ALSTYNE / M: WALTER BLAUFUSS (1919)

I know my lips have never met your lips in sweet caress;
Your hand has never touch'd my hand with thrilling tenderness;
You never spoke of love to me, and still somehow I know
  For love has made me wond'rous wise:
  Your eyes have told me so.

*Chorus:*
I saw your eyes,
Your wonderful eyes,
With lovelight and tenderness beaming;
They thrill'd me thru,
They fill'd me, too,
With wonderful dreams I am dreaming.

No need to speak,
No more shall I seek
For my heart has taught me their meaning;
And love has come at last, I know:
Your eyes have told me so.

[*repeat Chorus*]

# You Said It!

W: BERT KALMAR & EDDIE COX / M: HENRY W. SANTLEY (1919)

1. Talk about your sweetie sweet,
   There's a girl lives on our street
      That all the boys are trying,
      Just dying to meet.

   All the fellows hang about
   Waiting for her to come out,
   And when they lay their eyes on her
   You will hear them shout:

      *Chorus:*
      "Is she sort of cute and pretty?
      You said it!
      Would she shine in any city?
      You said it!

      "Has she got beautiful clothes?
      Has she got plenty of beaux?
      And has she lots of other things that nobody knows?
      You said it!

      "Would she make you spend your money?
      You said it!
      Would she fill your little heart with joy?

      "She's the very kind you bet
      Ev'ry fellow wants to pet;
      Is she very hard to get?
      You said it, boy!"

      [*Last stanza, 2nd time:*]
      "When you call her on the 'phone
      And she tells you she's alone,
      Would you leave your happy home?
      You said it, boy!"

      [*Last stanza, 3rd time:*]
      "All the wild men she just tames,
      Makes them call her pretty names;
      Could she capture Jesse James?
      You said it, boy!"

2. Ev'rybody is her slave,
   You should hear the way they rave;
   She tries her best to shake them
   And make them behave.

   There's a school across the way,
   And at recess ev'ry day
   You'll hear the schoolboys singing this
   While they are at play:

   [*to Chorus*]


# You Tell Me Your Dream
## (I'll Tell You Mine)
W & M: GUS KAHN & CHARLES N. DANIELS (1908)

1. When silver moonbeams are creeping,
   I'm always happy it seems;
   Into my world when I'm sleeping,
   Night brings its wonderful dreams.
      You dream of someone, and I wonder who;
      Oh, how I wish that I knew.

   *Chorus:*
   You tell me your dream,
   I'll tell you mine.
   My dreams are sweet, dear,
   With love divine.

   Why keep me waiting,
   Why let me pine?
   You tell me your dream,
   I'll tell you mine.

2. Oh, how I wish I had told you
   All of my dreams long ago,
   Now that I kiss you and hold you,
   Now that at last, dear, I know.
      I'll always dream of this wonderful day
      When my heart told me to say—

   [*to Chorus*]

# Zum Gali Gali

ISRAELI WORK SONG

Zum gali gali gali,
Zum gali gali;
Zum gali gali gali,
Zum gali gali.

Hechalutz le'man avodah;
Avodah le'man hechalutz.
Zum gali gali gali,
Zum gali gali;
Zum gali gali gali,
Zum gali gali.

Avodah le'man hechalutz;
Hechalutz le'man avodah.

# A CATALOG OF SELECTED
# DOVER BOOKS
## IN ALL FIELDS OF INTEREST

# A CATALOG OF SELECTED DOVER
# BOOKS IN ALL FIELDS OF INTEREST

CONCERNING THE SPIRITUAL IN ART, Wassily Kandinsky. Pioneering work by father of abstract art. Thoughts on color theory, nature of art. Analysis of earlier masters. 12 illustrations. 80pp. of text. 5⅜ x 8½. 23411-8 Pa. $4.95

ANIMALS: 1,419 Copyright-Free Illustrations of Mammals, Birds, Fish, Insects, etc., Jim Harter (ed.). Clear wood engravings present, in extremely lifelike poses, over 1,000 species of animals. One of the most extensive pictorial sourcebooks of its kind. Captions. Index. 284pp. 9 x 12. 23766-4 Pa. $14.95

CELTIC ART: The Methods of Construction, George Bain. Simple geometric techniques for making Celtic interlacements, spirals, Kells-type initials, animals, humans, etc. Over 500 illustrations. 160pp. 9 x 12. (Available in U.S. only.) 22923-8 Pa. $9.95

AN ATLAS OF ANATOMY FOR ARTISTS, Fritz Schider. Most thorough reference work on art anatomy in the world. Hundreds of illustrations, including selections from works by Vesalius, Leonardo, Goya, Ingres, Michelangelo, others. 593 illustrations. 192pp. 7⅛ x 10¼. 20241-0 Pa. $9.95

CELTIC HAND STROKE-BY-STROKE (Irish Half-Uncial from "The Book of Kells"): An Arthur Baker Calligraphy Manual, Arthur Baker. Complete guide to creating each letter of the alphabet in distinctive Celtic manner. Covers hand position, strokes, pens, inks, paper, more. Illustrated. 48pp. 8¼ x 11. 24336-2 Pa. $3.95

EASY ORIGAMI, John Montroll. Charming collection of 32 projects (hat, cup, pelican, piano, swan, many more) specially designed for the novice origami hobbyist. Clearly illustrated easy-to-follow instructions insure that even beginning papercrafters will achieve successful results. 48pp. 8¼ x 11. 27298-2 Pa. $3.50

THE COMPLETE BOOK OF BIRDHOUSE CONSTRUCTION FOR WOOD-WORKERS, Scott D. Campbell. Detailed instructions, illustrations, tables. Also data on bird habitat and instinct patterns. Bibliography. 3 tables. 63 illustrations in 15 figures. 48pp. 5¼ x 8½. 24407-5 Pa. $2.50

BLOOMINGDALE'S ILLUSTRATED 1886 CATALOG: Fashions, Dry Goods and Housewares, Bloomingdale Brothers. Famed merchants' extremely rare catalog depicting about 1,700 products: clothing, housewares, firearms, dry goods, jewelry, more. Invaluable for dating, identifying vintage items. Also, copyright-free graphics for artists, designers. Co-published with Henry Ford Museum & Greenfield Village. 160pp. 8¼ x 11. 25780-0 Pa. $10.95

HISTORIC COSTUME IN PICTURES, Braun & Schneider. Over 1,450 costumed figures in clearly detailed engravings—from dawn of civilization to end of 19th century. Captions. Many folk costumes. 256pp. 8⅜ x 11¾. 23150-X Pa. $12.95

STICKLEY CRAFTSMAN FURNITURE CATALOGS, Gustav Stickley and L. & J. G. Stickley. Beautiful, functional furniture in two authentic catalogs from 1910. 594 illustrations, including 277 photos, show settles, rockers, armchairs, reclining chairs, bookcases, desks, tables. 183pp. 6½ x 9¼. 23838-5 Pa. $11.95

AMERICAN LOCOMOTIVES IN HISTORIC PHOTOGRAPHS: 1858 to 1949, Ron Ziel (ed.). A rare collection of 126 meticulously detailed official photographs, called "builder portraits," of American locomotives that majestically chronicle the rise of steam locomotive power in America. Introduction. Detailed captions. xi+ 129pp. 9 x 12. 27393-8 Pa. $13.95

AMERICA'S LIGHTHOUSES: An Illustrated History, Francis Ross Holland, Jr. Delightfully written, profusely illustrated fact-filled survey of over 200 American lighthouses since 1716. History, anecdotes, technological advances, more. 240pp. 8 x 10¾. 25576-X Pa. $12.95

TOWARDS A NEW ARCHITECTURE, Le Corbusier. Pioneering manifesto by founder of "International School." Technical and aesthetic theories, views of industry, economics, relation of form to function, "mass-production split" and much more. Profusely illustrated. 320pp. 6⅛ x 9¼. (Available in U.S. only.) 25023-7 Pa. $9.95

HOW THE OTHER HALF LIVES, Jacob Riis. Famous journalistic record, exposing poverty and degradation of New York slums around 1900, by major social reformer. 100 striking and influential photographs. 233pp. 10 x 7⅞. 22012-5 Pa. $11.95

FRUIT KEY AND TWIG KEY TO TREES AND SHRUBS, William M. Harlow. One of the handiest and most widely used identification aids. Fruit key covers 120 deciduous and evergreen species; twig key 160 deciduous species. Easily used. Over 300 photographs. 126pp. 5⅜ x 8½. 20511-8 Pa. $3.95

COMMON BIRD SONGS, Dr. Donald J. Borror. Songs of 60 most common U.S. birds: robins, sparrows, cardinals, bluejays, finches, more—arranged in order of increasing complexity. Up to 9 variations of songs of each species. Cassette and manual 99911-4 $8.95

ORCHIDS AS HOUSE PLANTS, Rebecca Tyson Northen. Grow cattleyas and many other kinds of orchids—in a window, in a case, or under artificial light. 63 illustrations. 148pp. 5⅜ x 8½. 23261-1 Pa. $5.95

MONSTER MAZES, Dave Phillips. Masterful mazes at four levels of difficulty. Avoid deadly perils and evil creatures to find magical treasures. Solutions for all 32 exciting illustrated puzzles. 48pp. 8¼ x 11. 26005-4 Pa. $2.95

MOZART'S DON GIOVANNI (DOVER OPERA LIBRETTO SERIES), Wolfgang Amadeus Mozart. Introduced and translated by Ellen H. Bleiler. Standard Italian libretto, with complete English translation. Convenient and thoroughly portable—an ideal companion for reading along with a recording or the performance itself. Introduction. List of characters. Plot summary. 121pp. 5¼ x 8½. 24944-1 Pa. $3.95

TECHNICAL MANUAL AND DICTIONARY OF CLASSICAL BALLET, Gail Grant. Defines, explains, comments on steps, movements, poses and concepts. 15-page pictorial section. Basic book for student, viewer. 127pp. 5⅜ x 8½. 21843-0 Pa. $4.95

THE CLARINET AND CLARINET PLAYING, David Pino. Lively, comprehensive work features suggestions about technique, musicianship, and musical interpretation, as well as guidelines for teaching, making your own reeds, and preparing for public performance. Includes an intriguing look at clarinet history. "A godsend," *The Clarinet,* Journal of the International Clarinet Society. Appendixes. 7 illus. 320pp. 5⅜ x 8½. 40270-3 Pa. $9.95

HOLLYWOOD GLAMOR PORTRAITS, John Kobal (ed.). 145 photos from 1926-49. Harlow, Gable, Bogart, Bacall; 94 stars in all. Full background on photographers, technical aspects. 160pp. 8⅜ x 11¼. 23352-9 Pa. $12.95

THE ANNOTATED CASEY AT THE BAT: A Collection of Ballads about the Mighty Casey/Third, Revised Edition, Martin Gardner (ed.). Amusing sequels and parodies of one of America's best-loved poems: Casey's Revenge, Why Casey Whiffed, Casey's Sister at the Bat, others. 256pp. 5⅜ x 8½. 28598-7 Pa. $8.95

THE RAVEN AND OTHER FAVORITE POEMS, Edgar Allan Poe. Over 40 of the author's most memorable poems: "The Bells," "Ulalume," "Israfel," "To Helen," "The Conqueror Worm," "Eldorado," "Annabel Lee," many more. Alphabetic lists of titles and first lines. 64pp. 5$\frac{3}{16}$ x 8¼. 26685-0 Pa. $1.00

PERSONAL MEMOIRS OF U. S. GRANT, Ulysses Simpson Grant. Intelligent, deeply moving firsthand account of Civil War campaigns, considered by many the finest military memoirs ever written. Includes letters, historic photographs, maps and more. 528pp. 6⅛ x 9¼. 28587-1 Pa. $12.95

ANCIENT EGYPTIAN MATERIALS AND INDUSTRIES, A. Lucas and J. Harris. Fascinating, comprehensive, thoroughly documented text describes this ancient civilization's vast resources and the processes that incorporated them in daily life, including the use of animal products, building materials, cosmetics, perfumes and incense, fibers, glazed ware, glass and its manufacture, materials used in the mummification process, and much more. 544pp. 6⅛ x 9¼. (Available in U.S. only.) 40446-3 Pa. $16.95

RUSSIAN STORIES/PYCCKNE PACCKA3bl: A Dual-Language Book, edited by Gleb Struve. Twelve tales by such masters as Chekhov, Tolstoy, Dostoevsky, Pushkin, others. Excellent word-for-word English translations on facing pages, plus teaching and study aids, Russian/English vocabulary, biographical/critical introductions, more. 416pp. 5⅜ x 8½. 26244-8 Pa. $9.95

PHILADELPHIA THEN AND NOW: 60 Sites Photographed in the Past and Present, Kenneth Finkel and Susan Oyama. Rare photographs of City Hall, Logan Square, Independence Hall, Betsy Ross House, other landmarks juxtaposed with contemporary views. Captures changing face of historic city. Introduction. Captions. 128pp. 8¼ x 11. 25790-8 Pa. $9.95

AIA ARCHITECTURAL GUIDE TO NASSAU AND SUFFOLK COUNTIES, LONG ISLAND, The American Institute of Architects, Long Island Chapter, and the Society for the Preservation of Long Island Antiquities. Comprehensive, well-researched and generously illustrated volume brings to life over three centuries of Long Island's great architectural heritage. More than 240 photographs with authoritative, extensively detailed captions. 176pp. 8¼ x 11. 26946-9 Pa. $14.95

NORTH AMERICAN INDIAN LIFE: Customs and Traditions of 23 Tribes, Elsie Clews Parsons (ed.). 27 fictionalized essays by noted anthropologists examine religion, customs, government, additional facets of life among the Winnebago, Crow, Zuni, Eskimo, other tribes. 480pp. 6⅛ x 9¼. 27377-6 Pa. $10.95

FRANK LLOYD WRIGHT'S DANA HOUSE, Donald Hoffmann. Pictorial essay of residential masterpiece with over 160 interior and exterior photos, plans, elevations, sketches and studies. 128pp. 9¼ x 10¾. 29120-0 Pa. $12.95

THE MALE AND FEMALE FIGURE IN MOTION: 60 Classic Photographic Sequences, Eadweard Muybridge. 60 true-action photographs of men and women walking, running, climbing, bending, turning, etc., reproduced from rare 19th-century masterpiece. vi + 121pp. 9 x 12. 24745-7 Pa. $12.95

1001 QUESTIONS ANSWERED ABOUT THE SEASHORE, N. J. Berrill and Jacquelyn Berrill. Queries answered about dolphins, sea snails, sponges, starfish, fishes, shore birds, many others. Covers appearance, breeding, growth, feeding, much more. 305pp. 5¼ x 8¼. 23366-9 Pa. $9.95

ATTRACTING BIRDS TO YOUR YARD, William J. Weber. Easy-to-follow guide offers advice on how to attract the greatest diversity of birds: birdhouses, feeders, water and waterers, much more. 96pp. 5³⁄₁₆ x 8¼. 28927-3 Pa. $2.50

MEDICINAL AND OTHER USES OF NORTH AMERICAN PLANTS: A Historical Survey with Special Reference to the Eastern Indian Tribes, Charlotte Erichsen-Brown. Chronological historical citations document 500 years of usage of plants, trees, shrubs native to eastern Canada, northeastern U.S. Also complete identifying information. 343 illustrations. 544pp. 6½ x 9¼. 25951-X Pa. $12.95

STORYBOOK MAZES, Dave Phillips. 23 stories and mazes on two-page spreads: Wizard of Oz, Treasure Island, Robin Hood, etc. Solutions. 64pp. 8¼ x 11. 23628-5 Pa. $2.95

AMERICAN NEGRO SONGS: 230 Folk Songs and Spirituals, Religious and Secular, John W. Work. This authoritative study traces the African influences of songs sung and played by black Americans at work, in church, and as entertainment. The author discusses the lyric significance of such songs as "Swing Low, Sweet Chariot," "John Henry," and others and offers the words and music for 230 songs. Bibliography. Index of Song Titles. 272pp. 6½ x 9¼. 40271-1 Pa. $9.95

MOVIE-STAR PORTRAITS OF THE FORTIES, John Kobal (ed.). 163 glamor, studio photos of 106 stars of the 1940s: Rita Hayworth, Ava Gardner, Marlon Brando, Clark Gable, many more. 176pp. 8⅜ x 11¼. 23546-7 Pa. $14.95

BENCHLEY LOST AND FOUND, Robert Benchley. Finest humor from early 30s, about pet peeves, child psychologists, post office and others. Mostly unavailable elsewhere. 73 illustrations by Peter Arno and others. 183pp. 5⅜ x 8½. 22410-4 Pa. $6.95

YEKL and THE IMPORTED BRIDEGROOM AND OTHER STORIES OF YIDDISH NEW YORK, Abraham Cahan. Film Hester Street based on *Yekl* (1896). Novel, other stories among first about Jewish immigrants on N.Y.'s East Side. 240pp. 5⅜ x 8½. 22427-9 Pa. $7.95

SELECTED POEMS, Walt Whitman. Generous sampling from *Leaves of Grass.* Twenty-four poems include "I Hear America Singing," "Song of the Open Road," "I Sing the Body Electric," "When Lilacs Last in the Dooryard Bloom'd," "O Captain! My Captain!"–all reprinted from an authoritative edition. Lists of titles and first lines. 128pp. 5³⁄₁₆ x 8¼. 26878-0 Pa. $1.00

THE BEST TALES OF HOFFMANN, E. T. A. Hoffmann. 10 of Hoffmann's most important stories: "Nutcracker and the King of Mice," "The Golden Flowerpot," etc. 458pp. 5⅜ x 8½. 21793-0 Pa. $9.95

FROM FETISH TO GOD IN ANCIENT EGYPT, E. A. Wallis Budge. Rich detailed survey of Egyptian conception of "God" and gods, magic, cult of animals, Osiris, more. Also, superb English translations of hymns and legends. 240 illustrations. 545pp. 5⅜ x 8½. 25803-3 Pa. $13.95

FRENCH STORIES/CONTES FRANÇAIS: A Dual-Language Book, Wallace Fowlie. Ten stories by French masters, Voltaire to Camus: "Micromegas" by Voltaire; "The Atheist's Mass" by Balzac; "Minuet" by de Maupassant; "The Guest" by Camus, six more. Excellent English translations on facing pages. Also French-English vocabulary list, exercises, more. 352pp. 5⅜ x 8½. 26443-2 Pa. $9.95

CHICAGO AT THE TURN OF THE CENTURY IN PHOTOGRAPHS: 122 Historic Views from the Collections of the Chicago Historical Society, Larry A. Viskochil. Rare large-format prints offer detailed views of City Hall, State Street, the Loop, Hull House, Union Station, many other landmarks, circa 1904-1913. Introduction. Captions. Maps. 144pp. 9⅜ x 12¼. 24656-6 Pa. $12.95

OLD BROOKLYN IN EARLY PHOTOGRAPHS, 1865-1929, William Lee Younger. Luna Park, Gravesend race track, construction of Grand Army Plaza, moving of Hotel Brighton, etc. 157 previously unpublished photographs. 165pp. 8⅞ x 11¾. 23587-4 Pa. $13.95

THE MYTHS OF THE NORTH AMERICAN INDIANS, Lewis Spence. Rich anthology of the myths and legends of the Algonquins, Iroquois, Pawnees and Sioux, prefaced by an extensive historical and ethnological commentary. 36 illustrations. 480pp. 5⅜ x 8½. 25967-6 Pa. $10.95

AN ENCYCLOPEDIA OF BATTLES: Accounts of Over 1,560 Battles from 1479 B.C. to the Present, David Eggenberger. Essential details of every major battle in recorded history from the first battle of Megiddo in 1479 B.C. to Grenada in 1984. List of Battle Maps. New Appendix covering the years 1967-1984. Index. 99 illustrations. 544pp. 6½ x 9¼. 24913-1 Pa. $16.95

SAILING ALONE AROUND THE WORLD, Captain Joshua Slocum. First man to sail around the world, alone, in small boat. One of great feats of seamanship told in delightful manner. 67 illustrations. 294pp. 5⅜ x 8½. 20326-3 Pa. $6.95

ANARCHISM AND OTHER ESSAYS, Emma Goldman. Powerful, penetrating, prophetic essays on direct action, role of minorities, prison reform, puritan hypocrisy, violence, etc. 271pp. 5⅜ x 8½. 22484-8 Pa. $7.95

MYTHS OF THE HINDUS AND BUDDHISTS, Ananda K. Coomaraswamy and Sister Nivedita. Great stories of the epics; deeds of Krishna, Shiva, taken from puranas, Vedas, folk tales; etc. 32 illustrations. 400pp. 5⅜ x 8½. 21759-0 Pa. $12.95

THE TRAUMA OF BIRTH, Otto Rank. Rank's controversial thesis that anxiety neurosis is caused by profound psychological trauma which occurs at birth. 256pp. 5⅜ x 8½. 27974-X Pa. $7.95

A THEOLOGICO-POLITICAL TREATISE, Benedict Spinoza. Also contains unfinished Political Treatise. Great classic on religious liberty, theory of government on common consent. R. Elwes translation. Total of 421pp. 5⅜ x 8½. 20249-6 Pa. $10.95

MY BONDAGE AND MY FREEDOM, Frederick Douglass. Born a slave, Douglass became outspoken force in antislavery movement. The best of Douglass' autobiographies. Graphic description of slave life. 464pp. 5⅜ x 8½. 22457-0 Pa. $8.95

FOLLOWING THE EQUATOR: A Journey Around the World, Mark Twain. Fascinating humorous account of 1897 voyage to Hawaii, Australia, India, New Zealand, etc. Ironic, bemused reports on peoples, customs, climate, flora and fauna, politics, much more. 197 illustrations. 720pp. 5⅜ x 8½. 26113-1 Pa. $15.95

THE PEOPLE CALLED SHAKERS, Edward D. Andrews. Definitive study of Shakers: origins, beliefs, practices, dances, social organization, furniture and crafts, etc. 33 illustrations. 351pp. 5⅜ x 8½. 21081-2 Pa. $10.95

THE MYTHS OF GREECE AND ROME, H. A. Guerber. A classic of mythology, generously illustrated, long prized for its simple, graphic, accurate retelling of the principal myths of Greece and Rome, and for its commentary on their origins and significance. With 64 illustrations by Michelangelo, Raphael, Titian, Rubens, Canova, Bernini and others. 480pp. 5⅜ x 8½. 27584-1 Pa. $9.95

PSYCHOLOGY OF MUSIC, Carl E. Seashore. Classic work discusses music as a medium from psychological viewpoint. Clear treatment of physical acoustics, auditory apparatus, sound perception, development of musical skills, nature of musical feeling, host of other topics. 88 figures. 408pp. 5⅜ x 8½. 21851-1 Pa. $11.95

THE PHILOSOPHY OF HISTORY, Georg W. Hegel. Great classic of Western thought develops concept that history is not chance but rational process, the evolution of freedom. 457pp. 5⅜ x 8½. 20112-0 Pa. $9.95

THE BOOK OF TEA, Kakuzo Okakura. Minor classic of the Orient: entertaining, charming explanation, interpretation of traditional Japanese culture in terms of tea ceremony. 94pp. 5⅜ x 8½. 20070-1 Pa. $3.95

LIFE IN ANCIENT EGYPT, Adolf Erman. Fullest, most thorough, detailed older account with much not in more recent books, domestic life, religion, magic, medicine, commerce, much more. Many illustrations reproduce tomb paintings, carvings, hieroglyphs, etc. 597pp. 5⅜ x 8½. 22632-8 Pa. $12.95

SUNDIALS, Their Theory and Construction, Albert Waugh. Far and away the best, most thorough coverage of ideas, mathematics concerned, types, construction, adjusting anywhere. Simple, nontechnical treatment allows even children to build several of these dials. Over 100 illustrations. 230pp. 5⅜ x 8½. 22947-5 Pa. $8.95

THEORETICAL HYDRODYNAMICS, L. M. Milne-Thomson. Classic exposition of the mathematical theory of fluid motion, applicable to both hydrodynamics and aerodynamics. Over 600 exercises. 768pp. 6⅛ x 9¼. 68970-0 Pa. $20.95

SONGS OF EXPERIENCE: Facsimile Reproduction with 26 Plates in Full Color, William Blake. 26 full-color plates from a rare 1826 edition. Includes "TheTyger," "London," "Holy Thursday," and other poems. Printed text of poems. 48pp. 5¼ x 7. 24636-1 Pa. $4.95

OLD-TIME VIGNETTES IN FULL COLOR, Carol Belanger Grafton (ed.). Over 390 charming, often sentimental illustrations, selected from archives of Victorian graphics—pretty women posing, children playing, food, flowers, kittens and puppies, smiling cherubs, birds and butterflies, much more. All copyright-free. 48pp. 9¼ x 12¼. 27269-9 Pa. $7.95

PERSPECTIVE FOR ARTISTS, Rex Vicat Cole. Depth, perspective of sky and sea, shadows, much more, not usually covered. 391 diagrams, 81 reproductions of drawings and paintings. 279pp. 5⅜ x 8½. 22487-2 Pa. $9.95

DRAWING THE LIVING FIGURE, Joseph Sheppard. Innovative approach to artistic anatomy focuses on specifics of surface anatomy, rather than muscles and bones. Over 170 drawings of live models in front, back and side views, and in widely varying poses. Accompanying diagrams. 177 illustrations. Introduction. Index. 144pp. 8⅜ x11¼. 26723-7 Pa. $9.95

GOTHIC AND OLD ENGLISH ALPHABETS: 100 Complete Fonts, Dan X. Solo. Add power, elegance to posters, signs, other graphics with 100 stunning copyright-free alphabets: Blackstone, Dolbey, Germania, 97 more–including many lower-case, numerals, punctuation marks. 104pp. 8⅛ x 11. 24695-7 Pa. $8.95

HOW TO DO BEADWORK, Mary White. Fundamental book on craft from simple projects to five-bead chains and woven works. 106 illustrations. 142pp. 5⅜ x 8. 20697-1 Pa. $5.95

THE BOOK OF WOOD CARVING, Charles Marshall Sayers. Finest book for beginners discusses fundamentals and offers 34 designs. "Absolutely first rate . . . well thought out and well executed."–E. J. Tangerman. 118pp. 7¾ x 10⅝. 23654-4 Pa. $7.95

ILLUSTRATED CATALOG OF CIVIL WAR MILITARY GOODS: Union Army Weapons, Insignia, Uniform Accessories, and Other Equipment, Schuyler, Hartley, and Graham. Rare, profusely illustrated 1846 catalog includes Union Army uniform and dress regulations, arms and ammunition, coats, insignia, flags, swords, rifles, etc. 226 illustrations. 160pp. 9 x 12. 24939-5 Pa. $10.95

WOMEN'S FASHIONS OF THE EARLY 1900s: An Unabridged Republication of "New York Fashions, 1909," National Cloak & Suit Co. Rare catalog of mail-order fashions documents women's and children's clothing styles shortly after the turn of the century. Captions offer full descriptions, prices. Invaluable resource for fashion, costume historians. Approximately 725 illustrations. 128pp. 8⅜ x 11¼. 27276-1 Pa. $11.95

THE 1912 AND 1915 GUSTAV STICKLEY FURNITURE CATALOGS, Gustav Stickley. With over 200 detailed illustrations and descriptions, these two catalogs are essential reading and reference materials and identification guides for Stickley furniture. Captions cite materials, dimensions and prices. 112pp. 6½ x 9¼. 26676-1 Pa. $9.95

EARLY AMERICAN LOCOMOTIVES, John H. White, Jr. Finest locomotive engravings from early 19th century: historical (1804–74), main-line (after 1870), special, foreign, etc. 147 plates. 142pp. 11⅜ x 8¼. 22772-3 Pa. $12.95

THE TALL SHIPS OF TODAY IN PHOTOGRAPHS, Frank O. Braynard. Lavishly illustrated tribute to nearly 100 majestic contemporary sailing vessels: Amerigo Vespucci, Clearwater, Constitution, Eagle, Mayflower, Sea Cloud, Victory, many more. Authoritative captions provide statistics, background on each ship. 190 black-and-white photographs and illustrations. Introduction. 128pp. 8⅞ x 11¾. 27163-3 Pa. $14.95

LITTLE BOOK OF EARLY AMERICAN CRAFTS AND TRADES, Peter Stockham (ed.). 1807 children's book explains crafts and trades: baker, hatter, cooper, potter, and many others. 23 copperplate illustrations. 140pp. 4⅝ x 6.
23336-7 Pa. $4.95

VICTORIAN FASHIONS AND COSTUMES FROM HARPER'S BAZAR, 1867–1898, Stella Blum (ed.). Day costumes, evening wear, sports clothes, shoes, hats, other accessories in over 1,000 detailed engravings. 320pp. 9⅜ x 12¼.
22990-4 Pa. $16.95

GUSTAV STICKLEY, THE CRAFTSMAN, Mary Ann Smith. Superb study surveys broad scope of Stickley's achievement, especially in architecture. Design philosophy, rise and fall of the Craftsman empire, descriptions and floor plans for many Craftsman houses, more. 86 black-and-white halftones. 31 line illustrations. Introduction 208pp. 6½ x 9¼.
27210-9 Pa. $9.95

THE LONG ISLAND RAIL ROAD IN EARLY PHOTOGRAPHS, Ron Ziel. Over 220 rare photos, informative text document origin ( 1844) and development of rail service on Long Island. Vintage views of early trains, locomotives, stations, passengers, crews, much more. Captions. 8⅞ x 11¾.
26301-0 Pa. $14.95

VOYAGE OF THE LIBERDADE, Joshua Slocum. Great 19th-century mariner's thrilling, first-hand account of the wreck of his ship off South America, the 35-foot boat he built from the wreckage, and its remarkable voyage home. 128pp. 5⅜ x 8½.
40022-0 Pa. $5.95

TEN BOOKS ON ARCHITECTURE, Vitruvius. The most important book ever written on architecture. Early Roman aesthetics, technology, classical orders, site selection, all other aspects. Morgan translation. 331pp. 5⅜ x 8½. 20645-9 Pa. $8.95

THE HUMAN FIGURE IN MOTION, Eadweard Muybridge. More than 4,500 stopped-action photos, in action series, showing undraped men, women, children jumping, lying down, throwing, sitting, wrestling, carrying, etc. 390pp. 7⅞ x 10⅝.
20204-6 Clothbd. $27.95

TREES OF THE EASTERN AND CENTRAL UNITED STATES AND CANADA, William M. Harlow. Best one-volume guide to 140 trees. Full descriptions, woodlore, range, etc. Over 600 illustrations. Handy size. 288pp. 4½ x 6⅜.
20395-6 Pa. $6.95

SONGS OF WESTERN BIRDS, Dr. Donald J. Borror. Complete song and call repertoire of 60 western species, including flycatchers, juncoes, cactus wrens, many more–includes fully illustrated booklet.       Cassette and manual 99913-0 $8.95

GROWING AND USING HERBS AND SPICES, Milo Miloradovich. Versatile handbook provides all the information needed for cultivation and use of all the herbs and spices available in North America. 4 illustrations. Index. Glossary. 236pp. 5⅜ x 8½.
25058-X Pa. $7.95

BIG BOOK OF MAZES AND LABYRINTHS, Walter Shepherd. 50 mazes and labyrinths in all–classical, solid, ripple, and more–in one great volume. Perfect inexpensive puzzler for clever youngsters. Full solutions. 112pp. 8⅛ x 11.
22951-3 Pa. $5.95

PIANO TUNING, J. Cree Fischer. Clearest, best book for beginner, amateur. Simple repairs, raising dropped notes, tuning by easy method of flattened fifths. No previous skills needed. 4 illustrations. 201pp. 5⅜ x 8½. 23267-0 Pa. $6.95

HINTS TO SINGERS, Lillian Nordica. Selecting the right teacher, developing confidence, overcoming stage fright, and many other important skills receive thoughtful discussion in this indispensible guide, written by a world-famous diva of four decades' experience. 96pp. 5³/₈ x 8¹/₂. 40094-8 Pa. $4.95

THE COMPLETE NONSENSE OF EDWARD LEAR, Edward Lear. All nonsense limericks, zany alphabets, Owl and Pussycat, songs, nonsense botany, etc., illustrated by Lear. Total of 320pp. 5⅜ x 8½. (AVAILABLE IN U.S. ONLY.) 20167-8 Pa. $7.95

VICTORIAN PARLOUR POETRY: An Annotated Anthology, Michael R. Turner. 117 gems by Longfellow, Tennyson, Browning, many lesser-known poets. "The Village Blacksmith," "Curfew Must Not Ring Tonight," "Only a Baby Small," dozens more, often difficult to find elsewhere. Index of poets, titles, first lines. xxiii + 325pp. 5⅝ x 8¼. 27044-0 Pa. $8.95

DUBLINERS, James Joyce. Fifteen stories offer vivid, tightly focused observations of the lives of Dublin's poorer classes. At least one, "The Dead," is considered a masterpiece. Reprinted complete and unabridged from standard edition. 160pp. 5³⁄₁₆ x 8¼. 26870-5 Pa. $1.00

GREAT WEIRD TALES: 14 Stories by Lovecraft, Blackwood, Machen and Others, S. T. Joshi (ed.). 14 spellbinding tales, including "The Sin Eater," by Fiona McLeod, "The Eye Above the Mantel," by Frank Belknap Long, as well as renowned works by R. H. Barlow, Lord Dunsany, Arthur Machen, W. C. Morrow and eight other masters of the genre. 256pp. 5⅜ x 8½. (Available in U.S. only.) 40436-6 Pa. $8.95

THE BOOK OF THE SACRED MAGIC OF ABRAMELIN THE MAGE, translated by S. MacGregor Mathers. Medieval manuscript of ceremonial magic. Basic document in Aleister Crowley, Golden Dawn groups. 268pp. 5⅜ x 8½. 23211-5 Pa. $9.95

NEW RUSSIAN-ENGLISH AND ENGLISH-RUSSIAN DICTIONARY, M. A. O'Brien. This is a remarkably handy Russian dictionary, containing a surprising amount of information, including over 70,000 entries. 366pp. 4½ x 6⅛. 20208-9 Pa. $10.95

HISTORIC HOMES OF THE AMERICAN PRESIDENTS, Second, Revised Edition, Irvin Haas. A traveler's guide to American Presidential homes, most open to the public, depicting and describing homes occupied by every American President from George Washington to George Bush. With visiting hours, admission charges, travel routes. 175 photographs. Index. 160pp. 8¼ x 11. 26751-2 Pa. $11.95

NEW YORK IN THE FORTIES, Andreas Feininger. 162 brilliant photographs by the well-known photographer, formerly with *Life* magazine. Commuters, shoppers, Times Square at night, much else from city at its peak. Captions by John von Hartz. 181pp. 9¼ x 10¾. 23585-8 Pa. $13.95

INDIAN SIGN LANGUAGE, William Tomkins. Over 525 signs developed by Sioux and other tribes. Written instructions and diagrams. Also 290 pictographs. 111pp. 6⅛ x 9¼. 22029-X Pa. $3.95

CATALOG OF DOVER BOOKS

ANATOMY: A Complete Guide for Artists, Joseph Sheppard. A master of figure drawing shows artists how to render human anatomy convincingly. Over 460 illustrations. 224pp. 8⅜ x 11¼. 27279-6 Pa. $11.95

MEDIEVAL CALLIGRAPHY: Its History and Technique, Marc Drogin. Spirited history, comprehensive instruction manual covers 13 styles (ca. 4th century through 15th). Excellent photographs; directions for duplicating medieval techniques with modern tools. 224pp. 8⅜ x 11¼. 26142-5 Pa. $12.95

DRIED FLOWERS: How to Prepare Them, Sarah Whitlock and Martha Rankin. Complete instructions on how to use silica gel, meal and borax, perlite aggregate, sand and borax, glycerine and water to create attractive permanent flower arrangements. 12 illustrations. 32pp. 5⅜ x 8½. 21802-3 Pa. $1.00

EASY-TO-MAKE BIRD FEEDERS FOR WOODWORKERS, Scott D. Campbell. Detailed, simple-to-use guide for designing, constructing, caring for and using feeders. Text, illustrations for 12 classic and contemporary designs. 96pp. 5⅜ x 8½. 25847-5 Pa. $3.95

SCOTTISH WONDER TALES FROM MYTH AND LEGEND, Donald A. Mackenzie. 16 lively tales tell of giants rumbling down mountainsides, of a magic wand that turns stone pillars into warriors, of gods and goddesses, evil hags, powerful forces and more. 240pp. 5⅜ x 8½. 29677-6 Pa. $6.95

THE HISTORY OF UNDERCLOTHES, C. Willett Cunnington and Phyllis Cunnington. Fascinating, well-documented survey covering six centuries of English undergarments, enhanced with over 100 illustrations: 12th-century laced-up bodice, footed long drawers (1795), 19th-century bustles, 19th-century corsets for men, Victorian "bust improvers," much more. 272pp. 5⅜ x 8¼. 27124-2 Pa. $9.95

ARTS AND CRAFTS FURNITURE: The Complete Brooks Catalog of 1912, Brooks Manufacturing Co. Photos and detailed descriptions of more than 150 now very collectible furniture designs from the Arts and Crafts movement depict davenports, settees, buffets, desks, tables, chairs, bedsteads, dressers and more, all built of solid, quarter-sawed oak. Invaluable for students and enthusiasts of antiques, Americana and the decorative arts. 80pp. 6½ x 9¼. 27471-3 Pa. $8.95

WILBUR AND ORVILLE: A Biography of the Wright Brothers, Fred Howard. Definitive, crisply written study tells the full story of the brothers' lives and work. A vividly written biography, unparalleled in scope and color, that also captures the spirit of an extraordinary era. 560pp. 6⅛ x 9¼. 40297-5 Pa. $17.95

THE ARTS OF THE SAILOR: Knotting, Splicing and Ropework, Hervey Garrett Smith. Indispensable shipboard reference covers tools, basic knots and useful hitches; handsewing and canvas work, more. Over 100 illustrations. Delightful reading for sea lovers. 256pp. 5⅜ x 8½. 26440-8 Pa. $8.95

FRANK LLOYD WRIGHT'S FALLINGWATER: The House and Its History, Second, Revised Edition, Donald Hoffmann. A total revision–both in text and illustrations–of the standard document on Fallingwater, the boldest, most personal architectural statement of Wright's mature years, updated with valuable new material from the recently opened Frank Lloyd Wright Archives. "Fascinating"–*The New York Times*. 116 illustrations. 128pp. 9¼ x 10¾. 27430-6 Pa. $12.95

PHOTOGRAPHIC SKETCHBOOK OF THE CIVIL WAR, Alexander Gardner. 100 photos taken on field during the Civil War. Famous shots of Manassas Harper's Ferry, Lincoln, Richmond, slave pens, etc. 244pp. 10⅝ x 8¼. 22731-6 Pa. $10.95

FIVE ACRES AND INDEPENDENCE, Maurice G. Kains. Great back-to-the-land classic explains basics of self-sufficient farming. The one book to get. 95 illustrations. 397pp. 5⅜ x 8½. 20974-1 Pa. $7.95

SONGS OF EASTERN BIRDS, Dr. Donald J. Borror. Songs and calls of 60 species most common to eastern U.S.: warblers, woodpeckers, flycatchers, thrushes, larks, many more in high-quality recording. Cassette and manual 99912-2 $9.95

A MODERN HERBAL, Margaret Grieve. Much the fullest, most exact, most useful compilation of herbal material. Gigantic alphabetical encyclopedia, from aconite to zedoary, gives botanical information, medical properties, folklore, economic uses, much else. Indispensable to serious reader. 161 illustrations. 888pp. 6½ x 9¼. 2-vol. set. (Available in U.S. only.) Vol. I: 22798-7 Pa. $9.95
Vol. II: 22799-5 Pa. $9.95

HIDDEN TREASURE MAZE BOOK, Dave Phillips. Solve 34 challenging mazes accompanied by heroic tales of adventure. Evil dragons, people-eating plants, blood-thirsty giants, many more dangerous adversaries lurk at every twist and turn. 34 mazes, stories, solutions. 48pp. 8¼ x 11. 24566-7 Pa. $2.95

LETTERS OF W. A. MOZART, Wolfgang A. Mozart. Remarkable letters show bawdy wit, humor, imagination, musical insights, contemporary musical world; includes some letters from Leopold Mozart. 276pp. 5⅜ x 8½. 22859-2 Pa. $7.95

BASIC PRINCIPLES OF CLASSICAL BALLET, Agrippina Vaganova. Great Russian theoretician, teacher explains methods for teaching classical ballet. 118 illustrations. 175pp. 5⅜ x 8½. 22036-2 Pa. $6.95

THE JUMPING FROG, Mark Twain. Revenge edition. The original story of The Celebrated Jumping Frog of Calaveras County, a hapless French translation, and Twain's hilarious "retranslation" from the French. 12 illustrations. 66pp. 5⅜ x 8½. 22686-7 Pa. $3.95

BEST REMEMBERED POEMS, Martin Gardner (ed.). The 126 poems in this superb collection of 19th- and 20th-century British and American verse range from Shelley's "To a Skylark" to the impassioned "Renascence" of Edna St. Vincent Millay and to Edward Lear's whimsical "The Owl and the Pussycat." 224pp. 5⅜ x 8½. 27165-X Pa. $5.95

COMPLETE SONNETS, William Shakespeare. Over 150 exquisite poems deal with love, friendship, the tyranny of time, beauty's evanescence, death and other themes in language of remarkable power, precision and beauty. Glossary of archaic terms. 80pp. 5$\frac{3}{16}$ x 8¼. 26686-9 Pa. $1.00

BODIES IN A BOOKSHOP, R. T. Campbell. Challenging mystery of blackmail and murder with ingenious plot and superbly drawn characters. In the best tradition of British suspense fiction. 192pp. 5⅜ x 8½. 24720-1 Pa. $6.95

THE WIT AND HUMOR OF OSCAR WILDE, Alvin Redman (ed.). More than 1,000 ripostes, paradoxes, wisecracks: Work is the curse of the drinking classes; I can resist everything except temptation; etc. 258pp. 5⅜ x 8½. 20602-5 Pa. $6.95

SHAKESPEARE LEXICON AND QUOTATION DICTIONARY, Alexander Schmidt. Full definitions, locations, shades of meaning in every word in plays and poems. More than 50,000 exact quotations. 1,485pp. 6½ x 9¼. 2-vol. set.
Vol. 1: 22726-X Pa. $17.95
Vol. 2: 22727-8 Pa. $17.95

SELECTED POEMS, Emily Dickinson. Over 100 best-known, best-loved poems by one of America's foremost poets, reprinted from authoritative early editions. No comparable edition at this price. Index of first lines. 64pp. 5$\frac{3}{16}$ x 8¼.
26466-1 Pa. $1.00

THE INSIDIOUS DR. FU-MANCHU, Sax Rohmer. The first of the popular mystery series introduces a pair of English detectives to their archnemesis, the diabolical Dr. Fu-Manchu. Flavorful atmosphere, fast-paced action, and colorful characters enliven this classic of the genre. 208pp. 5$\frac{3}{16}$ x 8¼. 29898-1 Pa. $2.00

THE MALLEUS MALEFICARUM OF KRAMER AND SPRENGER, translated by Montague Summers. Full text of most important witchhunter's "bible," used by both Catholics and Protestants. 278pp. 6⅝ x 10. 22802-9 Pa. $12.95

SPANISH STORIES/CUENTOS ESPAÑOLES: A Dual-Language Book, Angel Flores (ed.). Unique format offers 13 great stories in Spanish by Cervantes, Borges, others. Faithful English translations on facing pages. 352pp. 5⅜ x 8½.
25399-6 Pa. $8.95

GARDEN CITY, LONG ISLAND, IN EARLY PHOTOGRAPHS, 1869–1919, Mildred H. Smith. Handsome treasury of 118 vintage pictures, accompanied by carefully researched captions, document the Garden City Hotel fire (1899), the Vanderbilt Cup Race (1908), the first airmail flight departing from the Nassau Boulevard Aerodrome (1911), and much more. 96pp. 8⅞ x 11¾. 40669-5 Pa. $12.95

OLD QUEENS, N.Y., IN EARLY PHOTOGRAPHS, Vincent F. Seyfried and William Asadorian. Over 160 rare photographs of Maspeth, Jamaica, Jackson Heights, and other areas. Vintage views of DeWitt Clinton mansion, 1939 World's Fair and more. Captions. 192pp. 8⅞ x 11. 26358-4 Pa. $12.95

CAPTURED BY THE INDIANS: 15 Firsthand Accounts, 1750-1870, Frederick Drimmer. Astounding true historical accounts of grisly torture, bloody conflicts, relentless pursuits, miraculous escapes and more, by people who lived to tell the tale. 384pp. 5⅜ x 8½. 24901-8 Pa. $8.95

THE WORLD'S GREAT SPEECHES (Fourth Enlarged Edition), Lewis Copeland, Lawrence W. Lamm, and Stephen J. McKenna. Nearly 300 speeches provide public speakers with a wealth of updated quotes and inspiration–from Pericles' funeral oration and William Jennings Bryan's "Cross of Gold Speech" to Malcolm X's powerful words on the Black Revolution and Earl of Spenser's tribute to his sister, Diana, Princess of Wales. 944pp. 5⅜ x 8⅜. 40903-1 Pa. $15.95

THE BOOK OF THE SWORD, Sir Richard F. Burton. Great Victorian scholar/adventurer's eloquent, erudite history of the "queen of weapons"–from prehistory to early Roman Empire. Evolution and development of early swords, variations (sabre, broadsword, cutlass, scimitar, etc.), much more. 336pp. 6⅛ x 9¼.
25434-8 Pa. $9.95

AUTOBIOGRAPHY: The Story of My Experiments with Truth, Mohandas K. Gandhi. Boyhood, legal studies, purification, the growth of the Satyagraha (nonviolent protest) movement. Critical, inspiring work of the man responsible for the freedom of India. 480pp. 5⅜ x 8½. (Available in U.S. only.) 24593-4 Pa. $8.95

CELTIC MYTHS AND LEGENDS, T. W. Rolleston. Masterful retelling of Irish and Welsh stories and tales. Cuchulain, King Arthur, Deirdre, the Grail, many more. First paperback edition. 58 full-page illustrations. 512pp. 5⅜ x 8½. 26507-2 Pa. $9.95

THE PRINCIPLES OF PSYCHOLOGY, William James. Famous long course complete, unabridged. Stream of thought, time perception, memory, experimental methods; great work decades ahead of its time. 94 figures. 1,391pp. 5⅜ x 8½. 2-vol. set.
Vol. I: 20381-6 Pa. $14.95
Vol. II: 20382-4 Pa. $14.95

THE WORLD AS WILL AND REPRESENTATION, Arthur Schopenhauer. Definitive English translation of Schopenhauer's life work, correcting more than 1,000 errors, omissions in earlier translations. Translated by E. F. J. Payne. Total of 1,269pp. 5⅜ x 8½. 2-vol. set.
Vol. 1: 21761-2 Pa. $12.95
Vol. 2: 21762-0 Pa. $12.95

MAGIC AND MYSTERY IN TIBET, Madame Alexandra David-Neel. Experiences among lamas, magicians, sages, sorcerers, Bonpa wizards. A true psychic discovery. 32 illustrations. 321pp. 5⅜ x 8½. (Available in U.S. only.) 22682-4 Pa. $9.95

THE EGYPTIAN BOOK OF THE DEAD, E. A. Wallis Budge. Complete reproduction of Ani's papyrus, finest ever found. Full hieroglyphic text, interlinear transliteration, word-for-word translation, smooth translation. 533pp. 6½ x 9¼.
21866-X Pa. $12.95

MATHEMATICS FOR THE NONMATHEMATICIAN, Morris Kline. Detailed, college-level treatment of mathematics in cultural and historical context, with numerous exercises. Recommended Reading Lists. Tables. Numerous figures. 641pp. 5⅜ x 8½.
24823-2 Pa. $11.95

PROBABILISTIC METHODS IN THE THEORY OF STRUCTURES, Isaac Elishakoff. Well-written introduction covers the elements of the theory of probability from two or more random variables, the reliability of such multivariable structures, the theory of random function, Monte Carlo methods of treating problems incapable of exact solution, and more. Examples. 502pp. 5³/₈ x 8¹/₂. 40691-1 Pa. $16.95

THE RIME OF THE ANCIENT MARINER, Gustave Doré, S. T. Coleridge. Doré's finest work; 34 plates capture moods, subtleties of poem. Flawless full-size reproductions printed on facing pages with authoritative text of poem. "Beautiful. Simply beautiful."–*Publisher's Weekly.* 77pp. 9¼ x 12. 22305-1 Pa. $7.95

NORTH AMERICAN INDIAN DESIGNS FOR ARTISTS AND CRAFTSPEOPLE, Eva Wilson. Over 360 authentic copyright-free designs adapted from Navajo blankets, Hopi pottery, Sioux buffalo hides, more. Geometrics, symbolic figures, plant and animal motifs, etc. 128pp. 8⅜ x 11. (Not for sale in the United Kingdom.) 25341-4 Pa. $9.95

SCULPTURE: Principles and Practice, Louis Slobodkin. Step-by-step approach to clay, plaster, metals, stone; classical and modern. 253 drawings, photos. 255pp. 8⅛ x 11.
22960-2 Pa. $11.95

THE INFLUENCE OF SEA POWER UPON HISTORY, 1660–1783, A. T. Mahan. Influential classic of naval history and tactics still used as text in war colleges. First paperback edition. 4 maps. 24 battle plans. 640pp. 5⅜ x 8½. 25509-3 Pa. $14.95

THE STORY OF THE TITANIC AS TOLD BY ITS SURVIVORS, Jack Winocour (ed.). What it was really like. Panic, despair, shocking inefficiency, and a little heroism. More thrilling than any fictional account. 26 illustrations. 320pp. 5⅜ x 8½. 20610-6 Pa. $8.95

FAIRY AND FOLK TALES OF THE IRISH PEASANTRY, William Butler Yeats (ed.). Treasury of 64 tales from the twilight world of Celtic myth and legend: "The Soul Cages," "The Kildare Pooka," "King O'Toole and his Goose," many more. Introduction and Notes by W. B. Yeats. 352pp. 5⅜ x 8½. 26941-8 Pa. $8.95

BUDDHIST MAHAYANA TEXTS, E. B. Cowell and others (eds.). Superb, accurate translations of basic documents in Mahayana Buddhism, highly important in history of religions. The Buddha-karita of Asvaghosha, Larger Sukhavativyuha, more. 448pp. 5⅜ x 8½. 25552-2 Pa. $12.95

ONE TWO THREE . . . INFINITY: Facts and Speculations of Science, George Gamow. Great physicist's fascinating, readable overview of contemporary science: number theory, relativity, fourth dimension, entropy, genes, atomic structure, much more. 128 illustrations. Index. 352pp. 5⅜ x 8½. 25664-2 Pa. $9.95

EXPERIMENTATION AND MEASUREMENT, W. J. Youden. Introductory manual explains laws of measurement in simple terms and offers tips for achieving accuracy and minimizing errors. Mathematics of measurement, use of instruments, experimenting with machines. 1994 edition. Foreword. Preface. Introduction. Epilogue. Selected Readings. Glossary. Index. Tables and figures. 128pp. 5³/₈ x 8¹/₂. 40451-X Pa. $6.95

DALÍ ON MODERN ART: The Cuckolds of Antiquated Modern Art, Salvador Dalí. Influential painter skewers modern art and its practitioners. Outrageous evaluations of Picasso, Cézanne, Turner, more. 15 renderings of paintings discussed. 44 calligraphic decorations by Dalí. 96pp. 5⅜ x 8½. (Available in U.S. only.) 29220-7 Pa. $5.95

ANTIQUE PLAYING CARDS: A Pictorial History, Henry René D'Allemagne. Over 900 elaborate, decorative images from rare playing cards (14th–20th centuries): Bacchus, death, dancing dogs, hunting scenes, royal coats of arms, players cheating, much more. 96pp. 9¼ x 12¼. 29265-7 Pa. $12.95

MAKING FURNITURE MASTERPIECES: 30 Projects with Measured Drawings, Franklin H. Gottshall. Step-by-step instructions, illustrations for constructing handsome, useful pieces, among them a Sheraton desk, Chippendale chair, Spanish desk, Queen Anne table and a William and Mary dressing mirror. 224pp. 8⅛ x 11¼. 29338-6 Pa. $13.95

THE FOSSIL BOOK: A Record of Prehistoric Life, Patricia V. Rich et al. Profusely illustrated definitive guide covers everything from single-celled organisms and dinosaurs to birds and mammals and the interplay between climate and man. Over 1,500 illustrations. 760pp. 7½ x 10⅛. 29371-8 Pa. $29.95

*Prices subject to change without notice.*

Available at your book dealer or write for free catalog to Dept. GI, Dover Publications, Inc., 31 East 2nd St., Mineola, N.Y. 11501. Dover publishes more than 500 books each year on science, elementary and advanced mathematics, biology, music, art, literary history, social sciences and other areas.

X 1-20-04
Donation